THE ART OF
TROLLING

THE ART OF TROLLING

———

TEXT AND PHOTOGRAPHS
BY

KEN SCHULTZ

THE STEPHEN GREENE PRESS
LEXINGTON, MASSACHUSETTS

First published in 1987 by The Stephen Greene Press, Inc.
Published simultaneously in Canada by
Penguin Books Canada Limited
Distributed by Viking Penguin Inc.,
40 West 23rd Street, New York, NY 10010.

Photographs by the author.
Line drawings by Mary Jane Schultz.

LIBRARY OF CONGRESS CATALOGING-IN-PUBLICATION DATA
Schultz, Ken.
The art of trolling.
Includes index.
1. Trolling (Fishing)   I. Title.
SH457.7.S38   1987   799.1'2   86-25749
ISBN 0-8289-0622-X

Printed in the United States of America
by The Alpine Press
set in Goudy Old Style by Rainsford Type
produced by Unicorn Production Services, Inc.

To Kristen, Alyson, and Megan — all eager anglers

ACKNOWLEDGMENTS

Many fishermen, guides, and charter boat captains have shared their boats and angling expertise with me, and I thank them all. Bill Kelley, who is an exceptionally able and hard-fishing Lake Ontario skipper, deserves special notice for his efforts and assistance. Thanks also to Dr. Mike Voiland of Sea Grant, who helped many times with my big water education; to Roger Tucker, who still fishes with me even though I disparage his downriggers; and to my wife, Mary Jane, who provided the accompanying illustrations.

CONTENTS

INTRODUCTION

In some ways, trolling is an enigma. Nonfishing folk don't have the vaguest idea about this aspect of angling. When friends who don't fish or don't know much about fishing asked me what kind of book I was writing, I eventually just responded that it was "a fishing book" and changed the topic. After trying to explain to others what trolling is all about, and seeing the incomprehensive look on their faces, I stopped talking about trolling and its nuances. A recent cartoon in a national sporting magazine sums up the situation well. The cartoon shows two fellows on a bridge. One has a rod and tackle box in his hands; the other has a bow and arrow pointed at a particularly hairy and ugly troll who is running out from under the bridge. The fisherman is saying, "M'gosh! You actually meant . . . trolling!"

So who cares what nonanglers think? Does it surprise you to know that in some fishing circles there is a stigma attached to trolling? Visit the heart of southern bass country and ask the best bass fishermen how to troll for bass. They can't tell you because they scoff at the prospect of using their 70 mph glitter machines that cost $18,000 for such a low-brow activity. The best striped bass fishing guide whom I know — one of the best in the country — will positively have nothing to do with trolling. He says that he's interested in "catchin', not ridin'."

Trolling is banned as a musky fishing technique in some northern Midwest lakes, not as a fisheries management tool but as an appeaser of vocal anglers who despise the technique and deem it to be "unsporting." Trolling is a prohibited fishing technique in nearly all bass fishing tournaments; "too easy" is the rationale I heard from one major promoter. Diehard fly fishermen who cast for stream trout would no more try trolling for trout in lakes than they would let a monkey play with their wispy $200 fly rod. A significant number of cast-and-retrieve boat and shore anglers think trolling is about as exciting an endeavor as watching paint dry.

So that's what some angling brethren think of trolling: dull, easy, unsporting, demeaning. As you may realize, however, many people fear what they don't know, and many nontrolling anglers have never trolled, have not trolled with anyone who has mastered the technique in a sporting way, or are simply uncomfortable with the prospect of getting out on the big water and trying something that they are un-accustomed to doing.

And what about the major press? How do they treat the subject of trolling? Like something they are obligated to cover once in a while! Major outdoor periodicals have, by and large, ignored the fine points of trolling; it just doesn't have the charm of other types of fishing. Only recently have they paid attention to some modern aspects of trolling and the latest equipment that makes it a challenging and sporting activity. Although they run an article about, say, how to use downriggers for trout in lakes one month, they are still likely in the next issue to publish an article that has an "I-just-discovered-that-trolling-is-a-good-way-to-fish" theme, supported by two paragraphs of information on laid-back lure dragging, five paragraphs on what a neat idea this is, and ten paragraphs of anecdotal experiences. Then they may not have an article about trolling again for eight months. In essence they revert to the old school of thought.

So why would I write a book about this no-respect sport? For several reasons. Enigmas, stigmas, neglect, and ignorance notwith-standing, there are *many, many* people who troll for some or most of their fish. Trolling is *the* way to catch trout and salmon on lakes and reservoirs. It is *the* method on some musky waters. It is a valued technique for most walleye anglers, an overlooked method for black bass fishermen, an increasingly important means of catching striped bass, and a form of fishing that has taken on a greater dimension in the entire world of sportfishing even if there are fishermen who choose not to troll or who choose to ignore it as a viable technique. Additionally, trolling is a grossly misunderstood form of fishing, and many trollers simply aren't going about it very well. To most fishermen, trolling is the art of dragging any old lure or bait at an indeterminate distance behind a boat at an unknown depth, in an unplanned fashion — and with generally unproductive results. That's boat riding. It's a sure way to wash the paint off your lures. It's a good way to get a tan and see the lakeside. But it's not trolling.

This book rejects the old school of thought on trolling. It doesn't make trolling seem any more or less complicated than it need be, and it doesn't promise any more or less than the technique of trolling can deliver. Trolling the modern way appeals to anglers who want to know more about the fish that inhabit the wide open places and the environment that they inhabit. Modern trolling also lures those who want to master the challenge of catching fish — and especially big fish — that are often far out of reach in the aqua abyss. Today, trolling can be accomplished with tackle that complements, not constrains, the fish. As a result of the emergence of new tackle and techniques and of the stocking of large and desirable species of open-water game fish in big lakes and impoundments, there are more people than ever gravitating toward trolling to take advantage of the opportunities that exist. And there's a need, I think, for a book that covers the whole spectrum of how to troll in freshwater.

I think that trolling, done properly, is a very sporting and enjoyable way to fish. I will say, however, that it can be dull when you aren't catching fish, and it can be boring if you are doing the rod watching and someone else is pulling all the strings, that is, driving the boat, scanning the sonar, setting lines, changing lures, and so forth. If you really want to be challenged by trolling, you have to get out and do it, not let others do it for you. This book is geared toward that end. Personally, I get as much enjoyment out of rigging up lines, selecting successful lures, and finding and enticing fish, as I do in fighting them successfully. I get a kick when the rod starts bouncing and the call goes out, "Fish on!" You can have those same thrills and enjoy the same satisfaction when you understand what modern freshwater trolling is all about, which is what I hope this book shows you.

KEN SCHULTZ

1

DOWNRIGGERS

If you're not familiar with downriggers or don't really know what they mean to the technique of trolling, let me briefly explain other trolling systems so you can see how downriggers are different and what they essentially do. With this explanation, you will understand why they are functional trolling tools.

Make no mistake, downriggers are the best thing to hit the trolling scene since outboard motors were invented. They have not only revolutionized the trolling aspect of fishing in the past three decades, but they have made it a more sporting and fruitful endeavor and have helped bring more fun into what can at times be a lackluster activity.

In the predownrigger age, trolling basically consisted of the following methods, all of which will be reviewed in more detail later in this book:

Running an object on an unweighted nylon monofilament, braided Dacron, or fly line. Still popular where appropriate and known as flat-lining, this method is essentially for relatively shallow fishing, because the depth achieved is entirely dependent on the weight or diving ability of the object being trolled. To know how deep you are fishing, you must know the depth that object will attain depending on such factors as boat speed, line size, current, trolling line length, and so forth. Because most anglers do not learn to evaluate the depth that their trolled lures or bait actually attain, their efforts are often haphazard and their successes sporadic.

Running an object on a weighted line. Similar to the previous method, running an object on a weighted line simply involves using some type of weight (drail, split shot, keel, bell, or other types of sinkers) to get a lure or bait deeper than it would achieve unaided. The problem of knowing actual depth fished is essentially the same as with unweighted lines.

Running an object behind a lead-core line. In this system, the weight of the line causes the object being trolled to sink. Depth achieved depends on how much lead-core line is let out. Lead core is marked at intervals to let you know the length out; how much line you troll determines how deep your lure will run. Although this can be a more precise method of fishing than flat-lining, it still puts your lure or bait only at a general trolling depth. A lead-core line is not as comfortable to use as an unweighted line because lead-core line is strong and bulkier than nylon or Dacron. Lead core is neither stiff nor supple, and it dampens the fight of a fish.

Running an object behind a wire line. As with lead core, the weight of wire line causes the object being trolled to sink, and the amount let out determines the depth to be achieved. Wire can't be fished on any rod or reel. It requires stout tackle; is subject to kinking, crimping, and spooling difficulties; and does nothing to enhance the sporting nature of fish being caught because the tackle blunts the fight of the fish.

Running an object behind a diving planer. Because it pulls so hard when trolled, a diving planer is fished off of a very stout rod and is used with heavy line. Diving planers dive deep on a relatively short length of line, and the amount of line trolled essentially determines how deep the planer will dive. A planer trips when a fish strikes, so you don't have to fight it as well as the fish; nevertheless, the planer impedes the fight and activity of the fish somewhat.

Running an object behind a releasable cannonball sinker system. This is a deep-trolling system of traditional use on the West Coast for salmon fishing. A large cannonball-shaped sinker is used to get down deep, the sinker being released and dropping to the bottom when a fish strikes. You lose a lot of lead weight in this system and need stout, heavy-line tackle. You also don't often know the depth at which you're fishing when you're off the bottom.

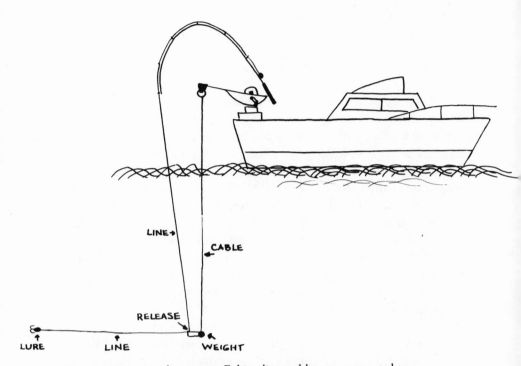

LINE→

CABLE

RELEASE

LURE   LINE   WEIGHT

Downrigging is a simple concept. Fishing line and lure are connected to a weighted cable via a release mechanism and lowered to a specific depth. When a fish strikes the lure, the line pops out of the release.

Each of the six systems mentioned can suffer from imprecise depth control; in other words, you often don't know exactly how deep you're fishing. When you do know, you either have an extreme amount of line out or you're using tackle that could subdue a submarine. Downriggers overcome all of these problems because they take the burden of getting a line to a specific depth away from your fishing line and put it on an accessory product. In brief, downriggers offer controlled depth presentation. Furthermore, they can be used with light and ultralight tackle, meaning that you can catch deep-dwelling fish on tackle that taxes your skills a little more and provides extra enjoyment.

There are enormous benefits of downrigger use, so much so that downrigger sales have grown markedly in the last decade. Downriggers started in the Great Lakes for trout and salmon fishing and spread inland for musky, bass, striper, and walleye use, as well as for inshore saltwater fishing and offshore big-game fishing. Downriggers are also being used in foreign markets. Although the aforementioned systems of fishing still are used — especially flat-lining and diving planer fishing — and have merit in certain situations, downriggers have relegated wire and lead-core line to ancient history among most regular and accomplished trollers.

Downriggers are not complicated fishing devices. The equipment components of downrigging include a reel, cranking handle, boom, cable, and pulley that are part of the basic product known as a downrigger; a heavy lead weight that attaches to the end of the downrigger cable; and a line-release mechanism that is located on or near the weight or at any place along the cable. In use, a lure that is attached to your fishing line is placed in the water and set at whatever distance you want it to run behind your boat. Then the fishing line attached to that lure is placed in the release. Fishing line and downrigger weight are lowered simultaneously to the depth you want to fish. When a fish strikes your lure, the fishing line pops out of the release and you play the fish on your fishing line, unencumbered by a heavy weight or strong cable.

Once you visualize the downrigger concept at work, you'll see that it is really quite simple. It's a piggyback system, somewhat like the NASA space shuttle, in which a plane is attached to a rocket to blast

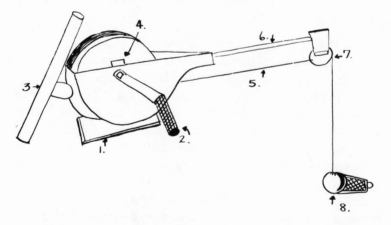

The components of a downrigger are: 1. base; 2. cranking handle; 3. rod holder; 4. line counter; 5. cable; 6. boom or arm; 7. pulley; 8. weight. Most models also include a clutch (not illustrated). Electric versions feature a motor housing and do not have the cranking handle.

into space but is separated from it to return on its own. With down-riggers, you piggyback your fishing line to a heavily weighted non-fishing line, and the two separate when a fish strikes.

Let's take a close look at the components of downrigging. Down-riggers come in manual or electric models. Many small boaters have manual downriggers or started with manual models and worked up to electric ones. Manuals come in small versions that clamp onto the transom or gunwales of boats or even into the oarlock receptacle, or in larger versions that are mounted permanently. Some are available in either right- or left-hand–crank versions. Electrics are generally made for permanent and sturdy mounting locations. Electrics are more expensive than manual downriggers, require power source hookup, and are more prone to malfunction. Because of their ease of use, they are invariably preferred by veteran trollers, however. Electric down-riggers are raised and lowered by flicking a switch, while manuals are always hand-cranked up. Some manual models are also cranked down (on some you can release clutch tension to lower a downrigger weight instead of handle-cranking it down).

Although you can often raise or lower a weight faster with a manual model than with an electric one, you can hit an automatic up switch on most electrics that retrieves the downrigger while you are tending to other things. Besides saving time, this is a convenience feature. Not all electrics are comparable in the speed at which they raise or lower (especially raise) a weight, however. It is often desirable to retrieve a weight as quickly as possible, particularly when a strong fish is on and near the boat, or to clear one side of the boat rapidly for landing a fish, but some electric downriggers are painfully slow at this.

If you're comparing features on different electric downriggers, don't just check the torque and speed of retrieve but note the amp draw of the units and see if there is an overload cutoff and circuit breaker reset switch. Also find out how hard it would be to turn the spool and recover the cable manually if your power should fail. On both electric and manual models, check to see how easy the slip clutch and drag assembly works. Only the smallest, cheapest units don't have this. On manual models, a handle that doesn't turn backward as the cable is lowered is preferable.

The length of the boom which carries the cable from the spool to a pulley, varies from short 1-foot arms to 8-foot ones, depending on the boat location and the need to spread out weights to cover the greatest possible horizontal range of water. To some extent, the length of boom used also depends on the size of the boat and on your ability to move freely around in it to tend regularly to line rigging and weight setting.

As a general rule, I find that as the boat size increases and the vertical distance from gunwale to water surface increases, so does the length of downrigger arm. Incidentally, the boom on some downriggers can be changed to different lengths, and in some products an extension can be bolted on. On small boats, such as 12- to 16-foot craft and bass boats, it is most common to use just two short-armed downriggers. On large boats, such as those with an 8- to 10-foot beam, as many as four 2- or 3- foot–armed downriggers may be spaced equally across the transom, with two longer-armed downriggers located partway up the gunwales and pointed perpendicular to the gunwale.

In boats with adequate room, the longer arms can be swiveled in to retrieve the weight or line release and to set fishing line in the release. Preferably the cable can be pulled inward via a retriever, a free-sliding pulley on the cable that is attached to a lanyard, when necessary. On some downriggers, the boom and spool assemblage pivots upward, raising the boom vertically to retrieve weight or line release. Most models are of a fixed nature and cannot pivot upward, although if mounted on a swivel base they can be moved to various side positions. I don't like the lift-up arms and find them awkward when rigging lines, especially in rough water as the boat is bouncing. The tendency for the ball to be raised too low and swing into the side of the boat, or too high and crash into your body, is a drawback to booms that are raised vertically.

At the end of a downrigger boom is a pulley that guides the cable as it extends downward to the water. This pulley should pivot from side to side because the cable usually extends back rather than from directly below the pulley when the boat is moving forward. Some type of cable guard should be mounted on the pulley to prevent the cable from jumping off the track. Some downriggers sport a hook on the underside of the spool frame, and this is convenient for attaching the downrigger weight (if it has a hole at the back end) or the snap at the end of the cable for in-transit storage. If you are moving from place to place and have the weight hooked up, you can simply unhook it and drop it in the water instead of having to reattach the weight to the snap.

Most downriggers in use today have a line counter in 1-foot increments to measure the amount of cable that has come off the spool. Some older transom-mount manuals don't have such a counter, but you can obtain one from the manufacturer as an accessory or mark the cable or count off spool revolutions to know how deep you are. Without a counter, however, you may forget the depth setting after awhile, especially if you have changed it a time or two without raising the weight. It is important to adjust the counter in accordance with the amount of cable between the pulley and the surface of the water. The counter should read zero when the weight is in the water just below the surface. If you don't adjust it in this fashion, the weight will be 1 to 3 feet shallower than the counter shows, and you'll constantly have to add to the indicated depth to know exactly how deep the weight is.

Some downriggers sport one or two rod holders that attach to the frame or base of the unit. Rod holders are critical to downrigging, so you should either have one or two mounted on the downrigger itself or have them located nearby. Place rod holders strategically and allow for more holders than you expect you will need when actually fishing, because extra holders come in handy when storing rods out of the way for fish-landing, rigging, running, and so forth.

Downriggers utilize braided steel cable, normally of 150-pound breaking strength, that does not stretch, meaning that the depth on the line counter will conform exactly to the length of cable set out. Spools are filled with approximately 200 yards of cable, though a greater length can be spooled provided that it is continuous, unspliced cable. Cable has a tendency to coil or kink, and can be weakened when it does. It can also be weakened in locales where line releases have been repeatedly set or where the cable has been nicked due to collision with some object. It's a good idea to check the cable periodically for signs of strand fraying or crimping and to cut off the affected area so you don't lose a downrigger weight and terminal hardware. This isn't too difficult to accomplish as long as you have metal sleeves and crimping pliers to make the change. If you lose a weight and terminal hardware in the water and don't have replacement materials, you can still jury-rig by running the cable through a heavy-duty snap swivel (or to the weight if you don't have a snap; however, you can't take the weight off readily when you do this) and tying a series of jam knots in the cable. Test the holding strength of this arrangement, be careful not to hang the weight on bottom, and rerig properly at the first opportunity ashore.

To minimize fraying and stress at the end of the line, you can use a rubber snubber that fits over the cable. This is very useful with electric downriggers that come up automatically and jam against the pulley if not stopped in time, which may cause the circuit breaker to pop. A snubber is also very helpful with coated coaxial cable that is used to transmit temperature from a sensor at the end of the cable near the weight. When this cable is frayed, nicked, or severely stressed at the terminal end, it will not give accurate temperature readings. Furthermore, coaxial cable, once cut, is hard to reconnect properly. Usually you must bring the downrigger to an electrical repair shop to get the sensor and cable properly mated. To minimize coaxial cable damage, you shouldn't use a line release that attaches on the cable.

The size of lead weight used in downrigging varies, although 10- to 12- pound weights are the norm. Heavy weights are needed to keep the cable directly below the boat or as close to this as possible for precise depth determination, especially if a wide-angle sonar transducer is used so that you can see your weights on a sonar machine, if there is current, and when you are trolling fast. Heavy weights are also necessary for fishing in very deep water. In relatively shallow water, in places where there is no current, and when you are trolling slowly, you can use a lighter 7- or 8-pound weight. Some small downriggers have a 2-pound weight because that is about all the compact unit can handle. Although I have successfully used these, I find it difficult to know the actual running depth of the light weight and to calculate approximate depth, which makes these light compact units less functional products. For shallow fishing and portability, however, they aren't a bad idea.

Weights are often referred to as cannonballs because the earliest models, and many current ones, are shaped like a round ball. A round ball with a stabilizing fin on the back is currently a popular weight, although weights are found in all configurations. Those shaped like a fish or a torpedo are fairly popular, and a current favorite with some anglers is a deep but slender-headed weight with a broad fin. I wish I could tell you that one kind tracked better than another (was less subject to side-to-side swaying), but I can't be definitive. I started out with solid and filled (with buckshot) torpedo weights but shun them now because they seem to sway more than cannonballs. I primarily

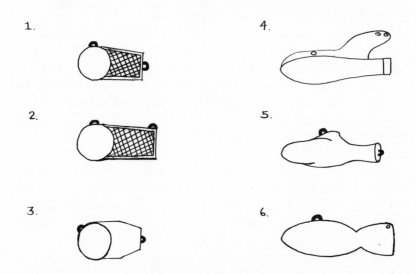

Popular styles of downrigger weights include cannonballs (1, 2, and 3); torpedo (4); and fish (5 and 6).

use cannonball-with-fin weights now and have no trouble with them, although I recently used heavy slender-fronted, wide-tail weights and thought they had little swayback (which I discuss later in this chapter) and tracked fine. My advice is to try different weights until you settle on what shape suits you, then have extras on hand.

Some of the manufacturer-supplied weights have a thick rubber or vinyl coating, which is a good characteristic. Coated weights don't mar your boat when they hit it or are dropped on the gunwale or deck, and they are easy to handle. They are no more efficient than uncoated weights, however, although their coloring lasts indefinitely. Painted lead weights lose their color in time. I fish with painted, unpainted, and half-painted cannonballs and can't say that one kind is best, although I like to paint mine lime green, chartreuse, or fluorescent orange. Some manufacturer-supplied weights are white, black, chartreuse, green, orange, and red. It is a fact that fish are often attracted to the trolled downrigger weight, so the question is whether the color or the vibration attracts them. I'm inclined to believe it's the latter, especially in deep water, and have no basis to say that color is especially important, although it doesn't seem to hurt.

Line releases are critical to the downrigging system and present a lot of room for experimentation — and also for problems. Line releases must be capable of freeing the fishing line when a fish strikes and also when the angler chooses to release it from above in order to retrieve the fishing line without bringing the weight in and manually releasing the line. To free a fishing line from above, you simply take the rod out of its holder, point the rod tip toward the water and reel up slack, then pop the rod tip upward as if setting the hook. If this procedure doesn't free the fishing line, the line was not properly set in the release or the tension was too high.

Easily adjustable tension settings are important in line releases, and having the right amount of tension is critical for catching fish. Practically, most fish that take a lure trolled behind a downrigger weight impale themselves with the hook(s) of that lure when they strike it and pull the fishing line out of the release. If the release is set too loosely, it will provide little resistance to help impale the hook in a fish. If it is set too tight, a small fish may strike the lure and not pop the line out of the release, causing the fish to be dragged for some distance before it is discovered. A tight release often cannot be freed by the angler when he wants to change lures.

There is, then, a proper middle ground that varies, depending upon the strength of line being used and the type of lure being trolled. When using light line, you have to set release tension fairly light so the line isn't broken if a big fish strikes the lure. When using objects that are heavy or that create a lot of resistance when pulled through the water, such as large deep-diving plugs or a dodger, the release tension must be set high enough so that the fishing line stays in the release and doesn't pop out without a fish striking, especially in rough water.

When you are experiencing frequent lost fish, either because the hooks pull out or the fish strike the lure and pop the release but fail to get hooked, try tightening the tension on your release and short-ening the length of line between the lure and the release. This problem occurs when fish are slapping at the lure or the release is set too light. You'll get a better strike-to-landing ratio by increasing tension and shortening the setback.

If you really want to get technical on this subject, conduct the following experiment on dry land. Take a top-quality spring scale and attach it to the end of a fishing line. Set the fishing line in your release, using a tension setting that you deem by feel to be just right. Have someone watch the release and holler at the precise moment that the line snaps out of the release. Watch the scale as you pull on it and see where the indicator lies at the moment your companion hollers. By doing this, you'll get a relative idea of how much pressure it takes to free the release at your chosen setting. Now conduct the same experiment with different tension settings, with different lengths of fishing line between the scale and releases, and with different strengths of line. Although this is not quite the same as using wet line in the water, because stretch and breaking strength of line differ, it is a reasonable comparison and may lead you to a better understanding of the tension settings that are useful for your fishing applications.

There are line releases that attach to your weight, to your downrigger cable at the weight, and to your cable at any location above the weight. I've progressed through a host of releases to some products that I'm currently satisfied with. The first releases I tried years ago were Mac-Jac products, which sport a spring clip that attaches to either the cable or weight and feature a nylon button that encircles your fishing line and is attached to the clip. The button has to be placed onto the fishing line before that line is attached to the lure, which can be inconvenient if you want to alternate a rod between downrigger use and flat-lining. You'd have to take the button off the line for flat-lining. Tension settings are largely uncontrollable with this setup.

After Mac-Jac's, I graduated to Riviera's adjustable tension release, which bolts onto the fin of the company's torpedo-shaped weight. Early models of this release featured a button that was placed over the fishing line and snapped into a grooved segment of the white plastic body of the release. The button had the same drawback as the Mac-Jac, so I bypassed it and placed the line directly into the back crevice between release halves. Tension is readily adjusted on this release, but I have had a lot of trouble with it when using light lines, like 4- through 10-pound test. Those lines often got frayed where they were placed in the release, resulting in seriously weakened line and/or breakage when a fish struck. For heavy lines, however, this release is adequate.

For a short while, I was also using the Penn snap-in release, which attached to the downrigger weight. This featured a rectangularly shaped buttonlike tab that was placed over the fishing line and snapped into a receptacle on Penn cannonballs. This suffered the same problem as other button-type releases and was nearly impossible to free from above. Buttons, incidentally, cause line twist because they hinder lure action when they are dragged through the water ahead of a lure. This happens when you free your line from above in order to retrieve and change lures. The long and short of button releases is that they are largely inadequate.

A release that I like a lot is the standard Roemer, which clamps to the downrigger cable. This is larger and more expensive than other releases, but it works extremely well. Fishing line is wrapped around a trigger that snaps open and frees the line when a strike is received. This standard Roemer is especially easy to trip from the boat and is very compatible with light-line use. It can also be readily removed from or located anywhere on the downrigger cable. I took some of my older models (the first ones sometimes pinched the cable and lead to strand separation, but that problem was solved), drilled a hole in them, and attached them to the fin of a cannonball weight — this worked well, although they were subject to breakage if the weight was dropped.

Releases attached to down-rigger weights and cables include (clockwise from the bottom): Clipper, Cannon, Roemer, and two Offshore versions. In the center is the Roemer Liberator, a device used to attach a second lure to one main fishing line.

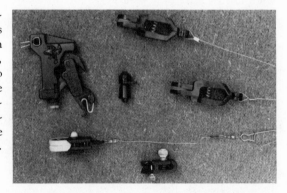

Another good release I've used lately is the Cannon Quick release, which has a short wire-leadered snap that allows it to be quickly affixed to a downrigger weight. Tension is easily adjusted and line is wedged into rubber-pad jaws. How far back you set the line will depend on what you are trolling behind it and on what strength line you use. The line doesn't need to be twisted (more on this subject shortly) when it is inserted into the release.

The Offshore release, which features a spring clamp with rubber pads at the end, has also proven effective for me and is very simple to use. There is no tension setting with this device; how far into the pads you set the fishing line determines the amount of pressure to keep it there and the force it takes to free the line. It, too, has a short length of wire line that snaps to the weight.

Recently I've had several occasions to use Clipper releases on boats belonging to friends, and have had good enough results with them to purchase a few. These are small and snap readily onto the downrigger cable. Fishing line is snapped into a clip, the release tension of which is controlled by a tension screw. I've had no trouble with line releasing out of these, although I have had some difficulty in getting the Clipper's cable-attachment rubber pads fixed on the downrigger cable so that it doesn't work free or fail to drop down when stacked (more on this shortly).

Obviously there is a good selection of releases to choose from, including some not mentioned here because I don't have much experience in using them. There are still some fishermen who don't use commercially produced releases at all, but employ rubberbands for this purpose. Numbers 14 and 16 rubberbands (available in quantity at office supply stores) are preferred by many, and these are attached to fishing line via a half hitch, then connected to a large snap that is affixed to a downrigger weight. Although I keep a supply of rubberbands on hand for occasional release use, I don't care for them much because their breaking strength varies greatly. When a fish strikes a line that is attached to a rubberband release, it must stretch the rubberband to its breaking point in order to separate fishing line and downrigger cable. Occasionally you'll catch a fish that is small and can't break the band; therefore, the fish will be inadvertently trolled for a long time. Sometimes it will be hard to snap the rubberband from above to retrieve the lure; at other times you'll get broken pieces of rubberband wrapped in your fishing reel, which can be messy when they melt or adhere to the line. Rubberbands left in the sun will lose their strength.

More than one fishing line may be used with a single downrigger cable and weight, with second or even third lines set at variable distances above the weight. This process is called stacking and is particularly useful for covering varied depths when you are unsure at what level to troll and are searching for fish. Releases used for stacked lines must be able to be placed anywhere on the cable and must pop free of the cable and slide down to the lower release or weight when a fish strikes or when the weight is raised. Otherwise, the release prevents the cable from being raised any further, which means you have to bring the cable in to you to free the release manually. This is more than inconvenient; it hampers efforts to clear tackle when a fish is on or near the boat and ready to be netted.

A number of manufacturers make releases that can be stacked and that function in this manner. Cannon and Offshore have stacker releases that work well. The Clipper can be stacked as is, though I find it hard to keep this release from sliding freely and view it better as a fixed release for use on the cable above the weight. The standard Roemer release is stackable and works well in this capacity provided that you do not set the cable clamp too tightly, which makes it impossible for the release to slip free down the downrigger cable.

One last point about some releases — you should twist the fishing line before putting it into the release. This may not be necessary for the Roemer, the Cannon, and a few others, but it is still a good idea to do so. Twisting is necessary because the line would slip freely through the release if it was merely snapped into place, meaning that (1) the lure might swim up to the weight and stay right behind it when you set the weight down; (2) a fish may not have enough resistance at the release to trip it properly, which could contribute to losing fish; and (3) the angler couldn't trip the release from above because the line might slip through the release. To prevent a line from slipping through the release, take the fishing line and make six or seven twists with it after the lure has been set back, then insert the twisted line or the loop created by twisting into the release. Although a few fishermen have complained that twisting weakens fishing line, I have not found this to be so, and see no line-quality related reason to avoid this practice.

I've devoted all attention so far in this chapter to the technical points of downriggers and the equipment used with them. Now I'd like to walk you through the mechanics of setting a line out with a downrigger.

Begin by opening the bail or by pushing the freespool button on your reel and letting your lure out to whatever distance you think it should be swimming behind the downrigger weight. Keep the reel in freespool with the clicker on if it's a levelwind reel and either loosen the drag or keep the bail open with a spinning rod. Bring the downrigger weight and line release close to the boat so you can reach them without stretching far overboard. Grab the line at the top of the rod and place it in the release, twisting the line first if necessary. Set the weight back overboard if you brought it onto the gunwale of the boat or swing the boom back to its proper position so the weight can be lowered. Take the rod in one hand and make sure that the line is not fouled at the tip and that it will freely depart the reel spool. Use your other hand to lower the weight, either by depressing the down switch on electric downriggers, by releasing clutch tension lightly, or by back-reeling manual downriggers. Stop the weight at whatever depth you want, as indicated on the line counter. Set the rod in a holder and reel up slack so that the tip is bowed over.

Other than changing the length of line between release and lure and altering the depth to fish, you will go through this same procedure every time you set a lure out with the aid of a downrigger. The depth to fish can vary from just below the surface to as deep as the line on your downrigger spool will allow. Determine depth to troll by checking temperature levels to see at what depth the thermocline or preferred temperature of your quarry or bottom habitat can be found. You can also pick what seems like an appropriate depth for the time being and wait until you find fish on your sonar equipment before making changes.

Sonar equipment is an essential accessory to use in conjunction with a downrigger. The purpose of downrigger fishing is to control the depth of your lures and to place them in specific places and at specific levels. You use sonar equipment to find bait fish or game fish and the levels at which they are located, as well as the depth of the bottom and other aspects of underwater terrain. Without sonar you are guessing as to the depth to fish and the depth of the water in which you are fishing. You also run the risk of hanging up your weight when the bottom gets shallower.

How far back to set your lines varies from a few feet to 200 feet, depending on the depth being fished and the species being pursued. You'll find information on trolling line lengths in later chapters. As a general rule, the deeper you fish the less line you need to have between weight and lure, and the shallower you set weights, the further you put the lines back. This is only a general guideline, however, because some fish can at times be caught shallow on short lines. Setback distance is something that requires experimentation and analysis under different conditions. It is to your advantage to fish with the shortest setback possible under the circumstances (water clarity, species, depth, and so forth), because this increases hook-setting efficiency, minimizes possible conflicts with other boats in heavily trafficked areas, and makes it easier to turn a boat and execute boat-maneuvering patterns.

To determine the length of line out, you can use one of several systems. With levelwind reels, you can count the number of "passes" that the levelwind guide makes across the top of the reel. Measure the amount of line that comes off the spool for one pass, then multiply that amount by the number of passes to arrive at a setback distance. Another system, used with levelwind reels possessing a line guide that locks in an open position and with spinning and fly reels, is to count "pulls." Start with the lure or fly in the water, hold the rod in one hand, and grab the line just ahead of the reel with your other hand. Pull off line in set increments, either as far as your arm will reach, or in 1- or 2-foot strips. Count the distance let out as you pull to arrive at setback length. A third method is to "sweep," by putting the lure in the water, pointing the tip back at the lure, and sweeping the rod toward the bow of the boat in a measured length. As the boat moves ahead, bring the rod tip back and then sweep forward again. If your sweep is 6 feet, multiply that by the number of sweeps you make to approximate setback length. Sweeping is a bit less accurate than using pulls or passes.

You can also judge setback distance by sight where surface lures are fished. Rough water, glare, and hard-to-see lures make this tough, and sometimes inaccurate. I often use this method, however, because I am good at judging distances and am often able to keep an eye on the lure being set back. Many people are not good at judging even short distances, however, and often grossly overestimate the distance that they have set a lure behind the boat. When I have other people set a line out by sight, I watch to make sure that they get it out approximately to the length I want. I've seen people set lures 40 feet away that they estimated were 75 feet away, and this misjudgment can sometimes be critical to angling success.

When you place the downrigger-set rod in a rod holder, it's important to do several things. Reel all the slack out, then pull on the line near the first rod guide while you turn the reel handle to bring the line from rod tip to release as tight as possible without pulling it out of the release. The rod should be well arched in an inverted **J** shape if properly set. This increases hookup efficiency as well as alerts the angler to a strike when the tip momentarily springs upward as the line is pulled out of the release by the strike of a fish.

In addition, the reel drag should be checked for proper setting and adjusted if not adequate. With levelwind reels that sport a clicker, the clicker should be in the on position, so if a fish strikes and takes

Rods set on downriggers should be cocked and bent over. The two rods on the left are stacked off the starboard gunwale downrigger, just barely visible; the right rod is set on the starboard transom downrigger, behind the angler.

line before someone spots the rod tip bouncing, the clicker will alert the angler that a fish is on and taking line off the reel.

Long rods, incidentally, are optimum for downrigger use, preferably having a long handle for rod holder insertion and an action that is not overly stiff. I've successfully used 6-foot rods for downrigger fishing, but prefer at least a 7-foot rod or, better, an 8- to 9-foot product. The stiffer the rod the harder it is to get the inverted J shape into it when rigging and the more likely that the tip will not be forgiving enough when rough water is encountered and both boat and downrigger weight are rocking and bouncing. This means that the stiff rod will often cause a false release. Even longer rods, including the 12-foot "noodle" rods preferred by some ultralight tackle anglers, can be used with downriggers. Long rods used in steelhead fishing can be adapted for downrigger use, but aren't quite as accommodating as more parabolic downrigger rods. I've used Fenwick's fiberglass Rigger Stiks and graphite Matrix downrigger rods and have had good success with them for big salmon and trout. Lately, I've also been using Daiwa KGX Kevlar/graphite downrigger rods for a broader range and size of fish, and I like them very much. Other products are available, however. Among noodle rods, the Loomis IM6 graphite 12-footer is proving to be a honey.

Reels used in downrigger fishing run a wide gamut, but, in general, where deep water is fished, long setbacks are used, or strong fish capable of stripping off a lot of line are found, you need a reel with plenty of line capacity and a good drag. Levelwind products are more functional for downrigger fishing (and all trolling) if they have a clicker. The smaller versions of Daiwa Sealine reels, the larger ABU-Garcia Ambassadeur, and the smaller Penn reels are examples of such products. Bait-casting reels are suitable for trolling for bass, walleye, and muskies although they usually don't sport a clicker. Ryobi, Daiwa, Shimano, Garcia, and others make useful bait-casting products. These reels can also be used for ultralight trolling and will hold plenty of light line. Spinning reels run an even wider range. I do a fair amount of light and ultralight trolling with 2- through 8-pound-test lines in places where great line capacity isn't a big factor but a good drag is. For this kind of trolling, I often use Garcia Cardinal, Childre Speed Spool, and Zebco Quantum reels with fine results, although there are other reels that are equally capable.

One thing I'm looking forward to in trolling reel developments is the day when there is a good-quality product that electronically displays line length and retains this information in memory while the reel is sitting idle. The Daiwa electronic reels that currently tell you how much line is out and how much is left on the spool would be great for trolling if they were able to retain that information and display it (they go into a battery-saving off mode when not used for a few minutes) the moment you pull a rod out of the holder to play a fish. Because of the precision involved in trolling line setbacks and distance to long-lined fish, I think the real future for such products is in trolling applications.

It is possible, as I mentioned when discussing releases, to fish two rods off one downrigger. You can even stack three, although I haven't had reason to do this because I have other downriggers to use and don't have a boatload of people with me. To set up a stacked line, you rig the first line as you would conventionally and as I described earlier. Once the first line has been placed in the release by the weight, lower the weight down 10 feet and attach the stacker release to the cable. Put the second lure out the desired distance and set the line in the stacker release. Place both reels in rod holders and leave the freespool clicker on, then place the boom in the proper position (if applicable) and lower the weight down to the desired depth. The two lines are now spaced 10 to 12 feet apart. Be sure to place rods in holders so that the lower line will not tangle with the upper line if a strike is received and if the fish immediately comes toward the surface. The setback for the upper line should be shorter than for the lower line, again to minimize interference if a fish strikes the lower one.

The vertical distance between the two lines is optional, although it probably shouldn't be less than 10 feet. Where very deep water is fished, a difference of 30 to 50 feet may be useful. Such a situation

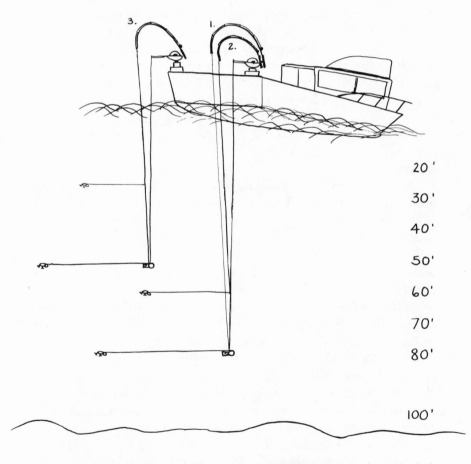

20 '

30 '

40 '

50 '

60 '

70 '

80 '

100 '

Here are two ways to fish two lures off a single downrigger, as well as a method of staggering four lures at varied depths. Rods 1 and 2 are stacked off one downrigger, with lures 20 feet apart. On rod 3, the main lure is fished at the depth of the downrigger weight and a slider rig is above it on the fishing line.

might be encountered when you are deep trolling near the bottom for lake trout, and also when you are running a second line off the same downrigger for salmon, which might be considerably higher in the water column and near the thermocline.

There is another option for fishing more than one lure on one downrigger, although it does not involve using two rods. Use sliders or cheaters. A slider is a lure that is affixed to a short leader and run down the fishing line. To rig it, tie a snap swivel to one end of a 3- to 5-foot length of line and attach a lure, preferably a spoon, to the snap swivel. Tie a snap to the other end, then clip it to a line that is already connected to a downrigger release below the boat. Carefully toss the lure into the water behind the main fishing line, and watch to make sure that it is not fouled. The slider rig will drift out of sight, ultimately to stop well above the lower release at a point where the main line is bowed most sharply in the water. When a fish strikes the slider lure, it pulls back on the main fishing line and pops the lower release. The rig slides down the main fishing line and stops at the snap or lure there. The exact depth of the slider rig will be unknown, but you'll have a second lure being fished on one line and one downrigger.

Slider rigs probably are of little value when the lower lure is fished less than 20 feet down. If you drop the lower lure down 12 feet and put a slider rig on, you'll see that the slider runs just below the surface; so at 20 feet, you might be getting the slider down only 8 feet or less, and there may be little reason to expect to get a fish on such a short line so close to the boat. One drawback to slider rigs is that you lose a lot of the fish that strike them because the hook doesn't get set well when they strike. On the other hand, sliders give you the opportunity to put a different type and color of lure out. If a slider gets a strike or catches a fish, this may entice you to change other lures being trolled or the depth at which you are trolling other lures. Sliders are particularly useful when trolling deep, when fish may be scattered at all levels, when you are unsure of what depth to be fishing but need to scour a lot of water, and when you have no idea of what color lure to use and need to wash many different patterns.

Another way to accomplish the same thing is to use a Roemer Liberator, which is a relatively new and virtually unknown type of slider. A short leader with a lure trailing it is attached to the Liberator via a snap swivel. The Liberator is set at any level on the fishing line prior to dropping the downrigger weight completely down. When a

How many downriggers you use and where you place them depend on the size and type of your boat, the number of people fishing, and your budget. Shown are small (bottom right), medium (bottom left), and big (top left and right) boat downrigger placements. Included are manual and electric models; long and short booms; fixed, swivel, and clamp-on base mounts; and two types of trolling boards. Note mounting locations and rod holder arrangements.

fish strikes the lure attached to this device, it trips the release located below at the level of the weight. The Liberator locks onto the main fishing line but releases to drop to the end of the line. This device allows more precise location of a cheater lure, increases lure separation abilities, and can be used to fish several lures off one main fishing line. It is primarily meant for use with medium to heavy lines.

I've gotten double trout and salmon hookups, on the slider lure as well as on the main lure, when using slider rigs. This is interesting from both a fish-playing and netting standpoint, especially when the fish are of decent size. Netting can be troublesome because the fish caught on a slider rig will be several feet behind the other fish. Once you net the lead fish, it's hard to get the trailing one, so it's best to get the trailing one first, except this isn't always possible. Such problems aren't encountered all that often in fishing, so it's something we'll all readily endure.

Incidentally, when using any type of slider arrangement, be careful that you do not exceed the number of lures, hooks, or hook points legally allowed per rod or per angler in the waters where you are fishing. Somewhere in each state or provincial fishing regulations, these numbers are specified. Additionally, be aware of the number of rods allowed per angler. In Canada only one rod is allowed per angler; in most states each angler can troll with two rods. American Great Lakes charter boat captains, many of whom fish out of 25- to 35-foot boats capable of holding five anglers plus captain and mate, technically can fish two rods per person. Big boat trollers have as many as six downriggers. Lines are stacked on several of them to get eight or nine rods deep, plus they'll fish one or two rods on diving planers and/or flat lines. It takes a good crew and good boat handler to work all this without major problems. I'm not going to detail big boat rigging setups; however, a few words about strategic downrigger placement for all boats are in order.

Downriggers are primarily located on and across the transom or near the transom on the gunwales. Transom-mounted downriggers face directly out the stern. The booms should be long enough to clear any trim tabs or swim platform that might be on the transom, and to enable the cable to clear an engine propeller (especially for an auxiliary motor) when seas are rough or when tight turns are made. In a four downrigger setup, there could be one unit on either corner perpendicular to the gunwales, and one on either side of the motor facing aft. This would give a good horizontal spread to the weights and trolling lines. In a six downrigger setup, there would be a unit on each gunwale a few feet ahead of the stern and perpendicular to the gunwale, and four properly spaced downriggers on the transom (including two on the corners), all of which face aft. Long booms would be used on the gunwale riggers to aid horizontal spacing. Small boats can locate downriggers wherever it is most convenient, especially if only one or two riggers are used and it is easy to get to them. It is still advisable, however, to place them as close to the stern as possible. If downriggers are mounted amidship and used for shallow fishing, there is a possibility that the trailing fishing line could be cut by the engine propeller on tight turns; so take this into account when considering what length of boom arm to buy and where to mount the downrigger.

Whether you use pedestal mounts, swivel bases, trolling boards, or the like depends on the interior arrangement of your boat, the amount of freeboard it has, your budget, and your personal taste. On small boats, and on some midsize and larger vessels as well, a trolling board is a great way to go. With small boats it offers versatility, portability, and removability for other types of fishing, and I describe a system for this later in the book. Swivel bases are really handy for gunwale and long-boom models, especially because you have to turn the boom in for docking and trailering as well as for setting lines sometimes. Some downriggers can be mounted in flush-mount rod holders and on rails, but if you are considering these I urge you to look at such options very carefully and with reservation. Some rails and flush-mount/through-the-gunwale rod holders simply don't have the strength to support a downrigger. You could be inviting trouble when trolling in big seas, when using the heaviest weights, or when hanging a weight on bottom.

With all but the shortest-armed downriggers, you'll find it handy to have some means of bringing downrigger cable, weight, and release close to the boat to set fishing line into the release. In earlier days, I used a good-quality snap attached to a rope, which in turn was tethered to a cleat to pull a cable to me. The snap slid down the cable as I pulled on it, which was prone to damaging the cable in time, plus I had to pull the weight into the boat. A better system came along in the form of the Cannon Retro-Ease Weight Retriever. It features a nylon pulley that doesn't abrade the cable and is attached to a lanyard. The lanyard runs through a snugging receptacle, so the line is held fast in the snugger and the weight can be dangled over the water while rigging is accomplished. When you lift up on the lanyard to free it from the snugger, the pulley rolls up the cable as the weight slides outward and into the water. The snugging receptacle can be mounted on the boat, on the downrigger pedestal, or on the downrigger frame, and the entire product can be used with any brand of downrigger.

As I've mentioned, the way in which you mount downriggers and the number used determine what horizontal spread can be achieved with lures presented on downriggers. If you troll only with two downriggers, you needn't be too concerned with rigging systems, other than to realize that you may want to keep the weights at different levels, use stackers or sliders to maximize your opportunities per line or per downrigger, vary drop-back lengths, and so forth. The more riggers you employ, however, the more you should be concerned with systems or patterns of operation, not only to cover the water well horizontally and vertically but also to facilitate fish-landing, to minimize line crossing and lure tangling, and to appeal more to some species of fish.

Boaters with four to six downriggers who fish large open waters can employ some variation of V patterns in terms of weight depth and lure drop-back length to avoid inconsistent, possibly confusing, and perhaps troublesome lure and line placement. Regarding depth, a V-down pattern would have the innermost weights set deepest, the weights to either side of them set shallower, and the outside weights set shallowest. A V-up pattern is just the reverse. An equal-depth pattern would see the weights all set at the same level. Regarding line-to-lure setback from the weight, a V-in pattern would see the innermost lures closest to the weight, the lures to either side of them farther back, and the outside lures farthest back. A V-out pattern is just the reverse. An equal-length setback would see all lures set at the same distance behind the downrigger weight.

Why would you want to adopt some type of pattern? It's like a plan. You always know relatively where your weights and lures are. The more rigs you troll, the harder it is to keep track of things. When a good fish strikes and lines are cleared, it is easy in the confusion to lose sight of what weight the successful lure was on, how deep that weight was, and how far the lure was set behind the release. When you know these matters, you can rerig immediately in a similar fashion. To fish with downriggers at discombobulated depths and setback lengths, and then to change them as you are trolling, invites hap-

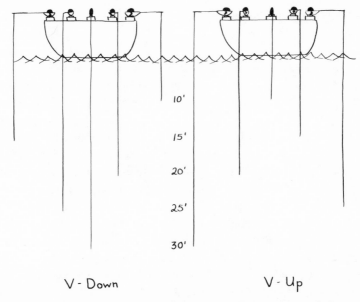

V - Down   V - Up

When using many downriggers, weights can be set systematically, with deepest weights in the middle (**V**-down) or on the outside (**V**-up).

hazardness to creep into your trolling style. That's not to say that you won't catch fish with staggered depths and setbacks, but you won't have the control over the situation that you could have, and you may spend unnecessary time undoing problems created by inefficient operation.

Because outside lures speed up and inside lures slow down on a turn — meaning that outside lures keep swimming high while inside lures rise or fall — and because the effects of this vary with the type of lure used — floating plugs rise while spoons and sinking plugs descend — it is important to do what you can to minimize the possibility of lines crossing over one another and tangling. Some fishermen troll for hours without checking their lures, only to find that they have been dragged in a tangle for who knows how much wasted time. The problems were the way in which they were set and how turns affected their movement. This not only happens when downriggers are used but when flat lines are trolled as well. To avoid tangling lines, you can employ two solutions: never turn or make only very slow and wide turns. Unfortunately both are impractical and such manipulation often fails to stimulate fish.

A V-down depth system is preferred by many fishermen who are aware of this rigging technique (a lot of anglers aren't). Deepest lines are directly below the boat. Shallower lines are more out of the boat's direct path of travel with this system, perhaps where fish that are spooked by boat passage or deeply set downriggers may have moved. The V-up, inverted V, system might be the better approach when you are after fish that are not spooked by the boat but are attracted to its noise or to the prop wash. Coho and Atlantic salmon are two such fish. An equal-depth presentation may be useful when fish are being caught only at a specific level, such as when they occupy a narrow-band thermocline and when you are not trying to locate fish by scouring all depth levels.

Regarding setback lengths, there is seldom much reason to use a V-out system. The V-in pattern is not only favored for the different downrigger depth settings, but also for flat-lining and planer board trolling, both of which are detailed in the following chapter. When fish are falling regularly to lures trolled at a fairly specific midrange distance behind downrigger weights (especially when depths are nearly the same), there is little reason to stagger them much, so equal-length setbacks can be used. With the V-in system, the inner lures will run under the outer ones when turns are made, and fish that are located on sonar directly below the boat may move up and out toward the lures set farther back. When used in combination with either the V-down or V-up depth settings, this setback system helps avoid line tangling when a fish strikes and releases deep lines from the release.

Naturally, you have to experiment with these patterns and see what's best for your type of fishing and boat. Where you fish only one or two downriggers, this is all academic, of course. Such patterns have their greatest use when you are trout and salmon fishing in mid- to large-sized boats, and the most common pattern is a V-down/V-in combination. Keep in mind that depth and setback distances are relative. A V-down system could see the shallowest depth trolled as 12 feet, the intermediate depth as 18, and the greatest depth as 24, which are not really significant variations, or it could see the same progression as 20, 40, and 60 feet. The same is true for setbacks. There are no limitations.

To close out this chapter, let's categorically and briefly focus on keys to successful downrigger use and some phenomena pertinent to their use.

Viewed from overhead, these lines are fished deep behind downrigger weights, with the shortest setback being in the middle and the longest on the outside. This system is preferred by many trollers.

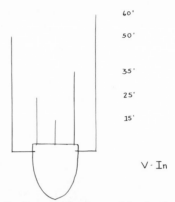

Cable kinking. The death knell for weights is cable kinking. Crimps, kinks, and frayed cable strands occur when cable pops off the spool or the pulley. Cut off defective areas and rerig at the first opportunity, even if you have to take a downrigger out of service for a few minutes while trolling. Keep repair items onboard.

Clutch. Be diligent about checking the clutch setting, especially if you will be trolling weights close to the bottom, when you are fishing in natural reservoirs, or when you are fishing where there are many bottom impediments or sharply changing bottom contours.

Swayback. Cable swayback — the tendency of downrigger cable to angle toward the stern of the boat — becomes more pronounced as you increase boat speed, encounter underwater current, or fish in fast-flowing rivers. Astute big lake trollers can tell when they've encountered underwater currents by noticing the increased angle of their cable as it enters the water. This swayback means that the weight is not running directly below the boat or at the level indicated by the depth counter. If it is important to know at what specific depth you are fishing (it usually is) by getting your lure down to a level where your sonar shows fish, you must make allowance for this. A chart that avoids guesstimating depth is made by Osprey and is detailed in chapter 5 as an accessory to trolling. The point is that you realize there are times when line counter indicated depth is not true depth.

Depth of diving lures. As with the swayback phenomenon, you must account for the depth achieved by diving plugs when you troll them behind a downrigger weight. If, for example, you want your lure

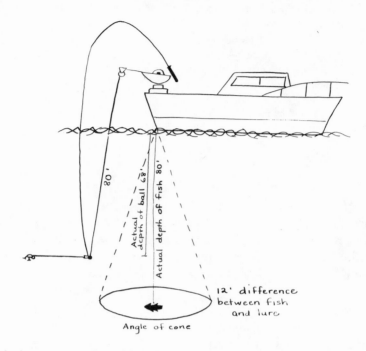

80'

Actual depth of ball 68'

Actual depth of fish 80'

12' difference between fish and lure

Angle of cone

If the boat is moving fast, if there is a lot of current, or if you are fishing very deep, a downrigger weight will not be as deep as the line counter reads because the weight and cable sway backward. As shown here, you might spot fish on your sonar under the boat at 80 feet deep and lower your weight until 80 feet of cable are out, but because of swayback you will not be at the 80-foot level. Thus, you have to let out more cable to account for this if your lure is running at the same level as the weight.

to run at 20 feet and you set a diving plug out to the 20-foot level as indicated on the line counter attached to your downrigger, that lure will be below the fish and will probably not be successful. If that diving plug runs 5 to 6 feet deep at the distance you have set it behind the downrigger weight, then you must set the weight down until the line counter reads 13 or 14 feet, no more.

Devices on the cable. It is common for many anglers to attach temperature and speed sensing probes to downrigger cables. These are usually part of lightweight torpedo-shaped tubes set just above the weight. Such devices can offer more drag resistance and increase cable swayback, a factor you should be aware of. Using heavy 12-pound weights can help minimize this. Such objects also make graph paper readouts a little confusing at times because, in concert with the weight directly below it, they help make a formidable streak across the paper that can obliterate fish or bait marks that may be at the same level.

Using sonar to watch your weights. Many downrigger fishermen like to use a wide cone angle transducer (32 to 50 degrees) to see their weights on their graph paper, video, or liquid crystal display (LCD) machines. This can be very valuable, but it can also give false impressions. The angle of viewing is very large at deeper levels, and sometimes the fish you see with a wide-angle transducer may not be directly below your boat; nonetheless, it allows you to see more of what is around you. Because so much of trolling has to do with locating fish and offering your lures at the levels at which those fish are situated, it makes sense to be using such equipment.

Working the fish you see on sonar. My Lake Ontario charter boat fishing friend, Bill Kelley, is a master at this. When fishing is slow and he marks a decent-size fish on his graph recorder, he runs to the downrigger that is nearest in depth to the level at which he saw the fish and lowers or raises the weight so it is just above the level of that fish. When he's especially hungry to catch a fish, Kelley waits a few moments for the lure to pass the fish, then jerks the rod out of its holder and pops the fishing line out of the release. He lets it flutter for a few seconds, then jigs it a time or two. If nothing happens, he retrieves the lure and resets it out. But he often (I'm not exaggerating) catches fish in some stage of this operation. That's working a fish!

Jigging a downrigger weight. Well, it's actually oscillating the weight, or simply raising and lowering it periodically. That's sort of what Kelley does, only he's working for fish that he's spotted on sonar. In downrigging you often (in fact, usually) catch fish that have not been spotted on sonar. In trolling, fish frequently follow a lure for considerable distances before striking or swimming away. One of the reasons why making turns and maneuvering in irregularly shaped patterns is a good tactic for trollers is because it imparts varying actions to lures. Changes in behavior can precipitate a strike; therefore, it's to your advantage to do whatever you can to make your offerings more attractive. Raising or lowering your weights may encourage strikes, just as pumping a rod with a spoon or fly on it is a good trick for flat-line fishing. Raising or lowering a downrigger weight periodically isn't

Lake Ontario captain Bill Kelley often catches deep-water fish that are well beneath his downrigger weights by lowering a weight and lure to fish that he marks on sonar.

much fun, however, but there is one downrigger that will automatically do this. I have one and have been using it very satisfactorily. Many other anglers, including charter boat captains, have gravitated toward this product.

Now almost three years old, the microcomputerized LCD-equipped Cannon Digi-Troll memorizes depth settings and automatically oscillates a trolling weight. As of this writing, the Digi-Troll is the only downrigger of its kind to do both these things. I know of no one using this product who doesn't think these features are the neatest trolling aids since the creation of fish hooks. In my experience, this product makes trolling with downriggers simpler and more functional.

The computerized built-in memory is convenient and produces more fishing time. When you touch the appropriate button, the Digi-Troll automatically lowers the downrigger weight to a preselected depth and stops it there. If you're fishing in a big boat with several of these downriggers, the memory feature saves fishing time by allowing you to tend other lines while the weight is being lowered. Moreover, it shows the depth to return to if you had a strike and pulled the weight up and can be overridden at anytime.

The oscillating feature is a functional fish-catching tool that influences lure depth and action. The downrigger can be programmed to cycle at various times from 5 to 90 seconds. In the cycle mode,

The Cannon Digi-Troll automatically oscillates a downrigger weight at programmed intervals.

the weight is raised then lowered automatically at the interval specified. Like me, most fishermen are running it at the shorter intervals.

This cycling raises and lowers the lure and speeds it up, in effect giving a trolled lure a dimension that can be achieved only by handholding the rod and jerking it, or by changing boat speed constantly. This downrigger in the cycling mode can help fishermen who are fishing for two species that require an incompatible lure speed. For example, you could run a slider rig and fish on the bottom for lake trout with the lower lure, as well as fish off the bottom near the thermocline for salmon with the slider. Lakers like a slow trolling speed that is not usually conducive to catching salmon. As the weight goes up and down when you are trolling slow and cycling the weights, both lures speed up by 1 ¼ miles per hour, and the slider spends at least one-fourth of its trolling time at a speed more preferable to salmon. If you assume that the boat is trolling at 1 ½ mph for lake trout, add 1 ¼ mph for cycling and you're up to salmon speed.

Watch the rod tips. If you make a habit of scanning your downrigger rods and watching for signs of behavior, you'll often see the rod straighten the moment a fish strikes and pulls the line out of the release. This means that you can get to the rod faster to set the hook and play the fish. You'll also see if a fish hits the lure but doesn't get hooked by noting how the rod suddenly dips without springing up. If the rod tip surges, it may be an indication that there is a small fish (bait fish or game fish) on it even though the release hasn't tripped.

One drawback to downrigger trolling is that you don't experience the thrill of the strike and the usual hook-setting response because you don't hold the rod in your hand. Another disadvantage is that if your lure is not working correctly, you seldom have any way of knowing it although the downrigger cable usually intercepts debris and keeps it from getting on your lure. Watching your rods may not overcome these points, but it can give you some clues as to what is going on.

Check your lure before setting it out. I discuss lures and lure usage in detail in another chapter, but because you lose touch with how your lures are working once you lower them on a downrigger weight, it's important to put them in the water and watch them swim before you set them out and before you attach the line to the downrigger release. Also, don't cast a lure out because it may become fouled. Put it in the water next to the boat and strip out the correct amount of line so you know it is working right. When there is a lot of surface debris, be careful that the lure doesn't snag debris before it gets lowered with the weight.

To clear or not to clear? You've got a whole bunch of lines set and you hook a fish. Do you keep moving? Do you pull in all lines and raise all weights? Many big boat trollers, particularly charter boat captains who fish a lot of lines, do not stop. They may slow down but they don't really want to rerig everything, so they try to maneuver the boat just right to land the fish without crossing lines, messing up

By bringing other lines in, swiveling downriggers so they are out of the way, and clearing rods out of holders, you can net big, active fish much easier.

their program, and having to pull it all in and reset. Small boaters with a few lines out don't have that problem and can usually pull in without too much trouble. I don't like to keep moving, especially for good-size fish. On a big boat, I try to determine how large the fish is. We may clear everything, or we may just clear one side of the boat and work the fish to that side for netting. This partially depends on the boat-handler's skills, the angler's fish-playing abilities, the size of the fish, and the amount of gear in use. With big fish, it's usually best to clear everything, put the boat in neutral, and maneuver the boat as necessary to maintain a desirable position on the fish.

A great trick when you're about to change lures. Do what Bill Kelley does when he's working a fish. Pop the line out of the release and let the trailing lure flutter. If it's a spoon, wait till the spoon rises to the surface and then retrieve it. If it's a plug, wait 10 seconds or so for it to swim up a bit, pump it once or twice, then bring it in. Many fish follow lures for a long distance. You'll be surprised just how many fish you can troll up with this technique, simply because the lure acted differently and a fish happened to be there to pounce on it.

Keep the boat straight. When setting lines out, it helps if you keep the boat straight, even if you're temporarily headed in a direction you don't want to go. A straight course while rigging minimizes line crossing and tangles.

Try downriggers in shallow water. Remember that downriggers are for controlled depth fishing, not exclusively for deep-water probing. You can set a weight 1 foot below the surface and get a diving plug down to a certain level, or you can set a spoon to run just under the surface and so on. You can be versatile enough to cover a broad range of trolling situations, including river fishing, drifting, and live-bait fishing.

Downriggers are made by about a dozen manufacturers. I've used most, but not all of them, and have much more experience with some than with others, so I'm reluctant to say that some are good and some no good. I have used Penn's fathom-master manuals for years without problems and consider them to be exceptionally good products. Penn's new electric is good, and notable for the high speed at which it raises and lowers the weight. Cannon's manuals are also excellent and their electrics, particularly the Digi-Troll discussed earlier, has set the industry standard in my opinion. Riviera, which was one of the pioneers in this field, has had problems with service and delivery for years and has lagged far behind in improvements and new modern product developments, so this company is not held in high esteem by many experienced trollers any longer. Big Jons, which I've used fairly often, are of good overall quality, though I do not like their swing-up booms. I've experienced no problems with the Walker downriggers that I've used on other people's boats.

When you shop, look at as many different downriggers as you can and compare carefully. Become familiar with the differences because these products are only going to become a more integral part of the trolling scene and will be increasingly functional and sophisticated as technology marches on.

2

FLAT LINES & SIDEPLANERS

For many people, trolling is not so much a means of making below-surface presentations with the aid of downriggers, weights, or some type of diving device as it is a relatively shallow water, ground-covering, "let the engine do the work" type of fishing.

The simplest trolling of any kind is to run a flat line. Flat lines are sometimes referred to as high lines, usually when trolled in conjunction with some type of deep-diving line. Flat lines are set straight out behind the boat; there are no heavy ball sinkers, downrigger weights, diving planers, or other devices to influence the depth attainment of the lure. Anyone with a rod, reel, line, and lure can run a flat line, and it is viewed as being a rather simple and easy thing to do. Most people who do some trolling in the course of their fishing run a flat line — but for hours on end without any regard to technique. To them, this is the epitome of what "trolling" is.

The keys to flat-line trolling productivity are the length of line you fish and how you manipulate your boat to position your lures or bait. The clearer the water, the shallower the fish, the spookier the fish, and the more local boat activity there is, the longer the line you need. Long lines are particularly important in inland trout and salmon fishing, where it is not uncommon to troll lures 200 to 300 feet behind the boat. If you're used to casting 50 or 60 feet to catch fish, such trolling distances seem outlandish. They're not.

Trolling even a long line straightforward for seemingly endless periods is boring, unimaginative, and unproductive. You have to alter the lure's path of travel regularly by turning, by steering in an S-shaped pattern, by driving in other irregular ways, or by increasing or decreasing the speed of the boat. This enhances your presentation by altering the speed and action of the lure and making it appear less mechanical and more susceptible to capture.

As you are making a flat-line trolling presentation, you have to consider where the fish are and how to get your lures close without alarming them. Fish that are in shallow water near shore or that are close to the surface in open water characteristically move out of the boat's path of travel because they are especially wary, perhaps even nervous. With few exceptions, you can't motor through the shallows and expect fish to stay around and/or to be exceedingly receptive to the offering you trail behind. This is one reason why you seldom see fish on a depth finder or graph recorder in less than 15 feet of water. Fish, particularly schools, swim off to one side of the boat as it approaches and are well outside the cone angle of the sonar device's transducer.

The fish may continue swimming away, they may stay where they are once they have moved, or they may return to their original location after the boat has passed. If your lure is trailing directly behind a

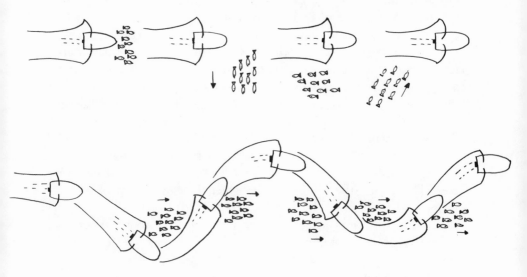

By using a very long line when flat-lining, you may intercept fish that have moved from the motor noise and then returned to position after the boat has passed (top). It may be more productive, however, to vary your course by making S curves, which help your lures come into contact with fish that they might have missed otherwise (bottom).

straight-moving boat, fish in the first two instances may never see your lure. If your line is too short, fish in the third instance may also not see it if they are slow to return to their position, or they may see it but associate it with the recently passed boat. This helps illustrate why a lure should be fished on a long line for some types of fish and how proper boat manipulation can bring lures into the range of fish that may not have been in the boat's path or that may have moved out of it.

This is particularly true concerning shallow fish. Although you might drift, row, use an electric motor, or cast for such fish, there are times when you must, or want to, cover a lot of territory. Perhaps the fish are well scattered. Perhaps the particular species you seek is nomadic. Perhaps you can make a better lure or bait presentation for a longer period of time and have a wider range of offerings if you troll.

There are a lot of shallow fish that can be caught by trolling, particularly in the spring. Line placement, lure presentation, and boat control are important matters in all trolling, but they are absolutely critical for shallow flat-line trolling success. There are some shallow water trolling strategies that work anywhere and for any species of fish for which flat-lining is practical or necessary.

The true test of shallow flat-line trolling is to make such presentations in nonopen-water areas. Near shore, around reefs or shoals or islands, along grass lines and weed edges, and so forth are hard places to reach effectively due to limited maneuverability, yet you may not have success if you don't reach them. Consider, for example, a lakeshore that drops off fairly sharply and has boulders or stumps submerged just under the surface. If you bring your boat too close to shore, your motor may hit these structures. You could try using an electric motor and steering around these objects, but this doesn't always work, and if the wind or current isn't favorable you would go nowhere. The only way to deal with this problem when flat-line trolling is to sweep in and out from shore and plan strategically advantageous approaches to such areas as points, sandbars, islands, shoals, channels, and the like. You may have to troll by many of these more than once and from different directions to cover the location effectively.

Flat-line trolling is not just for shallow water fishing, however. This information applies equally to trolling deep-diving plugs and, as far as boat manipulation to cover specific places and areas, to trolling

This Lake Ontario steelhead fell to a plug that was trolled on the surface off an outrigger that had a 180-foot-long setback.

of all types. Flat-lining can be accomplished with plugs that dive deep. I regularly flat-line large plugs for musky and northern Canada lake trout fishing, as well as smaller plugs on light line for trout, salmon, bass, and walleye. When fishing deeper water, however, you must know how deep your lures dive with various lengths and strengths of line, and you must pay a little more attention to the depth beneath you, and the lures behind you, while trolling.

There are devices that aid the technique of flat-lining substantially and make your presentations much more versatile. These are sideplaner boards. They are plastic or wooden surface-running planers that evolved on the Great Lakes for trout and salmon trolling. Sideplaner boards work something like a downrigger on the surface. A nonfishing line or cable tethers the planer (there are port and starboard models) to the boat and allows it to run at varied distances off to the side of the boat. One or more fishing lines are attached to the planer or tow line via release clips; you are free to fight a fish unencumbered when it strikes your lure and frees the fishing line from the release. Another type of planer, which is smaller, attaches directly to your fishing line and pops free when a fish strikes. This sideplaner has a fishing advantage in calm water, but must be retrieved after a fish is caught and, in my experience, makes hooking fish a little more difficult.

Sideplaners can be used in trolling for all kinds of fish. I have caught trout, salmon, pike, walleye, pickerel, bass, shad, and even a bullhead and a carp while using them. They can be effective for stripers, muskies, and saltwater fish. Sideplaners vastly increase your presentation capabilities because they allow your lures to pass near fish that may have been spooked by the passage of your boat (or may be spooked if you ran your boat near them) or that are in areas where you can't or don't want to take your boat.

How far you set the sideplaners out depends on how close you want your boat to get to shore, how far apart you want to spread your lures, how much room you have to fish, and how much boat traffic there is in the area. I usually run mine 80 to 100 feet out when boat traffic is moderate. They can be run out as much as 200 feet if you have a high anchor point in your boat for the planer line. Some fishermen use a 6- to 8-foot pole.

To use sideplaners, you must have a method of tethering them to your boat and retrieving them. You can use manual downriggers for that, but your range is limited because their arms are low to the water. And the wire downrigger cable poses problems that you don't have with Dacron tow line. When I first started using sideplaner boards, I hooked them up to my manual downriggers. It was easy to send the planer out simply by releasing the downrigger clutch. You are effectively limited to about 75 or 80' feet of tow line, however, because too much of the heavy cable is close to the water and will drag and flop into it, causing the releases to take extra punishment and possibly

Shown in the background are a double-runner Prince sideplaner board, single-runner Wille sideplaner board, and Prince dual retriever for planer boards. In the foreground is a Yellowbird planer (left) and a Rover planer (right), both of which are set on the fishing line but can be rigged to snap free of it when a fish strikes.

become fouled. Moreover, if you have to stop for any reason, you run the risk of having the line kink and twist, which so often happens to wire that is normally spooled and then freed of tension. I fished with a friend who was towing sideplaner boards off an electric downrigger with wire cable. When we stopped, the wire ballooned off the electric downrigger, and we had such a terrible mess to undo that we had to cut and reconnect the cable so as not to lose too much fishing time. I mention these points to show that using wire-cabled downriggers to tow planer boards is possible, but there are some limitations and problems inherent in them.

If you choose to remove the wire cable from your downriggers (especially if you have an old downrigger or two that are not regularly used), then you can use them fairly effectively for planer board trolling at short to medium distances from the boat. Downriggers with arms that swivel upward are especially conducive to this. I have a friend who took two old Big Jon manual downriggers, replaced the cable with Dacron, and locked the downrigger arms in the up position for planer board use. He is able to convert these units to downrigging if need be, so in a sense he gets double duty out of them. Most downrigger arms are permanently fixed in a near horizontal position, however, and are not usable in this way.

Several companies are making sideplaner retrievers, with two reels mounted on a single stand pole or with a single reel to be attached to the gunwale of a boat. I prefer a model that has a clutch, is sturdy, and well constructed. You don't want to have a retrieval reel that wobbles off-center, a pole that bends too easily, or a base that doesn't offer plenty of support.

You can fashion your own retrieval system with an old high-capacity levelwind reel or other reellike storage mechanism, spooled with 150- to 200-pound-test monofilament or Dacron and attached to a stand pole with a swiveling pulley at the top. I tried this a few years ago on a small boat and used 50-pound-test monofilament line to see if it would hold up. It did, probably because the pulling force of the sideplaner board didn't approach the breaking strength of the line. However, I'm convinced that heavier line is better from an abrasion-resistance standpoint and in the event of hanging the board up on some object. Most planer board tow line is made of braided Dacron in a highly visible green color. I think Dacron is used because of its very low stretch and comparably low diameter. I suspect that a very strong monofilament would do as well. Even though monofilament has the potential for stretching, the pulling force of the boards is not enough to make this happen. One drawback to Dacron tow line is that you occasionally get a fish hook stuck in the braids and have a hard time getting it out without cutting or slicing a strand; this would not happen with monofilament. The Dacron might last longer than the monofilament, however, and some releases may not slide down the line as easily on monofilament as on Dacron.

Ideally the sideplaner retriever or stand pole should be mounted as far forward in your boat as possible to get a high line angle to the board and to keep the boards relatively abreast, instead of well behind, the boat. On small boats, mount the poles as close to the bow as you can. On large boats, such as those with cuddy cabins that don't allow you to get up to the bow quickly, it's best to mount sideplaner retrievers on or near the gunwale, amidship, or flush to the cabin molding. Some big boaters mount a stand pole up on the bow, despite the difficulty of getting to it. They have plenty of releases so they don't often have to pull the boards in, and they use a loose tether (wrap a line around a cleat, connect a snap to the line, and snap it onto the tow line) to reach the tow line in order to clip a new release and line onto it.

Sideplaners exert a lot of pull on your boat. They act much like a rudder, especially for small, lightweight boats. When using one double-runner board in a small boat, you constantly fight the steering wheel and try to compensate to steer a straight course. The pull of the board turns the boat inward toward the board. If you want to fish off only one board (perhaps you're alone or want to get lures close to only one side, near shore, for example), it may be necessary to put the companion board out on the other side of the boat, but not use it, in order to offset the effect of the board being fished. With big boats, the effect of using just one sideplaner isn't much.

Some planers, incidentally, are available in double-runner models, that is, two boards spaced about 10 or 12 inches apart but bolted together to run as one unit. Double runners exert that much more pull and are principally for use in rough water with big waves. They run truer than single-runner models, however. Although I first started using singles, I haven't gone back to singles in several years because of the tracking and rough-water advantages of double-runner boards.

This starboard double-runner sideplaner is set about 50 feet away from the boat. The stand pole and retriever in the foreground are connected to the sideplaner, but the fishing line attached to it is not visible.

There will be times when you don't want to run planer boards because of the water conditions. In extremely rough water with high waves, planers do a lot of bouncing, which can knock the line out of the release if the tension isn't set tightly enough, or they conceivably can flip the planer over, which could cause a big problem. Planers in extremely rough waters can also lead to release fouling, particularly by having the release flop over behind the tow line. When that happens, you can't pop the line out of the release properly, especially if light line is being used.

Under windy conditions, sideplaners don't run as far off to the side of the boat as you might like, and releases may be hard to run down the tow line. When this happens, jiggle the fishing line or the tow line to bounce the release along, or turn the boat a bit so that the angle of pull of the trailing line forces the release down to the proper spot. Strong wind also causes a tactical boat-maneuvering problem when a good-size fish is hooked. If you catch a fish while heading downwind, you can, if you like, leave the motor in neutral and just play the fish in. When heading upwind, however, you cannot stop the boat because of the possibility of tangling lines, tow ropes, and the like. If the fish is really big or fights particularly well (especially when you are running from side to side), or if you are using very light line, you should play it while a companion retrieves the other lines and the boards and frees the boat for maneuvering and landing. If it's a small fish, you may be able to keep the boat headed into the wind, to move slowly with several stop-and-go actions executed by a partner, and to keep the other tackle out. If you're alone, you have to manage as best you can.

You can run lures any length behind a sideplaner that seems feasible. Because the lures are trolled well off to the side of the boat, and behind a relatively unobtrusive planer, they often don't have to be run as far back as when a flat line is used. You still need a lot of line on your reel, however, because your fishing line extends first to the release clip then back to the lure.

With sideplaners, a host of fishing combinations are possible. When fishing near-shore areas, you can run two or three strategically spaced lines off the shore sideplaner. On the open-water side of the boat, you have the option of running a surface or diving lure on a long flat line, running a lure deep via the downrigger, or running one

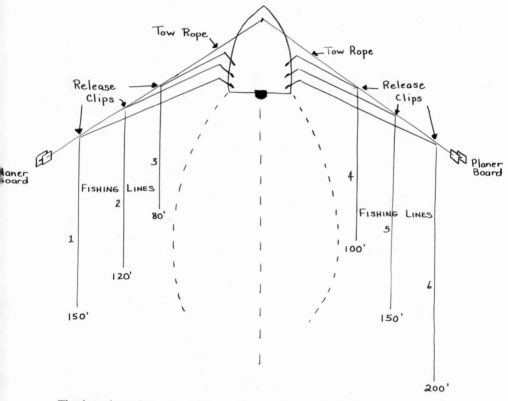

This hypothetical situation illustrates how six lines might be fished off two sideplaner boards. The inner lines are under the outer lines when rigged, so there is no need to move rods around when a fish is caught. The dotted lines represent the general fish-playing area. Note the V-in line setback pattern and the staggered setback lengths.

or more lures off the other sideplaner. Moreover, the amount of territory that can be covered is vastly increased. If you run two sideplaners, each 60 feet to either side of the boat, and have two fishermen in the boat, you might run four lines over a 40-yard span of water. If the bottom drops off sharply near shore, as it does in many inland lakes, you could be working over a few feet of water on the near-shore side of the boat and over 40 feet on the opposite side, presenting your lures to fish that would not ordinarily see them and would not be frightened by the passage of your boat. This example assumes that you can fish two lines per fishermen; as noted earlier, in some states only one line per angler is allowed.

Trolling strategies and boat manipulation techniques when using sideplaner boards are much like those described earlier for flat-lining. When you turn, however, the outside planer board increases its speed and the inside one slows or stalls. Because the fishing lines are well separated, there is less chance of entanglement when you turn, particularly if all lines are nearly the same distance behind the boat or if the inside planer board lines are not as far back as the outside lines.

When you attempt to make a sharp turn, however, you must be careful not to turn so sharply that the inside board lies completely dead in the water and the lures don't move. If you're in shallow water and using a sinking plug or a spoon, the motionless lure can settle to the bottom and get hung up. The release on the tow line can also get tangled when the board picks up speed. Furthermore, many fish strike a lure on a turn. If your lure is floating upward or fluttering down and a fish strikes it, there will be no tension on the fishing line or tow rope line. The release cannot be snapped or the hook set; therefore, the potential for losing a fish exists under this condition. If you must make a sharp turn, do so only as sharply as necessary to keep the board moving slightly forward, which keeps tension on the line.

Boat manipulation and turning when traffic is heavy is a little more complicated than usual when sideplaner boards are being fished. That's why many big boaters elect to run flat lines off outriggers and small boaters shorten the distance that they run boards away from the boat. If you haven't run your sideplaner into a collision with someone else's sideplaner, you've missed one of trolling's most embarrassing, aggravating, and mayhem-causing experiences. If a collision seems imminent, the worst thing you can do is turn the boat away because that causes the outside planer to speed up and arc outward a bit, making a collision all the more probable. You might turn inward, but then you'll have to sit still till the other boat passes. The best tactic is to reel the board toward your boat as quickly as you can.

Lines fished off sideplaner boards don't have to be run shallow, incidentally, and needn't feature just shallow-running plugs or spoons. You can use whatever lures are appropriate for the angling conditions; moreover, by adjusting the tension of the line release, you can troll a hard-pulling deep-diving plug or a line with weights on it. The keys to success, however, are knowing how deep those lures run at the length of line you have them set behind the planer board tow line and having the tension on the release set properly. The tension must be taut enough to withstand the force of hard-pulling diving plugs or the weight being trolled, so the line doesn't pull out of the release without being struck by a fish. Yet the line mustn't be so taut that it is hard to pull out on a strike or when freed by the fisherman.

There are a number of releases that are suitable for sideplaner board trolling, and they work under much the same principle as releases described for downriggers in the previous chapter, except that their position on the tow line is not fixed and is determined by the amount of fishing line you let off your reel. I have primarily used the spring-set Wille sideplaner releases with good results, although I recently have started fishing an Offshore spring-pad release connected to a wide snap and a Clipper release also. In addition to having reliable adjustable tension, releases used with sideplaner boards should clip onto the tow line and slide down it readily.

Three types of sideplaner board releases, clockwise from the top, include: a Halvorsen, a Clipper, and two Willes.

When you're fishing several lines shallow, you can experiment with their distance from the boat and with the distance the lures are set behind the tow line. Sometimes when I'm running two or three lines off one sideplaner and they are of a similar type (all minnow-imitation floating/diving plugs, for example), I may run them at approximately the same distance behind the tow rope to imitate a small school of bait fish. But I usually don't put short lines on the outside. If a fish were to strike a short outside line, there's a chance that it would cross over one or more of the longer inside lines after the hookup. I take this into account when setting lines out and try to arrange them so that a fish caught on the outside line will drop back clear of the inside lines, then be played up the unfished center alley. Perhaps it's coincidence, but most of my fish fall to the outside line.

One of the advantages to sideplaner board fishing is that if you have multiple lines on one side and the outermost one pops, you can slide the inner lines out, then put the released line back out as the inside line. This is all accomplished without having to pull fishing lines and the planer in. If you want to replace one lure without bringing the board and other lures in, you can pick up your fishing rod, reel up the slack, pop the fishing line out of the release, reel in the lure to be changed, reposition the other lines and releases on the tow rope, and set the new lure out in the inside position.

The drawbacks to using sideplaners are that (1) they require a little more equipment and cash outlay (though some trollers make their own planer boards) than flat-lining, (2) it takes some practice to get used to them, (3) it can be tough to work everything if you're alone in the boat, and (4) they pose logistical problems at times. Although they are interesting and productive to use, it's work, and the most efficient sideplaner board fishing is had when two or three people are in a boat and all are capable of setting lines and maneuvering the boat effectively as a team.

Those who find sideplaner boards too much trouble to use simply run flat lines. But when it is necessary to get your lures away from the boat; when you want to have the ability to cover a spread of territory with each passage of your boat; or when you troll some hard-to-reach places, close to a jetty or breakwall, for example, sideplaner boards will put your trolling lures over a lot of fish that you couldn't otherwise reach.

3

SPEED

A few years ago in mid-September, en route home after several days of fishing on Lake Ontario near Rochester, I stopped in Oswego, New York, at 7 AM to rendezvous with the father of a friend. This man had an old inboard runabout that he'd trailered hundreds of miles for his first try at salmon. I had promised to join him for a few hours to show him how to use his new downriggers and how to troll for salmon.

We launched his boat, rigged tackle, and made adjustments to his gear and downriggers. It was 8:30 when we finally put lines in the water. I was sorry that I didn't arrange to meet him earlier. Salmon activity is often best in the first hours of the morning, and I knew that we'd already missed the easy fish. The previous day in Rochester, I'd landed a 25-pound salmon before 6:30.

We began by working around the breakwalls at the mouth of the Oswego River, then got into a circular trolling pattern around the breakwalls and pier heads, joining a parade of about four dozen other boats. I set the downriggers and three lines that we trolled, then drove the boat. Nearly an hour went by without our taking a fish. I'd seen a few fish boated and was wondering what we were doing wrong, when I realized that our speed might have been too slow.

When I saw a charter boat land a fish and resume trolling, I maneuvered near it and adjusted our speed to keep pace with it. I reasoned that because the captain had just caught a fish, he would immediately resume trolling at the speed he'd just been traveling. There was no speedometer or trolling speed indicator in our boat, but there was a tachometer that read just over 600 rpms while I paralleled the charter boat, which was 50 rpms higher than we had been running. We broke away and maintained 600 rpms while working through areas that other boats had vacated.

Fifteen minutes later we landed a 12-pound chinook. When I left at noon, we had also caught a 22- , a 25- , and a 28-pound salmon. My friend's father, who had unsuccessfully fished the same place the day before, was thrilled.

I am convinced that there were two factors — other than having the right lure — that primarily contributed to our success. One of these was that we made an effort to repeatedly troll places that had the least amount of boat traffic. This is a fabulous trick when trolling a confined area with heavy boat traffic. Instead of following everybody else, break away from the pack and slip into those spots that have been momentarily rested. Heavy traffic spooks fish, and those that haven't heard a boat or seen a lure for a few moments may jump on the next offering.

The other factor is that we had exactly the right speed. When I was paralleling the charter boat and establishing a boat speed of 600 + rpms, we were headed away from the river, in essence partially downstream. When I headed toward the river and into the current, I nudged the throttle forward till the tachometer registered between 650 and 700 rpms, guessing that this would counter the effect of heading into the current and approximate the same boat speed that we had while being pushed by the current, or at least give the lure a similar action. This tactic must have been right because we caught two fish while heading out and two while heading in.

I didn't see another boat, including the charters, catch more than two fish, and most of the boats had no fish. Several anglers shouted to us as they passed, and asked what depth we were fishing, what lure, what color, and how far behind the downrigger weight we were running the lure, but I wonder if any of them were paying equal attention to their speed.

There are a number of ambiguous terms in fishing. "Deep" and "shallow," for example, if not discussed in relation to exact depth to be fished, are specious words. Water clarity is an aspect of fishing usually mentioned without definition; what is meant precisely by "clear," "stained," and "muddy" water?

Speed is another intangible and is an especially ambiguous term when applied to trolling: speed of retrieve when casting, speed of lure when trolling, speed of boat when trolling. What is fast? What is slow? How do you know if you're going at the right speed to catch fish?

Boat and lure speed while trolling is one of the most overlooked aspects of sportfishing. It is given very little attention by writers. Most anglers are unaware of the vital role speed plays in trolling, which perhaps partially explains why trolling is such a hit-and-miss proposition for so many people. The better, more successful trollers have a special understanding of the behavior of the fish they seek; of the size, color, and style of lure that appeals to those fish under various conditions; and of boat manipulation techniques for effecting a proper presentation. They also have a keen awareness of speed and how it relates to these other elements.

The better guides and charter boat captains have a sixth sense about speed. They intuitively know if they are at the right speed, or they rely on some instrument to gauge speed. Many anglers, however, troll in an unrefined and haphazard manner. They fail to recognize that boat and lure speed (there can be a difference, which is explained later) is an integral aspect of trolling and that they must be attentive to it.

The key point about trolling speed is not speed for speed's sake, not a fast speed because your quarry is accustomed to outhustling its prey, not a slow speed because the species being pursued won't run down an object moving quickly, but speed that *gets the right action out of your lures*. The swimming action of a lure, perhaps more so than shape or color, causes fish to strike. If it didn't, we might as well troll single- or treble-hooked pencils. They would have virtually no swimming motion, but they'd be cheap. Action is the key. It is determined by lure design and the speed with which the lure is pulled. The matter is as simple, and as complex, as that. The complexity arises when you consider all the variables that affect trolling speed and lure action. These include current, waves, wind strength and direction, type and weight of boat, power of engine, type of lure, and so forth.

Surely one of the greatest mistakes made by trollers is to fish at the same boat speed when heading into the wind as when moving with the wind. On an otherwise still body of water, you will go faster with the wind than against the wind, assuming that you never reposition the throttle. The same is true of current. Maintain a boat speed of 2 mph downstream, then turn around and head upstream at the same throttle setting. You may head upstream only at 1 mph, you

It's important that lures exhibit proper action when trolled and that boat speed be appropriate to achieve such action. This salmon was caught on an erratic swimming J-Plug capable of being trolled at fast speeds. Note the trolling speed indicator on the transom, which helps monitor boat speed.

may make no headway at all, or you may lose ground, depending on the strength of the flow; but you won't maintain the same speed unless you advance the throttle. Now throw some wind into this situation, or add varying wave heights, and think about the effect they would have. These factors affect the way your lure works and may explain why, on a particular day, you catch fish when trolling in one direction and not in the other.

Boat speed, however, must be compatible with the lures to be fished. Trolling lures are designed to be fished at a certain range of speeds. There is a particular speed at which each lure exhibits its maximum designed action. This is true of all lures, yet all lures do not run equally well at the same speeds. Some are more tolerant of slow or fast speeds, some can sustain a wide variation in speeds, and others have a narrow range of workability.

Plugs that don't wobble, that run on their side, that roll, that don't track true, that skip out of the water, or that don't have a natural swimming motion either need to be tuned to work properly or are being run too slow or too fast. Spoons that lie flat as they're trolled, that have a lazy wobble, that hang more vertically than horizontally, or that spin furiously aren't working right. You may find that a spoon will swim perfectly at a certain boat speed while a plug will hardly wobble at the same speed. The two should not be fished together.

Most trollers have experienced an occasion when one rod out of several consistently caught fish while the others had no action. Maybe the lure on that rod was at the magic depth or had the hot color, so you put other lures of that color out and/or more lures at the same depth. But still the one rod outproduced the others. Often that occurs because the lure on the productive rod was perfectly matched to the speed of the boat and exhibited the action that the fish wanted or that most accurately mimicked the movement of prey fish. The other lures may not have been swimming right because the boat was going too slow or too fast.

Trollers should habitually check the swimming action of every lure before they put it into the water, even lures that they have recently been fishing successfully. Put the lure in the water, point the rod tip at the water or lower it into the water with the lure several feet behind the tip, and watch the lure swim at the current boat speed. You can alter boat speed to get a lure to run well, but this might adversely affect other lures that you already have out.

Keep in mind that even though you may have achieved the proper speed for a particular lure, that speed may be inappropriate for the fish you seek. Thus, you have to experiment with different lures and different trolling speeds. The effective trolling speed varies by species and seasons. For example, you might troll plugs fairly slow for brown trout in the spring, then graduate to spoons and a faster speed when the water warms up. Lake trout, which are often caught deep, are known to favor a slow presentation, so you usually cannot fish slow for lakers and expect to catch other species of trout or salmon at the same time. It happens occasionally, but that's not the norm. You can troll for muskies at a much faster speed than for most other freshwater fish, but not all lures are conducive to high-speed work, and a lure that works best at a slow speed may not be attractive enough to a musky.

What you need is some reference point for trolling speed. Engine rpms are not a great gauge, but they are something to go by. In the absence of other reference points, you can use rpms to gauge speed when conditions are relatively calm. Stick with a certain rpm setting if you're catching fish. You have to alter rpms, however, when wind, waves, or current impede your forward movement. If you're using a lure that has caught fish at a certain rpm setting and if you encounter some force (current or wind) that is affecting your headway at that rpm setting, run the lure alongside the boat and watch how it behaves. Increase the throttle until you get the lure to run perfectly, then note the new rpm indication and try to maintain it.

Small boaters, including those with tiller steering, may not have a tachometer, so they have to guess at relative speeds or use some type of incremental measuring device. Some boaters fashion their own speed indicator by attaching one end of a 3-foot wire or heavy nylon monofilament leader to a 1-pound lead weight and the other end to an arrowlike indicator, which pivots along a plate that has incremental measuring units marked on it. The weight is dropped in the water and the arrow points to a spot on the plate, changing location as boat speed is altered. There are inexpensive, commercially made speed indicators that work in the same manner. Dura Pak produces a plastic Grizzly trolling speed indicator that clamps to the gunwale of a boat. Eagle Claw's Accu-Troll is made of metal and bolts to the transom or gunwale.

Units of measurement on these devices do not correlate to actual speed in statute or nautical miles per hour, but simply to the lines and numbers inscribed on the plate. When you put a lure in the water and get it to work properly, note the measurement unit and run the boat at a speed that keeps the arrow in the desired position.

For small boats without a lot of electronic gadgetry, the Accu-Troll is a helpful speed-indicating device.

More precise speed indications, based on nautical or statute miles per hour, are obtained by using relatively sophisticated electronic instruments powered by internal 9-volt batteries or 12-volt boat batteries. These sport paddle wheels are mounted on the transom; the paddle turns as the boat moves and relays speed in knots or miles per hour on a meter or digital display.

These instruments all measure boat and lure speed at or near the surface. In many trolling situations, this speed is the same, or nearly the same, as the speed of the lure down at the level you are trolling it and accurately provides the speed references that you need. There are times, however, when surface speed has no relation to speed of the lure.

If you have ever anchored your boat in a river and fished a lure on a fixed length of line behind the boat, you can readily appreciate this principle. This is how steelhead fishermen work downriver with plugs; it is also how shad fishermen use jigs or darts. The boat may be stationary, but the force of the current makes the lure swim. In effect, it's like trolling in place; the lure may actually be going nowhere, but the speed of the current is giving it action.

Imagine now that you are trolling up a river. The force of the current, in addition to the forward movement of your boat, could be making your lure swim wildly instead of working naturally. How do you know? If the water is fairly shallow, you can watch your lure swim beside the boat and be fairly certain that it will swim the same when you drop it a little deeper. But in a deep river, or where there may be back currents or varying flow patterns, you may not have the same speed down deep as you do on the surface. What if you are trolling up a tidal river when the tide is coming in? Does that negate the force of the current, and if so, how does that affect your lure? You might be slow trolling upriver at a boat speed of 1 mph and the tide is slowing the action of your lure. If you are slow trolling downriver when the tide is going out, it's conceivable that your lure might be hanging listlessly below your boat instead of swimming provocatively behind it.

These problems are not restricted to rivers and obvious current or tidal environments. It is well known that there are currents in the ocean. There are also currents in open-water portions of the Great Lakes and in many large inland lakes. Few big water anglers know this or understand its affect on fishing. Current in lakes and reservoirs can be caused by tributaries entering the lake, by dam releases ("pulling water"), by river outlets, and by wind and wave action. It may be obvious but is usually so subtle that a visual inspection of the surface — and measurements of speed at that level — gives no indication of the presence of current. In some of the Great Lakes, there is such a strong current at 50 or more feet of water that it is detectable by watching the action of downrigger weights and cables. At a slow rate of speed heading into the current, the weights and cables sway back. Going with the current, the weights and cables hang nearly vertically.

As in rivers, underwater lake currents affect the speed and action of trolling lures. It is possible for a boat to be moving at 2 mph while the lure is running faster. If the lure is not swimming at the proper speed, it may not catch fish. You can troll all day, change colors till you've surveyed the entire spectral range, have no success whatsoever, and have no idea why.

If you are flat-lining under such circumstances, you may be able to detect the influence of current by watching your lines and rod tips, but most of the time this will not be an indicator. You can determine the presence of strong current by watching a downrigger, but even then you don't know how it is influencing your lures.

There are several electronic speed indicators (from Weller, EMS, and Fish Hawk) that relay the speed of your lure or downrigger via sensors that attach to a downrigger cable above the weight and electrically transmit that speed to a readout. Some of these devices also indicate temperature and pH at the depth of the sensor and at the water surface. They are very expensive ($300 and up), and the first models of these devices performed poorly and achieved a bad reputation. I've used two; one never worked properly and the other had

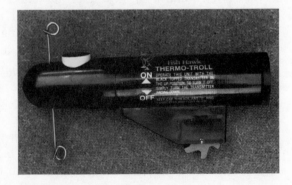

The probe of Fish Hawk's Thermo-Troll, which attaches on the downrigger cable above the weight, relays speed (via the paddle wheel) and temperature at the weight.

Weller's Troll Control, formerly called the Pro-Combinator, measures deep speed and temperature. Photographed in use, it indicates a deep speed of 2.1 knots.

an incomprehensible installation and instruction manual. Some still don't always work properly, but charter boat operators and avid private anglers are gravitating toward these as they try to learn what is going on at the level of their lure as well as on the surface.

An important point to remember when comparing boat speeds is that the speed recorded on one boat may not be comparable to the speed recorded on another boat. You may be catching fish while motoring at 550 rpms, for example, yet your buddy is not catching anything despite the fact that his tachometer has the same reading. Or, you may be catching fish while traveling at 2 1/4 mph while someone else is catching fish at 2 1/2 using the same lures. I find that gauges vary slightly and that boat speed is influenced by a host of factors, making speed comparisons difficult.

That's why you have to focus on the speeds that work well for your lures in your boat. If you do a lot of trolling, it is an excellent idea to make up a lure speed chart. Use a tachometer, an electronic speedometer, an incremental indicator, or whatever reference device that you have. Spend the time to run all of your different types of lures in the water beside the boat to find out what their ideal speed is, and learn what range of speeds they will tolerate. It may not be fun, but that information will be valuable, especially when you want to mix speed-compatible lures or change boat speed to accommodate your lure-changing activities.

Knowing the range of speeds that lures will tolerate is very helpful and may give you the impetus to change boat and lure speed to find what is preferred by fish on a given day. It is no accident that many fish, especially trout, are caught when boaters speed up or slow down and when they make turns. On a turn, unless it is very long and gradual, the lure on the outside of the turn speeds up and the lure on the inside slows down. The lure that slows down will sink if it is a spoon or sinking plug or rise if it is a floater. These changes in lure behavior often trigger strikes and may indicate that your speed was incorrect for the successful lure or that you needed a momentary change in boat and lure speed to trigger a strike from a curious fish, which you had no idea was following. I am certain that there are many fish that come in and look at trolled lures but aren't inclined to strike. Frequent alterations in speed, either by decreasing or advancing the throttle or by turning, are valuable tactics for the troller to employ.

Few fishermen have the problem of not being able to troll fast enough (though electric motor trollers headed into a wind and rowers may), but some encounter situations when they cannot troll slowly enough. Boat speed depends on boat size, weight, and engine power as well as on throttle setting. Some boats simply cannot troll slowly enough even at the lowest throttle setting, particularly if they are

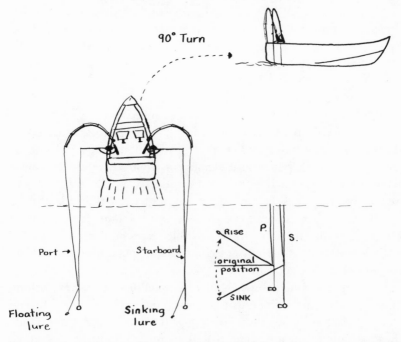

Changes in lure behavior often trigger strikes, which is why turns are an important trolling maneuver. This illustration shows what happens to floating and sinking lures on a turn and is applicable to any type of trolling, although downrigging is depicted here.

headed downwind. A light boat with a moderate-size engine will troll faster than many larger, heavier boats with powerful stern-drive or inboard propulsion. Some large outboard motors will not troll below 600 rpms and, on a moderate-size craft like a bass boat, will push that vessel along at a speed greater than is practical for the fishing to be done. In these instances, consider using an auxiliary motor (a 9.9 or 15 hp) if you have a big boat, a so-called trolling plate (which baffles thrust and stymies forward propulsion), or a sea anchor (a bag that is dragged alongside the boat) to troll slowly.

How should you gauge speed if you don't have some type of indicating device? Become a rod tip watcher when you flat-line (this is a good practice at all times because you can often tell if your lure has picked up some grass or leaf or other object that impedes its success); listen carefully to the sound of your engine; and watch the action of your lures. If you have a tachometer or some type of speed-indicating device but don't know what is a good speed to employ for the species you're after, experiment with different speeds until you catch a fish, then check your gauge to use the successful speed as a reference point.

No matter what kind of fish you troll for or what tackle and type of boat you use, you'll get more out of your lures by paying close attention to the speed at which they are working. This is easier to understand than it is to accomplish.

4

SONAR

Graph recorders and depthfinders are some of the best tools for anglers who fish from a boat and who troll. An outgrowth of sonar (short for sound navigation and ranging) applied by the military in World Wars I and II, today's electronic depth-finding and fish-locating equipment is helping anglers enjoy their sport and become more learned and proficient. So widespread has the use of these devices become in the last two decades that it is difficult to find a credible guide and virtually impossible to find a charter boat captain who do not possess one or more of these instruments. They would no sooner think of fishing without such tools than of driving an auto at night without headlights.

Why? Principally because sportfishing sonar is the boat angler's magic underwater eyes. With it, he can find concentrations of migratory, suspended, schooling, and nomadic fish, plus locate unseen habitat that may be attractive to bass. With sportfishing sonar devices, an angler can become accurately acquainted with the beneath-the-surface environment of a body of water in significantly less time than without it. In addition to these benefits, the use of sportfishing sonar allows an angler to navigate better, more safely, and quicker than he might otherwise.

Locating fish with sonar is no guarantee that they are the kind of fish you seek. On Lake Erie they could be sheepshead when you think they are bass; in a southern impoundment they could be channel catfish when you think they are stripers. Sonar also can't insure that you'll be able to catch fish, regardless of the extent of your knowledge and experience. There still is no substitute for angling savvy, skillful presentation, and knowledge of fish behavior and habits. This notwithstanding, there are many times when even the most skillful anglers can find fish but not catch them. And many fishermen are only moderately successful anglers despite their collection of electronic wizardry. Obviously, what you have is important, but less so than what you do with it.

How sonar instruments do what they do is immaterial to most fishermen. There are a few technical points about their operation, however, that will help you understand and use these machines to the fullest.

Sound travels at 4,800 feet per second through the water, which is four times faster than it travels through air. Sportfishing sonar instruments issue signals (pulses) at extremely swift rates, in some cases as many as twenty times per second. The greater the distance between transducer (the object that sends the pulses out and receives them) and bottom, the longer it takes for the pulses to bounce off it (or other objects between it and the bottom, including fish) and return. Nonetheless, the speed of operation is amazingly swift.

Transducers send out their pulses in a three-dimensional cone-shaped wave, not in a narrow band. Cone angles range from 8 degrees (most narrow) to 50 degrees (extremely wide). The diameter of these cones influences how much detail will be seen. An 8-degree cone has a 2-foot diameter when the water is 15 feet deep; it has a 4-foot diameter at a depth of 30 feet; and so forth. A 20-degree cone, which is more or less standard in freshwater, has a 6-foot diameter in 15 feet of water and 12-foot in 30. A 45-degree cone has a 13.5-foot diameter at 15 feet and 27-foot at 30.

I've had transducers that ranged from the least to the greatest cone angles on different boats I've owned and have found that the narrowest cones are most useful in extremely deep water, such as 150 feet or more. The widest cones enable you to see a lot more of what is beneath you, are especially useful for downrigger trolling and fishing directly below the boat, and work only at slow boat speeds. The medium-range cones are less specialized, have all-around functionality, and are best used in less than 100 feet of water.

Most trollers use an 18- to 20-degree cone angle and are satisfied with it. I've found it worthwhile to have two transducers connected via a switch box to the same sonar instrument, not only to change cone angles but also to have a backup in case one malfunctions. I first experimented with 8- and 20-degree cone angles but found the 8 to be too narrow for the predominantly less than 100-foot water that I

This graph recorder is equipped wth a 45-degree cone transducer, wide enough to view four downrigger weights below the boat, which it was doing when photographed.

was fishing in at the time. The graph recorder that I have now, a Lowrance X–16, has the capability of utilizing both 20- and 45-degree transducers, which is a good trolling arrangement. The only drawback to the superwide cone angle is that it takes in so much information, therefore, you may trick yourself into thinking that fish it details are directly below the boat when they may be well off to the side. As long as you remember that your field of view is so great when using the 45, you can switch back and forth, using it to give you a look at your entire downrigger presentation.

Many first-time users of sonar, and those who have switched from one brand to another, have difficulty getting their machines to provide optimum results, especially graph recorders. Most problems result from improper transducer installation and operator misuse.

Misuse usually centers around the control functions, particularly sensitivity and suppression. The sensitivity control, also called gain, is akin to volume. Many inexperienced sonar users keep this turned down too low, either because they are experiencing electrical interference or because they think a low setting is adequate. When the sensitivity is too low, sonar may fail to register key bait, fish, or bottom readings. When extremely low, only an indistinct bottom may be registered. On some units, a high sensitivity setting prompts a lot of false signals and distorted images, primarily due to the inadequacies of the machine.

On a flasher-style depthfinder, the sensitivity should first be turned up just enough to indicate bottom depth. Then it should be increased till a second reading, double the depth of the bottom, is recorded. This is an echo signal resulting from the sonar pulse going down to the bottom, bouncing back to the surface of the water, returning to the bottom, and bouncing back again. Adjust the sensitivity control so the echo signal is faintly distinguishable. As you move into deeper or shallower water, you'll have to increase or decrease sensitivity, respectively.

An echo signal on a graph recorder can be confusing and isn't practical for shallow water use. With these instruments, it is best to turn the sensitivity up high, usually at a two-thirds to three-quarter setting. Increase it till you have a strong, well-defined bottom marking. If you turn it too high, you may get black marks all over the paper or interference signals. Turn the sensitivity down slightly to avoid this. If you are getting no marks between the bottom and the surface or if the bottom is indistinct, the sensitivity setting is too low. If you increase or decrease depth or if water conditions change markedly, you may have to alter the sensitivity slightly. Good machines can detect algae, debris, tiny bait fish, and severe water temperature changes.

Suppression is a control function used to block unwanted and interfering noises from being registered. I rarely use any suppression on my sonar equipment so as to get the maximum "view" of what is below. The higher the suppression setting, the more you will block out fish signals. Suppression is best used when operating a boat at high speed because engine noise or boat movement over choppy water may result in distorted or wild signals. Increase suppression to block out interference signals so that you get a clear reading of bottom depth when running a boat at high speed. If you experience interference in normal, slow-boat operation, it could be due to a problem with the sonar instrument itself, improper transducer installation, or electrical interference from other objects in the boat.

Although there are other controls on some of these instruments, including depth or fish indication alarms, variable depth scales, and surface clutter suppression, graph paper speed is the most notable. Although slow paper speed conserves paper, it sandwiches details, making it more difficult to determine what is below. When you know what to expect, are continuously going over the same ground, or are interested only in depth, a slow paper speed is fine. When it is important to see the maximum amount of detail, run the paper at high speed.

I've had about six Lowrance graph recorders, including all of their microprocessor models and the current X–16 version, and have always found that the best results come from a mid to high sensitivity setting, little or no suppression, and medium to high paper speed. These graphs are excellent products and, at the risk of sounding biased, I'm often disappointed when comparing the performance of some other brands to the Lowrance graphs. Whatever graph recorder you have, it pays for you to experiment with the sensitivity and suppression controls and the paper speed at various depths and boat speeds to get the most out of your machine.

Although sonar devices seem like magic, there is nothing magical about interpreting their signals. Flashers are harder to read than graphs because signals disappear quickly, and flashers produce so many signals at times that you cannot digest the information quickly enough to interpret it. A flasher can tell you almost as much as a graph recorder, but you have to watch it virtually all the time and you need practice to confidently determine what every signal is.

Depth is gauged by watching the innermost part of the signal band. Often the bottom signal covers a range, say from 24 to 28 feet. The shallow edge of the band, in this case 24 feet, denotes the depth directly underneath. A hard bottom typically gives off a wide signal because it reflects transducer pulses better. A soft bottom produces a weaker signal and a narrow band. A hard bottom enhances the echo image while a soft bottom weakens it. A drop-off will appear as a wide series of signals, which is actually the transducer receiving several signals (remember the cone diameter) of varying depths at one time. A rocky bottom appears choppy and broken up, while a sandy bottom is solid. Even a sandy bottom can appear choppy if the boat is moving through substantial waves, which cause the boat and transducer to bob up and down. Weeds return a thin, pale signal; fish in weeds show up as brighter signals. A school of bait fish produces a flurry of short-duration signals. This is just a sampling of what to expect, but understand that you can become fairly adept at interpreting signals as long as you pay attention to the unit.

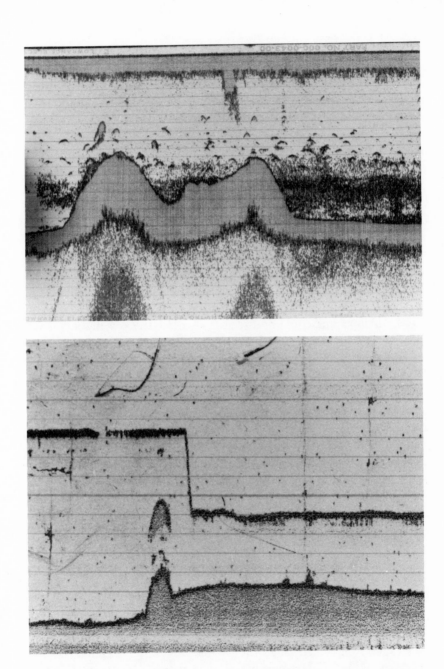

The paper at top was recorded on Keystone Lake, Oklahoma, with the scale set at a 60-foot depth. Shown is a hard bottom, lots of white bass and striped bass from 16 to 30 feet deep, and a strong temperature variance (colder water) below 30 feet. At bottom is how the graph recorder depicted a large single fish and a down-rigger weight that was lowered to it on a New York reservoir.

On a graph recorder the bottom is easily distinguished, and the strength of the impression on the paper is often indicative of the type of bottom, just as it is for flashers. Trees, stumps, boulders, drop-offs, and the like are all readily observed without having to watch the monitor continuously. Most graphs have a gray- or white-line feature, which issues a light band below the bottom that helps distinguish bottom terrain features. A lump that is filled in, for instance, might be grass, weeds, or a fish in direct contact with the bottom and ordinarily indistinguishable from the rest of the terrain.

Unlike flashers, some graphs can show you minute matter in the water, such as algae, heavy plankton concentrations, and sedimentation. These are readily observed in the upper layer of freshwater impoundments in the spring and appear as small specks. Some graphs also show the depth of the thermocline — a layer of water separating the warm upper and cold lower sectors — when this is well established in summer and fall in large lakes. This appears as a faint gray band, often speckled, and remains at a constant depth.

Fish signals appear on a graph as an arc unless the fish are very small, the paper speed is very slow, or the boat is moving very fast. This is because a fish is first picked up on the outer edge of the cone, then directly underneath it (the strongest pulse area), then on the outer edge as the boat passes over it. The strongest reading of the fish is seen as the center part of the arc. A partial arc means that a fish was moving either in or out of the cone when you passed by. A school of bait shows up as a big pod, which may be vertical or horizontal depending on the species. Sometimes you can decrease the sensitivity on a graph to separate individual fish.

It is very difficult to tell the specific size of fish detected with sonar because this varies according to the size of the fish, the speed of the boat, the paper speed on a graph, and the sensitivity setting. If you catch a fish out of a school that you've just marked on a flasher or graph, you may have some idea how fish size compares to signal size, but if any of these factors change as you continue fishing, it's a new ball game. Remember, small fish produce less intense signals of short duration and big fish produce wide signals that last longer on a flasher.

Determining size of fish is somewhat possible but determining species is not, although educated guesses based on extensive experience and knowledge of individual species behavior and certain environments can be accurate.

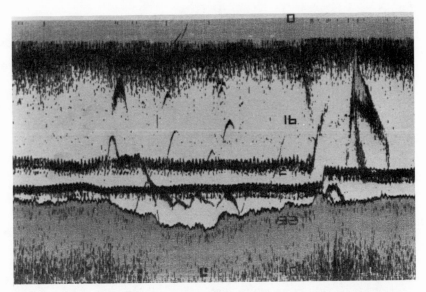

Printed on Lake Ontario, this graph paper readout depicts fish that streaked down, streaked up, and followed a lure that was run close behind a downrigger weight. The faint horizontal lines below the weights are those of diving plugs. One weight was retrieved. The other weight was raised when it almost struck bottom. Note that this was a rocky bottom, and also that there was a school of bait fish from 6 to 16 feet deep.

You can tell if fish are active or not, and thus potentially susceptible to angling. With some species, suspended fish are likely to be inactive, while others, situated on top of a stump or edge of a drop, may be waiting in ambush. At times on graph recorders, you can watch fish hit a jig worked vertically below the boat, or you can see fish follow a lure. I've watched fish come off the bottom, follow a trolled lure, strike it, then be played out of the cone angle up to the surface.

The newest sonar devices on the market, and catching on with increasing popularity, are the liquid crystal display recorders (LCRs). Many anglers have recently gone to these in preference to flashers and instead of having a graph recorder on their boat. The appeal of LCRs is based on economical price, no graph paper installation or expense to contend with, and no need to watch them constantly to see what's below. Thus, they are supposed to meld the good points of graphs and flashers without their disadvantages, though few anglers who depend on a graph are forsaking them for LCRs. Many fishermen who don't need a graph recorder, however, like an LCR for its graphlike screen information. Unlike flashers, you don't have to watch LCR recorders continuously.

With LCRs, signals appear at one side of the screen as you go over them, then cross the screen and disappear at the other end. Some of the better models have a screen update to recall a full screen's worth of information, memory storage, a zoom feature that narrows down the area being observed, an automatic depth-determining mode, and forward and reverse displays. I used a Humminbird 4000 for a year and was not terribly impressed with it other than for determining bottom depth. Placed alongside the Lowrance X–16, it didn't come close to displaying the information that showed on the graph. I'm now using a Humminbird 8000, which is a better machine and also has a memory recall and split screen capability. It shows downrigger weights, fish, and thermocline with good clarity. It's clear to me that these devices are getting more sophisticated and will someday show fish and bottom contours as well as the best graphs.

Many sonar units now offer bottom or any-depth closeup monitoring (a zoom feature), and some offer a dual-screen feature, but when the Humminbird LCR 8000 splits into left and right screens, sixteen memorized positions can be recalled on the left side. This unit helps find open-water structure in a way that can be otherwise done only with Loran, triangulation, or time-consuming searching. When navigating, you can recall a memorized scene and display it on the left side of the 8000 screen; while motoring, the scene below the boat is recorded on the right side of the LCR screen and when the two closely match up, you're in the right place. I saw the usefulness of this action while striper fishing recently in Texas and was able to use this unit to relocate an underwater hump that was attracting hybrid and striped bass. Another notable aspect of such a device is that a site confined to the LCR's memory can be shown on land or water to other fishermen, who can have a view of what kind of structure they should be seeking.

One disadvantage to LCRs is the difficulty of reading them in bright sunlight or from particular angles. It is often necessary to rotate or tilt them to be able to view the screen information adequately. Some anglers have difficulty distinguishing bottom characteristics (soft versus hard bottom), interpreting the signals (is that brush or small fish clustered together?), and discriminating between large and small fish or groups of small game fish and bait fish. This is because LCRs transfer signals into dots (pixels), most of which look like one another

Graph paper recorders (right) and paperless liquid crystal display recorders (left) are important tools for most trollers, especially downrigger fishermen. Many big boaters have two such sonar devices.

and are hard to interpret when they appear on or close to the bottom.

These units are going to become more sophisticated in the near future and will be more popular as anglers learn to use them. It took awhile for fishermen to learn to interpret flasher-style sonar; many people still use them merely to indicate depth and/or are not good at interpreting the signals they produce. The same pattern is emerging with LCRs, though such matters as transducer usage, transducer installation, sensitivity, and suppression functions are roughly the same. The liquid crystal display aspects of these units are present in many of the higher priced sonar, including the color videosonar used by big boat trollers. This trend is causing flasher-style sonar to become obsolete. When the display mechanisms become more sophisticated, graph paper recorders will fade away, too.

Another product that may be seen on some trolling boats in the near future, incidentally, is a talking depth sounder, which is a 4 x 5 x 5 box that annunciates how deep the water is below a boat. Actually it's an add-on, a device that attaches to almost any sonar instrument and offers an audible depth-reporting capability. Called Depth Talker, the device is used for depths up to 50 feet; I've used it once for trolling and think it may be useful to those fishing in fairly shallow water with irregular bottom terrain.

In learning to use sonar equipment, it is imperative that you develop some confidence in it from the start. After you've digested the instruction manual, take the time to experiment with it over known terrain. Bring your boat over shallow water near shore, where you know the depth, and check to see that the sonar reads accurately. Find a stump several feet down, and see how it registers on your machine. Go over a sandy bottom, a mud bottom, a rocky bottom.

Go out to deeper water and check the depth measurements against a hand line or measured fishing line if you are wondering about the depth-reading accuracy.

Rest assured that you don't have to employ sportfishing sonar devices to catch fish, but trollers find them to be an especially valuable fishing aid. If you are trolling with downriggers, trying to locate specific habitat, or trying to follow specific contours, you'll find some type of sonar to be essential.

TRANSDUCER INSTALLATION

Getting good readings from your sonar gear is important to interpreting what the machines read. Improper transducer installation leads to many problems and can hamper your fishing efforts. Through-the-hull transducers are best for fiberglass boats and should be installed in the sump on a smooth surface, without air bubbles in the epoxy bond,

Proper transducer installation is critical to sonar use. These transducers are mounted on the transom between strakes, with the 8-degree center transducer flush to the hull and the 20-degree transducers (on kickup brackets) below the hull.

and in a locale that is free from any irregularities in the hull. Large aluminum boats require transom-mount transducers installed midway between the hull strakes to minimize the effects of turbulence when the boat is underway. I like to use kickup brackets with these, which allow them to be installed below the hull line (they would be at the line on other brackets). A kickup bracket puts the transducer deeper to minimize the possibility of interference from air bubbles and also lets the transducer swing up if it contacts a rock, stump, or other obstacle.

Because improper transducer installation is the cause of much unit malfunctioning and because anglers have difficulty in learning to use these devices, some tips on how to correctly install transducers follow.

Position a transom-mount transducer so that no air bubbles will trail below it. Strakes, weld lines, and rivets, among other things, give off a bubble trail, especially at high speed. Find a location that permits clear water to flow below the face of the transducer, such as between strakes on an aluminum hull. The closer you are to the centerline of the hull, the better. It may be necessary to point the transducer up slightly; if pointed down, the flow of water may emit a bubble trail beneath. If there are heavy bubbles below a transducer, you'll get no readings.

When epoxying a transducer in the sump for through-hull shooting, keep it close to the centerline, to be sure it will read in heavy seas, and away from struts and supports. Place it at least 1 foot in front of the transom in small boats, several feet in large boats, due to the possible extra fiberglass layers that are applied in the hull-transom bondage.

In many fiberglass boats, it is best to have the transducer laid into the hull in the manufacturing process. I've had five boats that were so arranged; however, boats with an air space, foam, or balsa core are not conducive to through-hull mounting because sonar cannot pass through these substances. Transom-mounting is best for aluminum boats. Wide-angle transducers are not recommended for through-hull mounting, but I have had good results with a 45-degree transducer (for a Lowrance X–1550 computer graph) that was installed in the fiberglass of an 18-foot boat during construction.

How can you tell if your boat/transducer is suitable for through-hull transducer mounting? Put water in the bilge and take the boat out to 30 or 40 feet of water. Place the transducer on the hull in the bilge and turn the sensitivity of your flasher or graph back until you faintly receive a bottom signal. Move the transducer around to different locations until you get a better (stronger) signal. When you get a good spot, turn the sensitivity back again till you barely detect bottom, and try to find a better location. When you have the best possible spot, take the transducer out of the sump and place it overboard in the water. Compare this signal with the one you received from shooting through the hull. If the signals are the same, you can shoot through the hull. If the through-hull signal is significantly different, you should not shoot through the hull. If it is only slightly different and your usage will be primarily in shallow water or in freshwater up to 150 feet, then you'll still get good enough results when shooting through the hull.

Though manufacturers are loathe to suggest or approve it, you can cut a hole in the hull of aluminum or fiberglass boats and install the transducer so that its face makes direct contact with the water, which may invalidate the manufacturer's warranty. One method of doing this is to fiberglass a 2 x 4 to the inside of the hull, then cut a hole the size of the transducer through the hull and wood, and epoxy or fiberglass the transducer in.

If you are experiencing continuous electrical interference, it may be caused by an untuned engine sending extra electrical energy through the tachometer cable that is placed alongside the transducer cable. Try relocating the transducer cable.

5

TROLLING AIDS

It would be a gross understatement to say that things have changed a lot in the field of boats, general fishing tackle, trolling aids, gadgets, and electronic fishing and boating equipment in the past two decades. Actually there has been a veritable revolution. Most of the devices that people are using on their boats to help them troll weren't around in even crude forms 20 years ago, and new developments in equipment are progressing right now at a tremendous clip. The impact of microprocessors and digital displays on tackle and trolling aids is really only beginning. In the future, we'll see innovative devices that will make the current crop of goodies so antiquated that we'll wonder how we ever got by with what we now have.

Those who don't troll or don't understand much about modern trolling do not, and cannot, appreciate the usefulness of much of the modern-day equipment. As I stated in the introduction to this book, many people, including nontrolling anglers, are under the mistaken impression that trolling is accomplished from any old boat simply by placing some object on a line and dragging it an indeterminate distance behind a boat until a fish takes it. Although it is not my intention to make you feel that you must have all of the equipment available to trollers — much of which is very expensive — or that trolling need be a very technical exercise performed with a plethora of sophisticated equipment, I do want you to be aware of what's available and how it has great impact on the efforts of the modern-day troller.

If you think I'm making much ado about the usefulness of modern equipment, consider this analogy: while I was writing this book, I took my ten-year-old four wheel-drive truck to the cemetery and replaced it with a brand new vehicle. The new one could be shifted from two-wheel drive to four on the fly. Is that an improvement? I think so. The new truck gets almost twice the gas mileage that the old one got and is aided by electronic fuel injection. This simply wasn't possible ten years earlier. The new one has a microprocessor that tells me when to shift manual gear for maximum performance and fuel economy. Another modern innovation. There are other notable improvements that were not thought of or were not technically possible a decade earlier. Nonetheless, both vehicles accomplished the same objective: they got me where I had to go. The difference is that the new one does it better (and cost far more).

To a great extent, it's the same with boating and fishing gear for trolling. If you're new to modern trolling techniques, or to big water fishing, you'll be surprised to see how avid anglers have embraced the latest trolling aids.

Recently I fished for Lake Michigan salmon on a 36-foot boat that would have seemed like a science fiction vessel to our forefathers. Particularly fascinating was its ultrasophisticated four-color videosonar machine cabled to two television monitors. One monitor was on the bridge next to a long-range navigation (Loran) instrument. The other was in the cabin — larger than most bedrooms, incidentally — next to a video cassette recorder, near a stereo cassette/radio and another Loran unit, and in front of the galley, which featured a microwave oven. This videosonar reminded me of the Astrosmash Intellivision video game that my kids play. The only difference was that the videosonar fish blobs moved horizontally while the space game meteor blobs moved vertically.

Despite the fact that there were six electric downriggers, a platoon of rods, and a legion of lures on the boat and despite hooking about eight trout and salmon, this experience didn't feel quite like salmon fishing. It occurred to me that this boat belonged in the blue water of the Bahamas more than it did in the blue-green water of the Great Lakes. To be fair, however, and in recognition of the adage about men and boys and the price of their toys, I should note that the skipper, who catered particularly to corporate charters, had merely gone a little farther than his peers.

Near us on the lake were other boats, smaller and less pretentious, and though they didn't possess the comforts of the craft I was on, they were similarly equipped for fishing. Every boat had one or more video or graph recorder sonar devices. Every boat had downriggers, primarily

There is a plethora of aids available for trolling, and many of them do help make the task of finding, hooking, and landing fish — especially on large bodies of water — easier or more enjoyable.

electric. Every boat had a trolling speed indicator and temperature gauge, primarily electric. Some had Loran. Many of these devices were liquid crystal display (LCD) or microprocessor-equipped units, and it was impossible not to see clearly the silicon, electronic influence on the fishing scene, regardless of the expanse and expense of boat employed.

Though many an observer is likely to wonder "what will they think of next?" when perusing some of the sophisticated devices available to fishermen today, this is part of a progression toward satisfying the inquisitive and equipment-possessing disposition of many anglers. I have a hunch that not long after James Heddon, the father of the modern plug, had whittled a piece of wood into bait form and saw a fish take it that he was angling someplace and showed his catch off to a fellow who was dabbling something live with a reelless cane pole. I imagine that when Heddon showed the other man the strange looking artificial plug that was used to catch fish, the cane-pole angler shook his head and asked, "What will they think of next?"

While I have been extolling the virtues of some of the latest equipment, I also want to present the flip side of the equation so you can understand that not all that's new is good.

One of the keys to the acceptance of modern trolling aids, particularly of electronic equipment, has been their ability to work continuously and report instantly. Sonar devices, for example, are always reporting information while you are running the boat or fishing. A surface temperature gauge gives constant readouts regardless of what speed the boat is moving or what the operator is doing. Some meters, however, have largely necessitated hand-held operation, requiring you to stop and uncoil the sensing mechanism, drop it in the water, and take a reading. This must be done every place that you want to obtain information. In this age of instantly accessible information, many fishermen don't want to make periodic measurements when they could be fishing, even if there is a possibility that those measurements will put them in more productive areas, so they shun potentially useful products or those that are slow at doing their job. This includes electric downriggers that take a long time to raise a weight.

As much as we think some of the latest creations make a lot of sense, they're only functional tools when they work well and reliably. Not all gadgets are so blessed. A few years ago, I was fascinated with a new hand-held 9-volt battery-operated sonar gun that you simply stuck in the water and pressed the trigger to operate. I bought one but it worked erratically. I sent it back to the manufacturer twice but it always went goofy. I gave up on it disgustedly, but my kids had great success with it as a mock Star Wars stun gun.

Another dismal failure was an expensive deep-trolling temperature gauge that operated on a remote battery system using a tube attached to the end of a downrigger cable. The guage sent deep-water temperature readings up to a receiving unit. It, too, had a short life expectancy, repeatedly gave me 99 degree readings in 50 degree water, and was returned for repair until I deep-sixed it in dismay. That cost me thrice what the stun gun did and had no residual use.

There have been other toys that have brought more frustration and aggravation than simplification and assistance. Many guides or charter boat captains tell horror stories about "great" new products that seldom worked properly. Sometimes so-called "revolutionary" equipment is made available to the public before all the bugs have been worked out, or before it has seen rigorous in-the-field use. Employing consumers as guinea pigs or supplying products before their time not only hurts the name of the manufacturer of that particular product but also diminishes reception for similar, but better, products to come. Yet the trolling paraphernalia field has consistently had its share of products that didn't live up to their public relations, in part because the consumer has been so eager for it. As always, caveat emptor is the byword.

With those thoughts in mind, let's discuss the salient points about equipment that is most functional for a wide range of trollers, with comments where appropriate on their use, installation, and relative merits.

Boats. Some readers may be disappointed that I am not making a long and detailed analysis of boats for trolling or of the ideal boat for trolling. There are comments throughout this chapter on ways to set up a boat for trolling; but it would literally take a small book to talk about all aspects of boats and motors, and this is a book about trolling, not about boats.

I have trolled from almost all kinds of craft, including such uncommon trolling vessels as pontoon boats, houseboats, inflatables, and canoes. The bulk of my experience, however, is with more conventional fishing vessels. I started trolling by rowing a 12-foot wooden rowboat, graduated to trolling with an electric motor on an aluminum cartopper, then stepped up a 7.5 hp gas motor on a johnboat before I got really serious about things. I've owned half a dozen so-called bass boats within the past ten years and set every one of them up for serious trolling. I've spent many days on 18- to 28-foot boats on large bodies of water all over the country, and often I've trolled out of still larger craft. So I've been there.

Because most people fish out of small- to medium-size boats, I'm especially sensitive to using and outfitting such craft for trolling applications. The information I detail here relates to all trollers, however, even though some equipment or installation methods may not be economically practical for some small craft. The size of the bodies of water you fish; the water conditions you encounter, including wave height, distance to port, and current; the depth of your bank account; and the intensity of your interest in pursuing fish are the factors that determine what you fish from and how you are outfitted. I'll give you the options, but you'll have to take it from there.

I want to note, however, that if you are in the market for a boat that you will use primarily or exclusively for trolling, you must have a good idea of what your needs are before you shop. The pattern of boat ownership is typically to start small and modest and work your way up to bigger, more expensive, and more powerful craft. This is partially because anglers initially are conservative and want to keep their expenses down to where they can cope with the bank payments. This is practical, of course, but some people make their initial purchases partially due to ignorance. People often buy boats and then, after fishing in them for a season or two, decide that they are not fast enough, not roomy enough, have too much or too little freeboard, won't carry enough equipment, won't take rough water, and on and on. The more boats you fish on, the more fishing boat owners you talk to, and the more you observe at docks and marinas and launching ramps, the better informed you'll be — and the greater the chance

When you're scouting for a new boat or for new trolling equipment, it's a good idea to see different installation systems and to consider where and how your equipment will be placed. A trolling board, as shown here, is a good option to concentrate paraphernalia on some boats.

that you can peg your needs and reach some accommodation between your needs and what you are able to spend.

Keep in mind also that some boats are designed as fishing machines, especially the smaller ones, but that many boats are designed as pleasure boats. I have seen very few boats primarily designed for cruising that also make good fishing machines, except for some in the 35-foot yacht category. Nonetheless, how you outfit your boat and how you tailor it to be a trolling vessel are of utmost importance and are pertinent to any type of boat, whether it be a 12-foot aluminum cartopper, a 17-foot bass boat, or a 25-foot cuddy cabin machine.

I like a boat that is set up for serious fishing. Be it a johnboat, a bass boat, a cruiser, or a deep vee-hulled, big water vessel, a boat that is reasonably and properly outfitted for fishing is a pleasure. That's because I think of a boat as a tool. It has to get me where the fish are. It must weather the necessary water conditions. It must be reasonably comfortable to allow me to put in long hours. It must be versatile to handle a variety of angling pursuits. It should be designed so that nothing gets in the way of fighting and landing big fish. And it should have readily available boating and angling accessories. Those are the criteria that I recommend you start with.

Sonar. The previous chapter covers sonar use and installation thoroughly. The only other aspect of sonar that I want to address is how you can make sonar equipment portable in order to use it on other boats. I often fish in places where rented or borrowed boats are used and where sophisticated sonar equipment is wanting; I've even taken a graph recorder as far as the Arctic Circle. People who rent a boat at a vacation destination, or who travel to a wilderness lodge to fish for walleyes or lake trout, or who simply avail themselves of a boat belonging to someone who doesn't have sonar gear may want to bring their own sonar equipment for trolling or general fishing and boating.

There are portable models of flashers that will do the job, but suppose you want to take a unit off your boat? Some manufacturers have pack housings that make certain stationary units portable. For others, you'll need to purchase a spare electrical connection from the manufacturer, to which you can attach alligator clips for battery terminal connections. Be sure that you'll have a 12-volt battery where you're headed. Take the appropriate transducer off your boat or use another; lay it flat on the floor (in an aluminum boat) or in the bilge of the boat for nonhigh-speed use, or use a transducer bracket (sold in some stores and in mail-order catalogs) that clamps to the transom or gunwale of the boat. If the battery is strong and if you use it only to power the flasher or graph, it will work for many days without needing to be recharged.

I've used this method for taking graph recorders with me to places that have no means of recharging batteries, and I have used spare floatplane batteries for power. Another option is to find the appropriate size tackle box, fit the electronic unit, a wet cell motorcycle battery, battery charger, transducer bracket, and transducer all inside for ease of use and transportation.

The author has taken a portable downrigger and graph recorder, powered by a wet cell battery, to remote Canadian locales and successfully used them for deep lake trout trolling.

Downriggers. The use of downriggers, and such options as arm length, manual or electric operation, swivel or fixed base, weight type, and so forth is covered in chapter 1. In talking about trolling aids, I'd like to add a few more thoughts about installations and tell you how you can fashion an excellent, removable mounting system for small boat use.

Downriggers can be installed almost anywhere on a boat as long as there is sufficient base support to hold them. A handrail would not provide enough support, for instance, and a thin gunwale — as found on aluminum cartoppers — may or may not be adequate where small clamp-on downriggers are employed. You can beef up a wide thin aluminum gunwale with a long, strong piece of metal or wood, however, and be able to mount a downrigger base there. There is at least one downrigger, a Walker, that is specifically meant for small boats, and fastens to an oarlock.

Most of the time, downriggers are mounted along the stern or on the gunwales close to the stern and spaced adequately so that they provide opportune horizontal lure placement. You need to be able to retrieve weights readily and engage releases without interference. The length of the downrigger arm depends on how far apart you want to get your lures, what obstacles (platforms, trim tabs, coolers) you have to clear behind the boat, what is convenient for swinging cable and weight in for rigging, and any peculiarities of your boat design.

Small boaters who use their vessels for many types of fishing, including conventional casting or still-fishing, might want to use downriggers or rod holders for trolling but wouldn't want the inconvenience of permanent mountings or drilled holes in a boat that they might not keep more than a few seasons. I've been modifying boats that don't seem to be suitable for trolling and downrigger fishing in a temporary and flexible way for a decade. Bass boats, for example, make good trolling vehicles, though rod holders and downriggers are a burden when you are fishing for species that needn't be trolled. For this reason, I prefer readily removable equipment. By fastening downrigger plates to the appropriate transom areas of a bass boat, you can take them on and off with ease, but a better tactic is to utilize a trolling board system.

I've currently got a 16-foot aluminum boat that I've done this to and I'll explain how it works. The board itself is an extremely sturdy rectangular aluminum duct obtained from a friend in the construction

A two-downrigger trolling board, complete with rod holders, on a bass boat. The board is removed when the boat is not used for trolling. This is a great system for small boat owners who use their boats for many kinds of fishing.

trade. It is mounted on the gunwales via metal clamps and located just behind the bow casting deck. A downrigger on a swivel base is mounted at either end. Both downriggers have optional rod holders attached to them, and the board is also equipped with two fully adjustable Bystrom rod holders. Both the board and the attached equipment can readily be removed. The downriggers are turned inward and fastened to each other for travel. With this system, the downriggers and rods are directly in front of me at the console and can be observed. The only drawback is that the downrigger weights are close together due to the narrow beam of the boat, causing the attached lines to be directly under the boat. When fishing near the surface, you may cut a fishing line on the propeller if you turn as sharply as possible.

Sharp turning isn't a problem with a similar trolling board system I utilized on earlier fiberglass bass boats. I installed half-length handrails on the rear gunwales and made a trolling board out of 1 x 8 pine. Mounting plates were attached to the board so that two downriggers could be readily detached from the board. I put rod holders on the board, plus rail-mount models on each handrail. The board was fitted with rubber tire tubing or carpeting on the ends to keep it from scratching the fiberglass, was cut to fit from gunwale to gunwale without sticking out over the edges, and slid under the handrails and just behind the seats. The only disadvantages to this system on such a boat are that the rods are always to the rear and you can't get into the live well or storage compartments without moving the board. There is no problem with shallow fishing or sharp turns, however.

The last point I want to make about downriggers is to carry parts in your boat or tackle box to remake connections. If you snag a downrigger weight and break the cable, you obviously need to rig up again. But if the cable becomes kinked or frayed, you should cut the cable above the affected area and connect it anew to the snap. Keep a supply of connector sleeves, large (No. 10) stainless steel snap swivels, and U-shaped cable supports with you. A pair of crimping pliers will make sure that you cinch the tubes tightly. If you're caught in a pinch without the necessary parts, you can run downrigger cable directly through the eye of the weight and then tie it off securely, but this is for short-term use only. Be especially careful not to crimp, kink, or fray cable that attaches to thermal sensors at the end of the cable by the downrigger weight, because you'll probably have to send this back to the manufacturer for repair, one of the drawbacks to downrigger cable-connected temperature-sensing mechanisms.

Temperature gauges. One of the most important aids for trollers is some type of temperature gauge. For many trolling activities, including shallow spring fishing, deep-water fishing, and angling for salmon and trout, an ability to find preferred temperature levels is a big help in catching fish. I believe in temperature monitoring so much that I seldom fish out of a boat for any species of fish without having some means of taking water temperature.

I have a surface temperature gauge on my boat and I also carry a hand-held thermometer, which I keep in a tackle box and carry with me everywhere. The boat gauge reads only surface temperature (the sensor is on the transom and always in the water), but it is most valuable, particularly in the spring and fall when water temperature is changing on a sometimes daily basis. Surface water temperature, particularly when the water is warming up, is a strong indication of where you might expect to find fish and under what conditions the fish might become more active.

The other temperature gauge that I use is simply a pool thermometer. It's a sturdy, reliable thermometer that I purchased from a pool equipment supplier for less than ten bucks. It's hardy enough to be bounced around in my boat or tackle box, and I use it to check the surface temperature of the water (by leaving it tied to the boat and dangling in the water) or the temperature at any particular depth. To accomplish the latter, I tie the pool thermometer to a snap, lower it to a specific depth on fishing line, leave it for a few minutes, then reel it up quickly to read. Another method is to tie the thermometer to a manually operated downrigger weight and lower it with the weight to a known depth. To retrieve it, I crank the weight up furiously to be sure of getting an accurate temperature reading. The same thing can also be accomplished with an electric downrigger, but because this cannot be raised as quickly, it is more likely to cause the temperature to change slightly as the thermometer is raised slowly through warmer water levels on top.

There are portable, self-contained, battery-operated temperature probes that are attached to a hand-held meter and lowered on flexible rubber-coated cable to various depths. These can be used for surface and deep-water temperature readings. Probes have an advantage over thermometers because they can be lowered to various depths for readings without being raised constantly. The disadvantages are that they must be lowered into the water any time you want to check temperature, and the cable must be manually wound or cranked around the meter spool. The deeper you drop the probe the more cable you need on the unit and the more you have to wind and wrap. This is a mite inconvenient and occasionally uncomfortable when the water is cold and you're working with bare hands.

Inevitably deep trollers will want a unit that reports deep-water temperatures all the time while trolling. From a practical standpoint, the most functional way to monitor deep-water temperature would be to utilize a device (of necessity electronic) that reported temperature continuously, so you could measure it at any depth at any time while trolling, much the way a surface temperature gauge operates. To get deep continuous readings, however, you necessarily need to employ a downrigger. At present there are several ways of doing so.

The first of these, and probably the oldest, is to use the downrigger cable as a conduit for signals from a sensor just above the downrigger clip to a meter that attaches to the body of the downrigger on the boat. To my knowledge, the only manufacturer to have such a unit in use and production for many years is Riviera. Their Temp Troll comes in manual and electric versions.

Many trollers, including myself, have used the Temp Troll relatively successfully for years, although several problems have been continuously associated with the use of this device. First, if you snag the

Temp Troll weight on the bottom and snap the cable, you're out of commission entirely because of the special conductive coaxial cable used on the unit. You can't replace it with regular downrigger cable, plus you need a probe. The second problem is that downrigger cables are subject to getting pinched, crimped, or kinked. A severe kink is the death knell for a Temp Troll cable, and the unit either won't work or will give false readings. Thirdly, these units have been prone to sensor or meter malfunctions and are obviously useless as a temperature gauge when this happens. Finally, Riviera has not been known for correcting design problems with any of their downriggers, for having parts available, or for making speedy repairs and returns. If you need your Temp Troll unit to fish but have to send it to the manufacturer for who knows how long, you might tend to wait until the winter to get it repaired. But what do you do if it needs repairs in April or May?

I have a manually operated Temp Troll and have had pretty good luck with it, but I know many fishermen who have had problem after problem, although they liked the ability of this unit to check water temperature instantly at any depth when it was working properly.

There is another way to utilize the cable-sensor system, however. The Fishmate Thermocline Locator, manufactured by J&J Associates of Rochester, New York, is a clever add-on that can be adapted to any downrigger. Via a sensing instrument at the terminal end and a transmittal coaxial cable, the unit records water temperature at any depth to which the downrigger weight is lowered. You ship your downrigger to J&J, they replace the old cable with sensor-attached conductive coaxial cable, attach a female plug-in receptacle to your downrigger spool, and supply you with a 9-volt battery-operated hand-held meter. In operation, you lower your downrigger to a specific depth, plug the male connector of the meter into the downrigger spool receptacle, and wait a few moments for the unit to register the temperature. Unplug the two and lower the weight to a new depth, reconnect, and take a new temperature reading.

This costs upward of $200 plus shipping and is subject to much the same potential difficulties as the Riviera Temp Troll, although repairs and service time are much better. However, the Fishmate Thermocline Locator is a way to turn an existing downrigger into a vehicle for monitoring deep temperatures and does cost less than a Temp Troll or a different type of temperature-sensing device.

The other ways of obtaining deep, continuous temperature read-

This manual downrigger was transformed into a temperature-sensing unit with the Fishmate Thermocline Locator.

ings are through a large torpedolike probe that attaches to the downrigger cable just above the weight, has a 9-volt battery inside the probe, and sends temperature readings up to a meter with or without using the downrigger cable as a signal conduit. These devices now report speed as well, and for this reason I consider them in the following section.

Trolling speed and temperature indicators. The most expensive and sophisticated trolling speed and temperature indicators are those that report speed in knots or miles per hour and temperature continuously and at any depth level. If you are wondering why it may be important to know lure speed or whether lure speed can be different from boat speed, I suggest you reread chapter 4.

My first attempt at obtaining continuous deep speed and temperatures readings was unsatisfactory. I bought a Fish Hawk Model 650 Thermo-Troll, which sported a 9-inch-long tube/probe that attached to any downrigger just above the weight. The tube contained a 9-volt alkaline battery and sent temperature signals back to a transducer on the transom of my boat. The transducer was connected via electrical cable to a meter, which in turn was connected to my electrical system.

The unit reported only temperature. I was very dissatisfied with it because it regularly gave wacky readings. Even when I thought it might be working right, I didn't have faith in it and was double-checking it often with a pool thermometer. I sent it to the manufacturer for repair, but continued to have wild readings, like 99 degrees in 50 degree water, and eventually gave up on it with grave misgivings about this type of product.

Recently, however, I communicated with Fish Hawk and they took this unit back and replaced it with their latest Thermo-Troll, the Model 800 computer, which monitors deep-water temperature, surface water temperature, speed at the downrigger, and boat speed. It has a large probe, called a sensor/sender, which sports a paddle wheel on the bottom and a forward temperature sensor. A black cap on top of the tube transmits signals to a receiving transducer on the transom of the boat. The transducer sports a paddle wheel speed sensor and a temperature sensor and is connected by electrical cable to a digital liquid crystal display meter. An optional model also can provide surface and deep pH measurements.

Besides the fact that this device gives you a lot of valuable information, its biggest advantages are that signals are transmitted from probe to transducer and that there is no special downrigger cable to worry about. Another advantage is simple installation. The top of the transmitter probe is snapped to standard downrigger cable. The bottom is attached to a short length of 60-pound-test cable (supplied with the unit), which in turn is snapped to the downrigger weight. The receiving transducer obviously needs to be installed, but that isn't difficult.

A drawback to this system is that you could lose the probe/sensor if your downrigger weight is hung up, which could be a costly ($200) replacement. The lighter cable between probe and weight, however, should break before the main downrigger cable. I haven't hung mine up yet, but I assure you that when I get close to doing so I raise the weight as quickly as possible. Furthermore, I usually don't use the probe-equipped downrigger as the deepest of my downriggers to prevent a hangup.

Somewhat of a disadvantage is the fact that the probe/sensor is large and causes cable swayback, meaning that the weight is not directly below the boat and thus shallower than your depth counter indicates. The faster you troll the more your downrigger weight is likely to angle back anyway, regardless of whether a probe is attached to it. But the probe adds more resistance and does cause more swayback under normal conditions. A possible solution to this is to use a heavier weight, say a 12 pounder instead of a 10, or simply allow for swayback when determining depth.

Another speed and temperature-sensing device is the Weller Troll Control, formerly known as the Procombinator when it was manufactured by B. C. Electronics. Weller bought this a few years ago and made good strides in making it a more serviceable product. The Troll Control formerly had circuit board problems that lead to unreliable operation on some units.

The Troll Control reads speed and temperature at the depth of the downrigger weight and sports a 7-inch paddle wheel probe that is on the downrigger cable above the weight. Unlike the Fish Hawk unit, the Troll Control uses a special coated conductive cable that runs from the probe to the downrigger spool and then to a meter. There is also a rod to be installed horizontally across the transom in the water and connected to a black electrical lead, which in turn is attached to the meter. The meter is not connected to a boat's battery but has two internal 9-volt batteries; the probe also has a 9-volt battery inside it. Speed and temperature signals are transmitted through the wire to the meter.

This device works well and reliably when it has been installed correctly, but the installation instructions that came with the unit (TC 1000) I bought two years ago were vague and unhelpful. Later instructions were better illustrated and less confusing. One advantage to this device is that it does not have to be permanently mounted to work and doesn't require a large 12-volt battery for power, meaning that even small cartop boaters could employ the device or those who remove the downrigger from the regular boat for a wilderness trip, for example, could bring this device along and benefit from its use.

The disadvantages of possible probe loss and swayback exist with this unit, and it does not read surface temperature and speed simultaneously with deep temperature and speed, though you can raise the probe to the surface to measure these factors. The fact that the Weller Troll Control relies on signal transmission through the downrigger cable also poses loss and abrasion problems, the consequences of which I discussed earlier. Weller uses 100-pound cable between the weight and probe and 130-pound cable from downrigger to weight in an effort to minimize loss of the probe if the weight is hung up. The company advises using liquid neoprene or fingernail polish, anything nonconductive, to patch over frayed cable spots.

Still another manufacturer of speed indicators is Electro Marine Systems (EMS), which makes a series of speed indicators, including two that measure speed and temperature at any depth and connect to the downriggers. Their probe is 6 inches long and powered by an internal 9-volt battery. It is connected to nylon coated Berkley Steelon downrigger cable that leads to the downrigger. An analog (Penguin 1) or digital (Penguin 2) readout meter, connected to a 12-volt boat battery, provides simultaneous displays of speed and temperature at the depth of the probe, and there is a small antenna that attaches to the boom of the downrigger. The antenna amplifies signals sent from the probe without the need for a transducer.

Although I haven't personally used the Penguin unit, I think it's a good one and like the advantage of having simultaneous speed and temperature displays. I still view using the cable for signal transmission as being a less desirable alternative to wireless operation, although EMS says that the Penguin still works down to a depth of 50 feet (it ordinarily works to 200 feet) even if the cable is frayed, and points out that it only costs about ten bucks to replace this readily available

The EMS indicator on the left measures surface speed and temperature.

cable if necessary. They also note that installation of the entire system is very simple, can be accomplished in 20 minutes, and can be done on the water.

A good feature of this unit, incidentally, and one that similar devices don't have, is an automatically activated on/off probe switch. When the probe is lowered into the water, the battery starts it working and when it is raised out of the water the probe shuts off. With other devices, you have to remove the probe battery or turn the probe upside down. If you forget to do so, which I do often, you quickly lose 9-volt battery strength.

I see a burgeoning market for devices that incorporate speed and temperature sensors at the downrigger weight. Cannon confirms that it has been working on developing a wireless system to do just this and may have a product on the market shortly after this book is published. I know that EMS, Weller, and Fish Hawk are working to improve their units and to offer still more information in the process. As I noted in an October 1985 *Field & Stream* article, I'm looking forward to the day when there is a computer-operated device, preferably incorporated into a downrigger, that reports lure speed, water temperature, and light intensity at the depth of the downrigger weight. The device should work all the time and not be affected by cable kinking. Light intensity, salinity, and pH will probably be measured by these devices sometime in the future. Lake Systems just developed a product, the Multi-C-lector, which will do much of this.

In my opinion, the wave of the future in deep-water speed and temperature monitoring devices will be wireless, provided the probes/sensors work and are reliable. Easy installation, "user-friendly" operation, good instructions with illustrations, solid construction, and day-after-day reliability will be the keys to achieving mass acceptance and winning a place in the troller's heart. I don't mind saying that I still turn on my speed- and temperature-indicating devices each day with a bit of will-they-work-this-time apprehension. I don't feel that way about my sonar, downriggers, surface temp gauge, or other trolling tools.

To close out this review of speed and temperature indicators, let me mention that electronic devices that measure boat speed with or without surface temperature are also available from several sources. Electronic Marine Systems leads the field in this arena and formerly made the now-defunct Penguin brand analog speed indicator, which was distributed by another company. Sensing devices for these instruments are located flush to the hull/transom line and are available in analog or digital readouts.

I think it's very important to know boat speed, especially when you're using flat lines and fishing shallow in the spring. This is particularly true for small boaters who may not be employing a downrigger for shallow spring fishing. I know one charter boat captain who has two surface trolling speed indicators on the port and starboard sides of his transom, because he claims it helps him distinguish speed difference from one side of the boat to another when he is making turns (the inside lures slow down and the outside ones speed up on sharp turns). If this causes a strike, he claims that the speed on the appropriate side of the boat will clue him to what trolling speed the fish want the lures.

Fishermen with small boats, and those who don't want to go electronic, can use the Wright & McGill Accu-Troll to indicate relative boat speed. With this device, which clamps to the gunwale, a 1-pound weight hangs from the bottom of a swinging arm and is dragged through the water to indicate speed. The arm swimgs to an analog dial that indicates relative units of speed, not actual speed in nautical or statute miles per hour. Another device, the Grizzly speed indicator from Dura Pak, works in a similar fashion, but is not as durable as the Accu-Troll.

One last point about trolling speed indicators: they are not necessarily compatible. If someone tells you that he caught fish while going at 2 1/4 mph, it doesn't mean that when your unit indicates a speed of 2 1/4 that you are in fact traveling at exactly the same speed as him. Units differ from brand to brand. Your speed and someone else's may be compatible, but the only way to know for sure is to get next to that person and compare speed indicator readings. Use someone else's information as a guide, but try speeds above and below that to establish what works for you.

Loran. Short for LOng RAnge Navigation, Loran is a low-frequency land-based navigation system that big boat fishermen are using in coastal waters and in the Great Lakes. Some type of navigation system will become a greater force for anglers and boaters everywhere in time. Loran C, presently in use, allows boats to locate and return to specific places or relatively small spots, although its accuracy is just fair and depends on a number of factors. The wave of the future here will be when there are fairly economical high-frequency satellite navigation (SatNav) units that transmit directly from a satellite to a receiving unit on a boat and bypass present land-based transmittal stations. The degree of accuracy with this is thought to be much greater than Loran C — perhaps as precise as being within 3 meters of any target — and may work in all land- and water-based areas capable of receiving signals from a satellite. Even small boats on inland lakes will be able to pinpoint precise spots by "the numbers" with SatNav. There's talk of an even more sophisticated system that eventually will become available. In fact, a few expensive SatNav Lorans are now in limited production.

Big boaters and charter boat operators on the Great Lakes are increasingly turning to Loran use, despite its limitations, for helping them to return to places where they caught fish or located schools of fish. Loran also aids in navigating at dawn, at dusk, or in fog. Some Loran units are now being made for small boaters, too. When SatNav products become widely available at reasonable prices, more big water anglers will want to employ them to find fish. I'm not going to launch into a discourse on this subject because relatively few freshwater trollers are utilizing this equipment, but in the future it may be a much more significant part of the trolling scene.

Some other sophisticated electronic devices may also be part of the scene, though I doubt the practicality of them for the average troller. Be advised, however, that a growing number of Great Lakes skippers are using radio direction finders (RDFs), which allow them to locate the source of a radio transmission. When someone calls a pal over the radio, for instance, and says he's catching fish at "the same spot where we caught them last weekend," someone with an RDF will pick up that transmission and be able to pinpoint the direction from whence it came. That knowledge might send the interested party in the direction of the lucky angler to get in on the action. Some RDFs are used in conjunction with automatic scanners so they pick up any transmission on any VHF frequency. This shows you how serious some folks take their trolling.

Autopilots are another device that some big water anglers, again primarily charter boat captains, are using, not only to keep them on course at running speeds but also to give the opportunity to set lines at trolling speed without being at the steering wheel. If you have a big boat and a bulging wallet, maybe you will want something like this, too.

Planers. Anglers who troll for trout or salmon in the spring may find it necessary to get their lures well off to the side of their boat and behind it, in which case sideplaner boards become extremely functional devices. I discuss these in detail in chapter 2. Sea Skee (Wille Products) and Super Ski (Prince Mastercraft) are two of the more prominent planer boards. To utilize them, however, you need to have some system of retrieving the line that tethers them to your boat. Manual downriggers may suffice, but they have limitations for such usage. A variety of homemade retrieval systems have been applied to this endeavor, with the reels attached to the boat's gunwales. Cannon makes the Plane-R-Reel, a good product, that comes in permanent and clamp-on models for use with planer boards. Prince also makes a good retrieval system, and some other manufacturers are in this business.

There are sideplaners that fasten directly to your fishing line. The Yellowbird remains on the line but trips so you don't fight the board as well as the fish. The Rover (from Troll Sports Co.) can also be arranged to trip and stay on the line, but is primarily used in a manner that allows it to detach from the fishing line when a fish strikes so you don't have it dragging in the water as you play a fish. You do have to circle back to retrieve the board, however. Such systems don't require the equipment and expense of big boards, but you do need stouter tackle to run them.

Diving planers are discussed in chapter 13.

Releases. Release clips are essential to downrigger and sideplaner board fishing and are a relatively cheap but important component of trolling. The types of release clips and how they work are reviewed in chapters 1 and 2, but I want to stress that it is important to test these periodically. In your spare time, take a good-quality hand scale or force gauge, attach line to it, attach the other end of the line in the release clip as if you were fishing, and test it to see how much real force it takes to trip the release, which depends on the size of line used, the location of the line in the release, the tension setting, and the amount of line out. I think you'll find this exercise rather enlightening.

Consider that it might be worthwhile to avoid metal or plastic release devices altogether and simply use rubberbands. No. 14 or 16 rubberbands, available in bulk in office supply stores, are popular with some fishermen, but I think they may be too strong unless you are using heavy line (17 pounds and up) or particularly hard-pulling lures. You can use a rubberband as a release at the downrigger weight or to stack lines. Fold the rubberband over the fishing line, wrap one end of the band underneath the second and pull it taut, then connect it to the cable or to a snap on the downrigger or cable end.

Because of the elasticity of rubberbands and monofilament line, it is often hard to snap your fishing line out of them, so you frequently have to pull the downrigger up before freeing the line. Another drawback is that rubberbands are hard to use with light lines. I am also highly suspicious of their breaking strength. For instance, I took four new and unused No. 16 rubberbands and applied a force gauge to them to see how much pressure it took to break them. The first broke at 13 pounds, the second at 9, the third at 9 1/2, and the fourth at 8 1/2. The range from 8 1/2 to 13 bothers me, not to mention that 8 1/2 is a lot of tension.

Trolling plates. Trollers who need to move slowly, but whose big engines don't allow them to do so, can utilize a trolling plate that baffles the propeller and ably serves to impede forward momentum. Several companies make them. With the plate in the up position, the boat can be run at high speeds without impairment; when down the plate slows boat speed. Several companies make such devices. Mine, the Happy Troller (Idea Development Co.), has a rudder on it, has

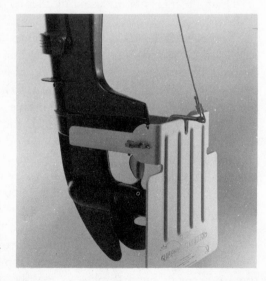

A trolling plate, shown in the operating position, slows a boat down significantly. It is raised for high-speed boat operation.

worked well for several seasons, and really cuts momentum down without sacrificing maneuverability.

Whenever I need to go slow, I use the trolling plate; on very windy days I use it when headed downwind but not when headed upwind. I take the plate off when I'm not using the boat for trolling. You do have to be careful that you don't bang the plate on an underwater obstruction, or that you don't forget that the plate is down when you're ready to plane out, which can damage it. These plates are spring-loaded and flip down for trolling by pulling a cord. You pull up on the cord to lock the plate in the up position. Some plates don't lock down into position right away, so it may be necessary to put your engine in reverse momentarily to lock the trolling plate into the down position.

Sea anchors. Many big boaters would rather not use trolling plates to slow them down, but at times, especially when there's a stiff tailwind, they might need to slow down. An auxiliary low-horsepower engine is one slow trolling option that also doubles as emergency propulsion if your main engine fails. It is especially useful on large bodies of water when you get well offshore and when the water gets especially rough. Another method is to utilize sea anchors, which are big bags that sailboaters and cruisers often use as a drag when drifting.

These large bags are made of ripstop nylon and may open up like an umbrella or a huge funnel when pulled through the water. They effectively slow momentum down and are attached to the gunwales of the boat. Sometimes one anchor will do but it may cause the boat to veer to that side, so you may need them on both sides anyway to maintain a slow speed. You must adjust the anchors for the amount of drag desired. I have used one of these products, Boat Brakes (Blue Harbor Inc.), on a friend's boat and am impressed with the way they collapse inward for easy retrieval as well as with the way they influence speed.

Steering devices. For big boat skippers, particularly for those who fish on the Great Lakes and spend a lot of time at the stern tending rigs and lines, the Cannon Helmsman offers remote-control steering capability. Electrically operated, the earlier models feature a long-cord remote switch, but the newest version is wireless. This device helps maintain boat control and is especially useful for keeping the boat straight when you set lines, fish alone, and/or fight a big fish, or when you maneuver to adjust lines. It doesn't work as well when the water is rough and when you're headed into the wind because many small steering adjustments must constantly be made. If you've got a large enough boat, and some extra bucks to spend, this is a nice trolling accessory to have. Some Great Lakes charter boat captains who don't have a mate use this device, while a few who have very large boats employ some form of autopiloting instrument.

Downrigger depth guide. The occurrence of cable swayback due to boat speed or current flow is discussed in chapter 1. The bottom line is that your downrigger weight and the lure attached to it may not be as deep as indicated on the downrigger's line counter. If the cable sways back significantly from a vertical position, the weight and lure will be shallower than the line counter indicates. This can have an adverse impact on your fishing success if you need to be fishing at a specific depth. An accessory that helps you calculate the exact depth under this condition is the Osprey Computrac Downrigger's Guide. This product features a clear plastic protractor that shows you the angle of swayback and a laminated chart to calculate actual depth. It's a clever accessory that downrigger fishermen who consistently experience swayback, and those who troll often in deep water, will find useful.

Marker buoys. Buoys are one item used frequently in conjunction with sonar equipment. Most big lake and deep-water trollers don't use marker buoys because they roam so widely, because the buoys aren't functional in really deep water, or because the placement of the buoys could interfere with trolling. However, boaters on small- to medium-size bodies of water, those who are looking to define specific and relatively shallow underwater structures or contours for trolling, and those who may be trolling to locate schools of fish that they will stop and cast to have good reason to use some type of marker buoy.

You can make your own marker buoys but there are good products in bright colors available from Lowrance and Humminbird, and these are nothing more than plastic floats and heavy weights with strong line attached to those weights. It is best to get a flat type of marker rather than a round barbell version because the former is more resistant to the effects of current, wind, and waves than the latter. Round markers can get blown quite a distance from the specific site they were supposed to identify, which does not happen with the square marker buoys. Incidentally, you might want to put your name on these buoys with a dark indelible marking pen. I've had curious pleasure boaters and sailors pick mine up.

Light meters/color guides. A lot of attention has been paid to lure colors in recent years, and a few devices measure light intensity and correlate this to lure colors that should be fished, suggesting that fish will strike the colors most visible under those conditions. The Color-C-Lector from Lake Systems Division is foremost of these and the product that has everyone's attention focused on this aspect of fishing. This is essentially a light intensity meter with a readout that corresponds to a color spectrum scale. The meter sports a probe that is lowered into the water and correlates the most visible colors to the clarity of the water. This device differentiates between muddy, stained, and clear water and registers the colors (and shades) that are most visible to fish under those conditions. It is 5 inches in diameter and 5 inches deep, and is water- and shockproof. I review the use of this meter for trolling, as well as the entire concept of trolling lure color selection, elsewhere in the book.

Lure storage systems. Most trollers store their lures in some type of tackle box. Because there are many good tackle boxes around and because this is such an obvious matter, I'm not going to dwell on that aspect of trolling equipment. One thing about trollers, however, especially trout, salmon, and musky fishermen, is that they possess a lot of lures and often use a lot of different lures in the course of a day's fishing. As a result, they tend to pile up lures that have been used or are about to be used on boat seats, decks, cooler tops, engine covers, and so forth. They like to have an array of tackle handy and accessible during the day, and often don't want to go through a compartmented tackle box and have to separate a handful of multihooked lures. Because of this, trollers often use or devise some lure and terminal tackle storage system that attaches to the interior of the boat and is convenient.

Devices for small boaters and small lure storage include the Weed

Master Snatch Box, which has a lid that locks lures in place plus a storage area inside; Berkley's Outdoorsman lure holder, which is a simple strip of foam and plastic; and the Action lure holder from Nautical Interiors, which has a half-dozen open slots that lures fit into.

An interesting alternative to traditional tackle box storage systems, and one used by some Great Lakes fishermen, is a soft compartmentalized cloth that keeps lures free of tangling and can be hung for easy access. Some homemade versions are in use. Commercially produced models, called Hangups (from Seahunter), are constructed of tough Dacron sailcloth and are covered with a clear, heavy vinyl sheet. They will not rot or mildew and are snagproof. Spoons, plugs, and other tackle items, such as dodgers or flashers, can be stored in individual compartments without tangling. Hangups can be folded and stored in a boat compartment or snapped under the gunwale. The vinyl keeps water off the lures. There are nine models of Hangups, each available in three sizes; the smallest is 6" x 13" and the largest is 16" x 25". Other similar models by the same manufacturer, called Dittys, sport carrying handles and Velcro closures.

Last but not least, I shouldn't overlook the highly sophisticated and ingenious lure storage system favored by many musky anglers: buckets and foam coolers! I'm kidding about this being sophisticated, but it is functional. Lures are hung head down on the inside of the cooler (not the outside, where hooks would inevitably snare things), with the rear hook stuck into the top of the cooler or draped over the lip of the bucket. Foam coolers are preferable because the hook can be imbedded in them, and they're cheap and expendable.

Rod holders. Rod holders for use while trolling come in many forms and are made by many manufacturers. In rod holders, I look for adjustability, ease of rod removal, sturdiness and stability, and placement options.

Some rod holders are mounted on downriggers and are not adjustable but are still very useful. Some are designed into the boat as through-the-gunwale holders. Some are mounted on trolling boards, handrails, or gunwales and are used for flat-line rods, downrigger rods, and planer board or outrigger rods; to serve many purposes well, these should be adjustable to different positions and angles.

These are nontraditional lure storage systems that are favored by some trollers.

For small boat and short rod use, I am particularly fond of Down-East Sportscraft rod holders. Made of corrosive-proof metal and fully adjustable, these durable holders come in clamp-on, rail, and flush-mount models. To release the rod, pull the handle upward and the top of the holder snaps open. A tube-type rod holder that I like is made by Bystrom; it stands straight up like a rocket launcher, swivels at the base under adjustable tension, and pivots to any angle.

The arrangement of fishing accessories via a board across the transom of a boat is fairly typical on many large trolling boats. Aluminum boards are manufactured by a few suppliers, and some anglers fashion their own from aluminum or wood. Two downriggers are usually mounted on the boards, with another two on the gunwales. Ample rod holders are placed on the board to allow rods in use to be within a narrow scope of vision and also to keep the lines clear of the motor to avoid cutoffs when turning sharply. Tube-type rod holders attached to the board or the downrigger are best here.

Stowing rods out of the way when not in use, such as when you are boating down the lake, makes good sense. There are various ways to do this, depending on the design of your boat. Open boats, center

Rods pop up out of Down-East holders, which are adjustable, extremely durable, and sturdy

consoles, and cutty cabin craft often sport through-the-gunwale or flush-mounted holders that keep the rods upright. This isn't practical for many small boats, and in some horizontal mounting is preferable. The decks of many small boats are often cluttered with rods, and many anglers leave these to bounce freely when the boat is moving at high speed. A snap-in floor holder securely retains them.

Propeller guard. A great accessory for anglers who fish shallow rivers or venture into uncertain waters is an outboard prop guard. OMC makes one for their 9.9 and 15 hp motors. The guard protects the propeller and part of the lower skeg. In appropriate situations, the motor is operated in the tilted shallow-water-drive position so it will kick up when it hits an object. Recently I bought one of the new Mercury 9.9 hp outboard motors especially made for trolling and fit the skeg and prop housing with the OMC prop guard. I had an old Mercury 7.5 hp motor that the OMC guard would not fit, but it appears that the latest Mercury motors are just different enough in the lower unit areas to allow such installation.

Some anglers have devised homemade guards, and you may see some of these on various rivers. I cut the fork from a pitchfork and hose-clamped it around the lower unit of my old 7.5 hp motor; this worked well as a guard but the engine performance was greatly impeded for nontrolling application, plus the guard didn't offer much protection if you backed into some object.

An OMC prop guard mounted on the author's 9.9 hp Mercury engine. The guard is particularly good for river fishing and keeps the propeller from contacting objects.

Electric motors and accessories. Those who strictly troll out of large boats, who do no casting, or who don't fish on lakes where outboard engines are prohibited may be surprised to see that I'm devoting some attention to electric motors in a trolling book. That's because they have no need for such devices. Many small lake fishermen, and those with small boats used for a variety of fishing applications, possess electric motors and use them for trolling. In fact, electric outboard motors are routinely referred to by many anglers and the general boating community as "trolling motors."

All electric motors are battery powered. Some run off just a single 12-volt battery; others run off 24 volts, requiring two 12-volt batteries; and some have the capability of running off either one or two 12-volt batteries. Not all electric motors are alike. Some produce considerably more thrust than others, which means that they are basically more powerful. There are such things as sustained thrust and initial thrust, however, the former being the power generated while underway and the latter being the initial startup power. Initial thrust is greater than sustained thrust. The amount of energy (designated as amperes or amps) consumed per hour by electric motors varies. This figure, when known, will tell you how many hours of continuous use you can get out of a battery at varied speeds.

Electric motors can get pretty technical, so the best thing to do is to check the specifications of these products and determine how much power you need and for how long you need that power in normal fishing circumstances. Generally, the heavier your boat and boatload, the more thrust you need. Another factor to consider is how much fishing you do in areas of substantial current or wind, which drains the reserves of a battery quicker than calm conditions.

On most fiberglass and many aluminum bass boats, an electric motor is mounted permanently on the bow, with the bracket support installed on the starboard to help put a little weight on that side and counterbalance the console and driver weight on the port side. If these are remotely operated with a foot pedal, they are relatively hard to control for trolling use. On small boats such as rowboats and johnboats, electric motors can be mounted on the front or back, but for convenience and best boat control while trolling, transom mounting is preferable, as is manual operation.

Small boats usually require the use of a single 12-volt electric motor only, though you can employ more than one motor at a time.

Some anglers who fish reservoirs where no outboards are allowed rig up two or three electrics in unison. There was a time when I had two small electrics of relatively low thrust, which I used together on a johnboat. They were hooked to two batteries and worked marvelously for trolling or for getting from one point to another fairly quickly.

One of the features you ought to look for in an electric motor is a breakaway bracket, where the shaft of the motor can slip back if it collides with an immovable object. This will save you from having bent shafts, damaged lower units, and extraordinary stress on the mounting bracket when you get into tricky shallow spots.

Another important feature is silence. Shallow water trollers who use electric motors can conceivably get much closer to fish than boaters with far noisier gas outboard engines. Not spooking fish is obviously advantageous. Some electrics are considerably noisier than others, however. Two Mercury Thruster Plus electrics that I've had were extremely noisy. Silvertrols were on the noisy side, too. The Minn-Kota was fairly quiet as was a Johnson electric I once had, but these and the Mercury were also pretty weak. The Motor Guide Perfector, which I now have, has plenty of power and seems to be only slightly noisier than the Minn-Kota.

If you're new to the electric motor scene, it will pay to shop around and compare features as well as price. Operate a few different models to compare all of their performance aspects. You should also look into the new battery-energy-saving and variable-speed control systems that most top-quality electric motors now have. This feature is called pulse-width modulation and is designed to extend battery life and provide more hours on the water. Pulse-width modulation is especially valuable to electric motor trollers who may spend many continuous hours draining a battery down.

Electric motors cannot be used without a battery. This is a seemingly obvious fact, yet one that many prospective first-time electric motor buyers overlook. You don't just buy an electric motor. You also need one or more batteries plus a means of recharging a battery. An electric motor does not automatically recharge the power source. In the course of a full day's fishing, you will likely drain the energy of a battery down considerably; therefore, it is necessary to recharge it frequently with a battery charger.

The best products for powering electric motors are deep-cycle batteries. Deep-cycle batteries are often called marine batteries, but

A hand-operated electric motor mounted on the transom is useful for slow trolling and when big engine noise is not desired.

not all marine batteries are deep cycled, so you should check to be sure that the batteries you obtain for electric motor use are deep-cycle products. These are constructed with special plates that allow them to be drawn down regularly and recharged; standard batteries are not meant to do this and do not have nearly the life of deep-cycle batteries when used for electric motor operation. I've used Gould Action Pak and Sears Marine Diehard deep-cycle batteries with good results for many years. For maximum performance, you are best off with the highest amperage batteries that you feel you can use — I've used 80 amps but prefer 105 — and a high-amp-capacity battery charger —at least 10 amps or more if you'll need to recharge dead batteries fully in several hours' time. For starting the outboard motor, you don't need a deep-cycle battery. A conventional automotive battery will do, but opt for a nondeep-cycle marine battery. I've had good use here out of Gould Super Crank, Sears Diehard, and Interstate products.

Battery box. Small boat fishermen who have several electrically operated accessories, such as a trolling speed indicator, temperature gauge, electric downrigger, sonar, and so forth, may find it worthwhile to use a product that helps them install a lot of options on one battery. The Power Station from Fishing Aids is a specialized battery box with a side-access electrical panel. Up to five accessories can be plugged into this simply by fastening the accessory's electrical leads to the appropriate plug and inserting the plug into the panel receptacle. This station is a particularly good idea for small boat trollers who have only one battery and want to avoid complex and permanent wire rigging.

Rods and reels. I cover the type of rods and reels that are useful for trolling applications in following chapters. There are no rods and reels that are suitable for any and all types of trolling. Musky trolling rods, for instance, are shorter and stiffer than those used for downrigger trolling for trout. Reel needs, too, vary widely even among anglers trolling for the same type of fish. For instance, you can use a light-duty spinning reel that holds over 200 yards of 8-pound-test line for brown trout trolling, a narrow-spooled bait-casting reel (as employed when casting for bass) that holds 180 yards of 8-pound-test line, or a large-capacity levelwind reel that holds over 300 yards of 14-pound-test line.

Line capacity and drag are the key factors to consider when selecting trolling reels. You must match these attributes to your abilities and the size of fish that you may encounter. It's also very helpful if your trolling reel has a clicker, as this can alert you to a strike.

One thing I do want to say about reels is the possibility of further advancements in electronic products and how they may be applicable to trolling. In 1985, Daiwa introduced the first microprocessor and liquid crystal display (LCD) equipped bait-casting reel, which was powered by two small batteries. This reel, the Tournament Procaster, uses an LCD panel on the front of the reel to denote the length of line cast, the speed of retrieve, the amount of line on the reel, the strength of line, the depth of the lure, and more via audible signals and programmable visual displays.

After using one of these reels for two seasons, I can say that I like it, but it's not what trollers currently need. When trolling, I have been using it to tell me exactly how much line I set out when dropping a lure back. This is where I see a big future in such products when they can retain that information. I expect these reels to be of value to striped bass, trout, and salmon fishermen, for whom it is important to set lines out a certain distance and to get lures down to a particular depth, when suitable models (with greater line capacity and clickers) become available and when they are able to revert from a battery-saving off mode into an operational one without losing stored information. Current models go into automatic battery-saving mode when not used for several minutes but lose information when the reel is picked up and the handle cranked.

6

LURES

As you know from having read my thoughts on downriggers, lure and boat speed, and sonar, I place great importance on having control over where and how you fish. The biggest mistake of trollers is fishing blind, not knowing *for certain* where the lure is, where the fish species they seek are, and how the lure is working. Monitoring such factors is the constant objective of guides and charter boat captains who troll, yet the nonpros, so to speak, often forget such matters or are too complacent about their activities to give it the attention it often deserves. Successful trolling — day in and day out — requires a lot of work, thought, and planning. One of the best Lake Michigan charter boat captains volunteered his thoughts on this subject one day when we worked hard for a great day's catch of trout and salmon by changing lures, trolling depths, and boat speeds constantly. "People say there isn't much to trolling," he said, "but I don't know of any type of fishing that requires more thought and calculation. At the end of the day I'm mentally whipped." Few trollers put the effort into a day's fishing that he does, but not very many get his results.

How you use your equipment — especially lures — is critical to all types of fishing, but especially so to trolling, considering that you are not casting, retrieving, or manipulating those lures by hand. They are nearly always worked out of sight; therefore, you must know what they are capable of doing, how to select type and color wisely, and how to get them to work to their fullest.

DEPTH

If you and I met one morning at the boat dock and I casually mentioned that there was at least one lure in my tackle box that would dive over 80 feet deep, I'm sure you'd raise your eyebrows. If I said the lure was a floating/diving plug straight out of the carton and told you this feat would be achieved without the aid of downriggers, lead-core or wire line, or weights of any kind — just the lure tied to nylon monofilament line — you'd say "bull," right?

Suppose I proposed to take any diving plug out of my box — or out of yours — and get it to run at least 50 percent and possibly 100 percent deeper than the manufacturer's packing sheet says it will run? Same provisions as before. Sound preposterous? Must be a gimmick? Neither. If you challenged me, I'd take your money, and your lure, every time. When you finish reading this section, you'll understand how such feats can be achieved. But achieving them is really unimportant. What *is* important is that your lure's depth attainment is based on a variety of factors, and by changing those factors you can give the lure a versatile depth capability.

Perhaps less than 10 percent of all trollers realize the full range of capabilities of their lures in terms of optimum speed (to get best action) and depth attainment. It's important to know that depth attainment is influenced by line diameter, length of line being trolled, design of lure, and boat speed. I proved the significance of these matters conclusively to myself in 1981 in an experiment that had eye-opening results. I detail the experiment next to support the foregoing statements and also to give you an idea of how you can do something similar for yourself.

My study took place over a three-day period on Tenkiller Lake in Oklahoma. With the technical assistance of Joe Hughes of Rebel Lures and Dick Healey and Ken Cowens of Lowrance Electronics, I tested a host of diving plugs to determine how deep they ran under varying conditions. I used three rods outfitted with different size nylon monofilament line (6-, 12-, and 20-pound test) and trolled from Hughes's boat. The same lure was run on each rod, being taken off the 20-pound outfit and tied to the 12 and so forth. The rods were placed in a holder and angled down so that the tip barely touched the water's surface.

To assure trolling consistent lengths of line, we joined four 75-

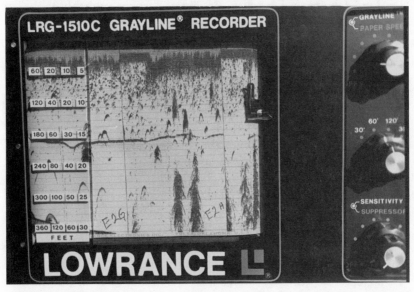

In a test of the depth attained by diving plugs under different circumstances, a tracking boat used a console-mounted graph recorder to find and follow the lures. One of the test results, shown on the graph paper, was a large lure that ran 31 feet deep at a boat speed of 550 rpms behind 22 feet of 12-pound-test line. When speed was increased to 850 rpms, the lure ran 30 feet deep, missing a submerged treetop by 6 feet.

foot sections of ski tow rope together and pulled that behind the trolling boat. Healey's boat was used to drop the lure at the appropriate length behind the trolling boat and to monitor lure depth. Using his company's 1510C graph recorder, which was the forerunner of the current Lowrance computerized graph, Healey would locate and track each lure — including the smallest, which was merely 2 1/2 inches from tail to tip — and report its depth via two-way radio to the trolling boat.

We began by running a battery of 36 tests on a few lures until a clear pattern emerged. These lures were tested for depth achieved with 75-, 150-, 225-, and 300-foot lengths out; for depth at 550, 850, and 1200 rpms at *each* length of line; and for depth under line-length and rpm conditions when using 6-, 12-, and 20-pound test. After running this comprehensive series on a few lures, we made selective, representative tests on other lures for comparative analysis. The results and their relevance to your fishing follow.

Line length. If I were an engineer, I could probably make an impressive technical statement about the laws of physics in regard to the correlation between length of line, angle from a horizontal plane, and water resistance. In fisherman's terms, however, *longer lines result in greater diving lure depth.* Most lures achieved an increase above 50 percent in depth with 300 feet of line out compared to 75 feet out. For example, I used a 6-pound line and 550 rpms boat speed with a Bagley Diving Bang-O-B (a lure, incidentally, that I've used very successfully for muskies, pike, stripers, and wilderness lake trout) that I ran 24 feet deep with 75 feet of line out, versus 39 feet at the greatest distance (see the accompanying chart). This is a 63 percent increase. Several lures reached or exceeded 100 percent, while a few recorded gains of less than 25 percent. The general finding was that diving plugs would run deeper if you let more line out.

There is, however, a point of diminishing returns. You cannot carry this finding to its extreme and let 500 feet of line out to obtain even greater depth. Beyond 225 feet, the rate of increase diminished. Although I did not test the effect of trolling with line lengths in excess of 300 feet, it is reasonable to assert that the drag pressure created by so much line will exert an upward influence on the lure, at which point it will begin to lose depth. The stronger the line, the more so this is true.

Moreover, it may not be desirable to have an exceedingly long line out, because this compounds the difficulties of hook-setting (due to line stretch) and fish-playing control. In fact, we found that the smallest and lightest lures, such as the bass family crankbait models, indeed did lose depth when we changed from 225 to 300 feet of line. Also, some baits seemed to surge with a short (75-foot) line out, presumably as the result of a combination of steep diving angle, lure size and shape, and line stretch.

Line stretch, incidentally, can be a factor in diving-lure usage, which is a relatively little-known or vaguely realized, phenomenon. For example, when we dropped a deep-running lure at the 300-foot marker, knowing that it would run in excess of 30 feet deep, we initially expected that the tracking boat would have to come a reasonable lineal distance closer to the trolling boat in order to graph the lure. This seemed a logical assumption considering the angle of the line when the lure was at 30 plus feet. However, strong-pulling lures on light line exerted enough pressure to stretch the line so that the tracking boat found itself nearly parallel to the 300-foot marker on the tow rope.

Keep in mind that these tests were conducted with premium-grade nylon monofilament line, most of which have the ability to stretch up to 30 percent without breaking. Heavy lines will not stretch as much in such circumstances as light lines will because it takes more pressure to effect stretch. Low-stretch line will obviously perform differently and may make your lure run a little deeper and a little closer to the boat than a comparable strength nylon monofilament line. Although the only cofilament line available as of this writing was DuPont Prime, and it wasn't available to the general public until early 1986, I've had two seasons of use with this line and can say that it makes a great trolling line because of the lower stretch (about 12 to 15 percent) and the ability to set the hook more efficiently even when long lines are trolled. I've already noticed that trolled fish hooked on Prime seem to take the lure more savagely, resulting in the rod popping up quickly and bouncing hard. It's the kind of strike that causes you to remark, "He really nailed that lure." It only seems that way, however, because of the low line stretch.

Line size. Aside from the previously mentioned aspect of stretch, there was a significant difference in diving depth between the three lines, the common denominator being that *lures dive deeper on light line than on heavy line*. This phenomenon is directly related to the thinner diameter of the light lines, which produce less drag in the water. The lighter line/greater depth tendency is magnified when longer lengths are employed.

There was not a single instance in any testing category where a light line failed to go deeper than a heavy line when the same lure was trolled. In the charts of the Spoonbill Minnow and Deep Bang-O-B, you'll notice this progression. In the case of the Bang-O-B, this varies from as little as 2 feet to as great as 16.

By carrying this test to an extreme, we were able to get two lures to troll at depths beyond 80 feet deep. The champion, Cordell's Striper Striker (the other one, in case you're wondering, was the Rebel Super Deep Minnow) reached 84 feet while trolling behind 300 feet of 6-pound-test line at an engine speed of 550 rpms. Amazingly the line never broke, leading me to theorize that if 4-pound line could be used without breaking (it's simply a matter of how much pressure this lure exerts), this lure might reach the 100-foot mark.

Of sixteen lures tested, nine reached or exceeded 30 feet deep on either 12- or 6-pound line; only two of these managed that on 20-pound line. And one lure, a 1/4-ounce medium-size crankbait that

Depth Chart, 5½-inch Rebel Spoonbill Minnow

Line length	75 ft.			150 ft.			225 ft.			300 ft.		
rpms	550	850	1200	550	850	1200	550	850	1200	550	850	1200
20-lb. line	10	9	9	11	9	9	11	10	10	11	10	10
12-lb. line	11	10	10	13	12	12	13	13	13	14	14	13
6-lb. line	13	12	–	16	15	15	17	17	16	20	18	–

Depth Chart, 5-inch Bagley Deep Bang-O-B

Line length	75 ft.			150 ft.			225 ft.			300 ft.		
rpms	550	850	1200	550	850	1200	550	850	1200	550	850	1200
20-lb. line	15	15	14	19	19	18	22	20	20	23	23	22
12-lb. line	18	17	17	23	23	20	26	23	22	31	31	26
6-lb. line	24	22	21	29	25	26	37	34	31	39	35	31

Depth Chart, Miscellaneous

Line length	75 ft.			150 ft.			225 ft.			300 ft.		
rpms	550	850	1200	550	850	1200	550	850	1200	550	850	1200
Cordell Deep-O/12 lb.	–	–	–	–	–	–	25	–	–	24	–	–
Cordell Deep-O/6 lb.	–	–	–	–	–	–	–	–	–	33	–	–
Rebel Deep Wee-R/12 lb.	–	–	–	–	–	–	18	–	–	20	–	–
Rebel Deep Wee-R/6 lb.	–	–	–	–	–	–	–	–	–	26	–	–
Rebel Deep Teeny-R/6 lb.	–	–	–	–	–	–	23	–	–	21	–	–
Rapala 5 in. Magnum/12 lb.	–	–	–	20	–	–	21	–	–	–	–	–
Rapala 5 in. Magnum/6 lb.	–	–	–	–	–	–	30	–	–	–	–	–
Cordell Striper Striker/12 lb.	30	–	–	49	–	–	56	–	–	66	–	–
Cordell Striper Striker/6 lb.	40	–	–	59	–	–	74	–	–	84	–	–
Rebel D99/12 lb.	–	–	–	–	–	–	18	–	–	19	–	–
Rebel D99/6 lb.	–	–	–	–	–	–	24	–	–	26	–	–
Crankbait Corp. 5-inch Fingerling/12 lb.	–	–	–	28	–	–	32	31	31	35	–	–
Fingerling/6 lb.	–	–	–	36	–	–	42	–	–	47	–	–
Rebel Deep Maxi-R/20 lb.	15	14	–	18	17	–	19	18	–	21	20	–
Rebel Deep Maxi-R/12 lb.	17	16	–	–	–	–	27	26	–	34	–	–
Rebel Deep Maxi-R/6 lb.	22	–	–	29	–	–	33	–	–	36	–	–

would ordinarily be used in casting and for scouring the bottom in 8 to 10 feet of water, reached 25 feet with 225 feet of 12-pound line out and 33 feet with 300 feet of 6-pound line out.

The important point here is not that you can obtain decompression-chamber–type depths, but that you have options with such capabilities open to you and that you can employ this information in your fishing. I learned long ago while fishing after ice-out for shallow trout that I could take a 4-inch floating/diving minnow plug, which ordinarily runs just a foot deep on a cast-and-retrieve, and get it down 6 to 8 feet deep by slow trolling it unweighted behind 200 feet of line. The Tenkiller study quantifies my trial-and-error education, but it graphically points out the options open to the thinking angler. Refer to the charts and you'll see what I mean.

To help illustrate the possibilities, however, consider this: if the water is clear and the fish are spooky and deep, you may need to use 200 to 225 feet of 6-pound line to get a certain lure to reach 30-foot-plus levels. If the fish aren't spooky and are within 20 feet of the surface, you can get away with 150 feet of 20-pound line. Or, if you're after large fish and want to use heavy line, you have the option of trolling just 75 feet of line to get down 15 feet and increasing the yardage as conditions warrant. All these options come while using the same plug.

At this point, I can imagine a diehard downrigger user saying, "But who cares about all this, when I can use my downrigger to place a lure at a specific depth?" That's partially true if you are using a plug on a very short line or if you are using a light lure that attains little or no depth on its own, like a flutter spoon, a spinner, or a nondiving plug. But suppose you receive information that the fish you seek are taking Tadpolly plugs at 25 feet and are fished 100 feet behind the downrigger. Do you set the downrigger at 25 feet? No, because you must take into account how deep the Tadpolly will dive with 100 feet of your line out. You don't know how deep that is, however. If you guess that it dives 10 feet, then set the downrigger weight at 15 feet, you may be right. But if, unbeknownst to you, the Tadpolly is diving 15 feet deep, you are actually fishing it 30 feet deep, 5 feet below the fish. The fish probably will not go down to take the lure and you may not catch anything, but all the while you are trolling the right lure at what you think is the right depth and wondering why you're not getting action.

When trolling a diving plug, you must take into account how deep that lure will dive behind the downrigger weight. This will vary with the length of fishing line used.

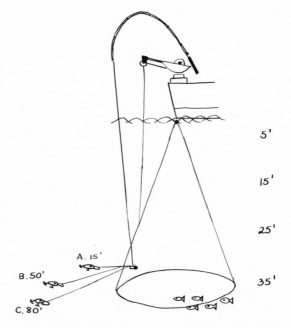

Speed. I discuss the relevance of speed in an earlier chapter and don't want to belabor this point, but it would be worthwhile here to detail briefly what this study showed relative to the speed aspect of trolling.

As with length of line and line diameter, there proved to be a strong relationship between boat speed and the diving ability of each lure. Simply put, *the greatest depth is achieved at the slowest speed* regardless of the length of line employed. Additionally, as speed increases, depth decreases.

The slowest speed of the trolling boat was 550 rpms. According to the trolling speed indicator that we hooked up to the boat, this was equivalent to between 1 1/2 and 2 1/2 mph. Yet not once did a lure dive deeper when speed was increased. All lures continued to perform satisfactorily at 850 rpms, and many lost little if any depth. At 1200 rpms, however, most lures lost appreciable depth. A few experienced erratic side-to-side movement, which made tracking and depth determination difficult, and a couple simply would not run properly at that speed. Although 1200 rpms is rather fast, many of the plugs trolled steadily at that speed, albeit with loss of depth.

This situation is akin to the diving ability of crankbaits used in cast-and-retrieve fishing. Although the length of line out is relatively short in this type of fishing, such as 50 to 70 feet, it is advantageous to retrieve the lure slowly to achieve maximum depth. In trolling, as our test proved, the only difference is having a longer, fixed length of line out.

Lure design. Among the lures we tested were products from five manufacturers, including Bagley, Cordell, Crankbait Corporation, Normark (Rapala), and Rebel. Testing results showed that some general observations could be applied to all lures and that lure weight, shape, lip design, lip angle, and line-tie location all contribute to the diving and running abilities of each lure, though to varying degrees.

Generally, all tested lures had acutely angled lips. In other words, they came close to the horizontal plane of the body of the lure. The deepest diving models very nearly protruded horizontally from the nose of the lure; thus, the less the angle, the deeper the lure dives.

There is a corollary between the size of the lip and diving ability, though it is not an absolute one. The lures with the greatest lip surface area generally were the better divers. The lip of the deepest running plug was 2 1/2 inches long and 2 1/4 inches wide at its greatest point, resulting in a massive surface area; yet the lure that ranked eighth in lip surface area ranked sixteenth in depth on 12-pound line. This lure, a Rebel 5-inch Spoonbill Minnow, is considerably lighter than lures with a larger lip surface area, and its long body has more of a tendency to create drag than a similar heavier model. On the other hand, a similarly shaped lure, the 5-inch Rapala Magnum, ranked thirteenth in lip surface area yet ninth in depth using 12-pound line. This lure, however, was the only sinking diver tested, and this aspect may have factored in the result.

Body shape was another element that played a difficult-to-assess role in depth attainment. The smallest crankbait tested, a Rebel Deep Teeny-R, which measured only 1 11/16ths of an inch long from tail to snout, not counting the lip, attained a trolled depth of 21 feet behind 300 feet of 6-pound line. It and other small crankbaits probably owed their diving accomplishments to a combination of small streamlined body shapes, light weight, and lips with large surface area in relation to lure body size. Two deep-diving lures present an interesting comparison in this regard.

The 5-inch Crankbait Corporation Fingerling and 3-inch Rebel Deep Maxi-R match up closely in weight, lip length, lip width, and lip angle and differ only in the fact that the former is 5 inches long

The old adage is that big lures catch big fish but here's proof that a little plug can catch a monstrous chinook salmon. You must know, however, how your lure swims at various speeds and how deep it is when you are trolling them regardless of their size. Marty Salovin caught this Lake Ontario fish on a blue-and-silver Hotshot, fished 6 feet behind a downrigger weight at 55 feet deep.

and somewhat slender while the latter is 3 inches long and bulbous. On 20- and 12-pound-test lines, the two are not far apart in depth, and, in fact, were nearly identical (35 and 34 feet, respectively) when run behind 300 feet of 12-pound line. On 6-pound line, however, the Crankbait lure outdistanced the other by a 25 percent margin. Apparently body shape is an influence dependent upon the contribution of other factors.

Still another point to consider regarding the depth attainment of plugs, especially when evaluating a lure you've never used before, is the matter of line-tie location. You can be sure that a lure with a line tie situated on the lip will run deeper than one with a line tie on the nose. The location of the line tie relates to the angle of pull. Most of the deeper running lures had line ties located on the lip, less than half the distance between the nose and the front edge of the lip. Therefore, it seemed that a combination of bulb-shaped lip with a line tie close to the nose resulted in a desirable diving plane and good depth achievement. Using this basic information, you can determine the relative diving ability of a new lure simply by observing it and comparing it to other lures that you may have experienced in trolling.

Other findings. No matter how promising any lure appears to be, it has an optimum action and speed. In order to get the most out of your lure, it must work properly, which often means that some tuning is required. Some of our lures could be run straight out of the box without needing tuning. The majority needed some refining, varying from very minor adjustment to extensive alteration. At least two samples were rejected because they could not be tuned to run properly. All lures were checked and tuned by the side of the boat prior to testing, which is how they should be treated when actually trolling. Some baits that are not tuned completely right will run fine at slow speeds, but become erratic at faster ones. A lure with debris on it is affected, too. We had one lure with a leaf on its bill that ran erratically between 19 and 24 feet deep. Some lures in this condition run awry yet stay down while others won't run at all and come up.

By watching the rpm and trolling speed indicators studiously, we noticed subtle changes in boat speed resulting from two factors. Movement in the trolling boat, resulting in a change in weight distribution, caused a minimal fluctuation in boat (and lure) speed. We were in a

17-foot fiberglass boat with a 140 hp engine. Speed decreased as much as 1 mph when one of us moved from the stern to the bow, which presumably lowered the bow and increased drag. More obviously, wind speed and boat direction relative to it affected the speed and location of the lure.

Finally, we found that it took a long time for some of the lures to reach their maximum depth under given conditions. Using 12-pound line, it took the deepest diving lure 28 seconds to reach 30 feet when we trolled 225 feet of line; 47 seconds to reach 40 feet; 60 seconds to reach 45 feet; and 84 seconds to reach 50 feet (all at 550 rpms). It leveled out shortly therafter at 56 feet. Later, using 200 yards of 6-pound line at 550 rpms, it took 85 seconds to reach 75 feet.

Why is this significant? Because it can take longer than you think for your lure to reach the level you want when flat-lining it. A boat that is averaging a speed of 4 mph is traveling at a rate of 5.86 feet per second. If it takes 85 seconds to reach the desired 75-foot level, you'll have traveled 499 feet by the time the lure reaches this level. On a more practical level, assuming that it takes 20 seconds to get a lure down to the desired 20- to 25-foot range, you'll go roughly 40 yards before your lure reaches its target level. There are instances when you must take this time factor into consideration, such as when you are making a critical approach to a specific location but just had a false release or just got debris on a lure and had to pull it in to clean it off and reset it. By the time you get this lure out and at the right level, you may have passed the school of fish you wanted to troll through.

I learned a lot and proved some suppositions by conducting this study. Most anglers who have put in a lot of hours trolling understand some or all aspects of these matters, although they may not be able to quantify them precisely or say that such-and-such lure will dive at X feet under certain conditions. They have a ballpark idea and this is enough to make their trolling efforts productive. But I think it's better to be able to say with come conviction exactly what your lures will do under certain circumstances and when used at different speeds and with different strengths of line. The more you understand these points and the more you know how these matters apply to the lures you fish and the species you fish for, the less mystery there will be to your trolling efforts and the more you will cut down on the amount of luck that it takes to be an effective troller.

TUNING

Trolling lures must run true to be effective. If they don't have the right action, they will probably not be as effective as they are capable of being; in fact, they may not be effective at all. Plugs, for example, must run straight on the retrieve, not lie on their side or run off at an angle; spoons must have the right wobble, not lay flat and skip. But lures don't always work just right. Some that have been working properly may run awry after you catch a fish on them, or someone steps on them, or they get bashed against a hard object. Some lures work perfectly right out of the box and some, especially plugs, do not. Moreover, you can buy a dozen identical plugs and find that several need alteration to work just right.

There are ways to accomplish this alteration, or "tuning," of lures to make them run true. It's not difficult, but it does take a few moments to accomplish, and it takes some observation to know when to work on a lure to make it troll better.

The majority of plugs have clear plastic bills of various lengths and shapes for diving. Into these bills are attached line-tie screws, and virtually all running problems center on these little screws. When a plug runs awry, it is the fault of the line tie. The line-tie screw must be placed vertical to the mean horizontal plane of the bill of the lure. Because this screw eye is positioned partially by hand at the manufacturing plant, the element of human error can be introduced. If the screw is placed a fraction of an inch out of position, the lure will not run perfectly true. Occasionally an assembler misaligns the screw, causing the product to need tuning.

A well-designed plug that sports a lip should have a good wiggling action. Some lures have a tight action and some have more of a wide wobble. Whichever action it exhibits, a lure should come back in a straight line to you while swimming or diving. The body of a plug should be vertical, not canted off to either side. It is important to get the lure running perfectly true; if it runs even a little bit off, it has an unnatural action that will likely cost you fish. This is not necessarily so of erratic swimming and darting cut-plug lures, such as the J-Plug, that have no lip or bill and appeal to salmon because of this erratic movement. It is a good idea to check each plug before you fish it. Tie it on your line, drop a few feet of line from the tip of the rod to the lure, then run the lure through the water next to your boat. If it does not run properly, adjust it immediately.

To adjust a plug, you need only a pair of pliers, preferably needle-nose, to bend the line-tie screw. If, as you watch the path of retrieve head-on, the lure is running to your right, you must bend the line-tie screw to the left (again looking at it head-on). If the lure runs left, bend the screw right. Adjust the screw in stages, bending it slightly then casting and retrieving once to see the change. Keep adjusting and changing until the lure runs true. In radical cases, you may have to bend the line-tie screw far from its original position. When bending the line-tie screw, be careful that you do not loosen it. The screw is merely epoxied in place and loosening may render the plug unusable. Sometimes you can take the screw out and reglue it using clear 5-minute epoxy.

Before you tune a lure that seems to run awry, make sure you are not trolling it too fast. All plugs have a top working speed beyond which they will not run properly. This speed is not the same for all lures.

Generally most plugs will not run very well if a tight knot is tied directly to the screw eye. For this reason, it is best to use a split ring or rounded snap, not a snap swivel, for connection. Most plugs are supplied with split rings or snaps, and your knot should be tied to this. Snap swivels may alter the action of these plugs, making perfect tuning a difficult task. A lure that is already tuned to work without a snap swivel may have to be retuned to work with it. Moreover, a snap swivel poses another possible problem point when fighting fish, and the least possible number of things that can go wrong the better. The only advantages to using a snap swivel are that it facilitates lure changing and prevents twist. Diving plugs don't induce twist, and snaps will ease the job of lure changing.

In addition, be aware of small things that might affect the way your lure trolls. Sometimes plugs can be sensitive to the slightest adornment. If you pull a lure through weeds and get a tiny confetti trailer on your hooks or line tie, you'll feel the action of the lure change if you have the rod in hand or notice a change in the movement of your rod tip. Something that gets on a lure trolled behind a downrigger weight usually goes undetected because the rod tip doesn't provide much of a clue, although at times you may notice the rod tip bow down momentarily when the object strikes your lure.

Tie a new knot on a bait that was running fine and the action may just be off due to the position of the knot. This is simply corrected by changing its position and realigning the knot, or by retying the knot and snugging it tight. You may also find that some plugs work best if you use a loop knot. With some deep-diving minnow-shaped plugs, such as the Rebel Spoonbill Minnow, I prefer to tie a loop knot directly to the line-tie screw or the split ring.

Some plugs seem to need more frequent tuning than others, and some small lures need more frequent tuning than large ones. Others never get tuned exactly right. It is not uncommon to make many attempts to modify a new lure before you get it running to your satisfaction.

Some of the foregoing comments about plugs and connections also apply to other lures. Spoons, spinners, and flies are also in the troller's repertoire. Spinners usually don't have much of a trolling problem except for the occasional bent shaft, which is obviously corrected if not too severe. Flies need to swim upright, and usually it's simply a matter of adjusting the knot location on the eye of the fly to achieve

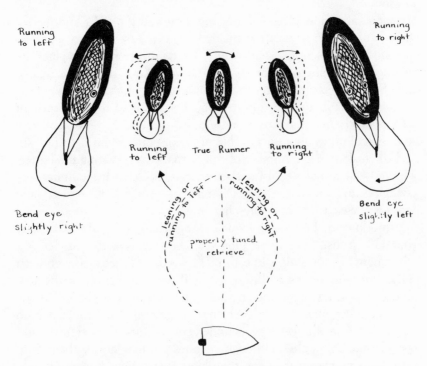

To tune a plug, you must bend the line tie in the opposite direction from which the lure is running astray. Do it in stages until you get the plug running in a straight-ahead, side-to-side wobble as it returns toward you.

this. Heavy-metal spoons don't usually get bent out of shape, but waferlike spoons do, and this sometimes requires adroit remodeling. A few thin flutter spoons can be bent at the tip and base to the left or right to modify their action. It pays at times to experiment with such maneuvers, if for no other reason than to compare actions. Remember to watch for line twist with these lures, and, in the case of spoons or spinners, use a good-quality snap swivel to offset twist.

There are some anglers, incidentally, who take seemingly serviceable lures and make minor adjustments to them — such as bending or shaving the lip or changing the hooks — that make the lures work exceptionally well. These secrets are not readily discerned, nor are the practitioners overly willing to divulge their handiwork. For example, one of the best musky trollers that I know is a devoted user of double-jointed Creek Chub Pikie Minnows. He may have caught more muskies over 40 pounds on these lures than any modern-day angler, and his techniques are partly antiquated, but his mastery of this particular lure and the nuances of fishing with it are two reasons for his success. This includes his hook changing and the use of a lip jig to bend both sides of the lip of this plug up at a slight angle. He uses the jig as a mask to determine when he has the lip bent into the precise position.

Another angler, a Great Lakes charter boat captain, has a way of modifying J-Plugs that consistently allow him to catch a dozen fish on that lure when others are only taking two to three fish on the unmodified version. I haven't seen the lure to evaluate what he does to it, and he doesn't let anyone except his charter parties see his modified plugs. However he alters them, I'm told they move slower with a wider tail waddle and with less frantic darting than the traditionally erratic parent lure.

There are all kinds of modification going on with lures, including some things that don't make the lure work better and may actually inhibit its success. Many striper anglers in the south are keen on using Whopper Stopper Hellbenders in conjunction with another lure. One method is to tie a short line and jig to the treble hook eyelet of the Hellbender and let this trail behind the plug. Another is to use the Hellbender as a diving planer by removing the hook and connecting link from the bill, passing the fishing line through a slip sinker then through the hole in the bill and attaching it to a split ring, then running a short line and lure behind the plug. In my opinion, it is very hard to know exactly what depth you are fishing under such an arrangement. Most anglers greatly overestimate the depth attained with this setup. If flat-lining, I prefer to run my line straight to the appropriate lure without intermediaries.

Perhaps the most common modification to trolling lures has nothing to do with the working action. It has to do with changing the lure's color or adding colors to it by using prism tape. But that brings us to the subject of colors in trolling lures, and I detail this later in the following section.

LURE COLOR

How we see color, how we think fish see it, and how this relates to the way we make trolling-lure color selections is an intriguing aspect of fishing. What type and color was your lure is a question routinely asked of a successful angler. No other topic fascinates anglers as that of lures and lure colors.

I've written before that lures are made to catch fishermen, that the best lure is only as good as the angler manipulating it, and that such factors as size, action, vibration, and color are critical in a complementary, not isolated, way to a lure's success. We've already talked about how to get the best swimming action out of your trolling lures, but we haven't discussed color, a topic that has particularly fascinated the general fishing public in recent years and is of special interest to those who troll for coho or chinook salmon, brown trout, steelhead, and muskies.

You've no doubt heard people say that so-and-so thinks like a fish. Sounds cute, but the fact is that no one thinks like a fish, nor is it possible to perceive things the way a fish does. That makes anglers' evaluations of the visual perceptions of fish, and the colors that appeal to fish, all the more curious.

You cannot discuss color without discussing light; color is an intangible property that is the result of reflecting light of different wavelengths. The duration of wavelengths produces the type of color that we see; the shortest wavelength visible to humans produces violet, while the longest produces red. Shorter (ultraviolet and X-rays) and longer (radio waves) wavelengths of light are invisible to the human eye. Colors are perceived differently above water than in the water, and their visibility is greater if they fluoresce. Fluorescence is the property of a substance that absorbs short wavelengths of light, particularly ultraviolet, and reemits longer and more visible wavelengths of light at a higher energy level.

Though we know a great deal about how we are affected by light and how we perceive colors, we can't say unequivocally that what we know about these subjects applies equally to fish. Therefore, anglers form theories and opinions based on experience and information provided by limited research.

It was once thought that fish were color blind and that they perceived colors in gradients of gray. Over the last century that opinion has changed. Researchers reported over 60 years ago that some fish could definitely perceive colors. Then it was thought that some species of fish could see color and some couldn't. Now it is conceded that most fish see color; only cave fish and extremely deep-dwelling ocean fish do not. Through the past 50 years, various researchers have reported that certain species of fish see through a yellowish, red, blue, or orange tint or screen. Some have postulated that the most important sense of a fish is its hearing, especially in turbid water. Now there is evidence that this may not be so and that fish can see far better than we thought even in turbid water.

What anglers think about this subject has been influenced greatly by these findings and by their own attempts to analyze natural conditions and the likelihood of a particular species of fish to act according to what seems to be sensible based on those conditions. Many anglers behave as if fish perceive colors exactly as we do; that's why lures are primarily made to catch fishermen. Some completely disregard the possible color perception of fish in making lure color selections. Some work strictly on the basis of natural forage imitation, figuring that if bait fish don't sport a chartreuse color, why fish with a lure that is contrary to nature? And others are ambivalent, vacillating between what looks good to them and what others seem to be having success with.

Despite the fact that we know more about our quarry and its sensory abilities than ever before, there are still some perplexing, fascinating, and unresolved questions. Perhaps the greatest puzzler is this: Why

do fish strike a lure that physically bears no resemblance to any naturally appearing food item? It happens all the time, of course. Some
lures simply act unlike any known forage, some have a form unlike
natural food, and some are colored unlike anything we know or see.
Yet they are effective fish-catchers, at times more productive than
another lure that in every way seems more representative of real prey.
The answer must be that for some reason they suggested food to that
fish. What that reason is, however, and what drew the fish's attention
in the first place are still questions that beg for answers.

Another mystery: How important is it to use a lure that is most
visible to the fish? At issue here is whether fish are acting principally
on the basis of visual stimuli, whether vision is subordinate to other
senses, or whether it matters under some conditions and not under
others. Researchers think they have some clues to answer these questions, and some insight into how fish perceive color and what makes
them respond to our offerings. But we may never *really* know about
these matters and perhaps we never should, because angling will cease
to be a sport, or be fun, when the puzzles have been solved. Nonetheless, some fish, particularly salmon and trout, appear to be sight
feeders almost exclusively, and a confirmed way to appeal to them is
to troll lures that have very high visibility under existing water and
light conditions and particular depths.

A vastly overlooked and underexplored mystery is where the most
prominent lure-attracting color should be located on a lure, especially
on a plug. Most predator and prey fish are dark on the top and light
on the bottom. Did nature make them light on the bottom to be less
conspicuous from below; did it make them dark on the top so they
would blend in with the environment when viewed from above; or
both? My experience is that game fish predominantly strike their prey
(and lures) from below. If they are coming from below, should your
aim be to imitate nature and have a light color at the bottom of your
lure? If so, what difference does it make what the top color is? On
the other hand, should your aim be to contrast nature and thus have
the most visible color on the bottom of the lure? This coloring system,
known as countershading, was tried unsuccessfully by one manufacturer several years ago, but more are picking up on this now.

What has been overlooked in this matter is the position of the
fish relative to the lure and the extent of visibility of that portion of
the lure. More and more I find myself questioning the importance of

Fish do perceive colors, and some fish seem more attracted to certain colors than to others. How important it is to use a color that is most visible to fish under existing water quality and light conditions is an aspect of lure selection that has been of increasing importance to trollers.

top colors on lures, especially in Great Lakes trolling. When someone reports that fish are taking a chrome plug with green ladderback tape on the top, I pause to wonder. Most of the charter boat captains and guides that I discussed this with agree with me that fish predominantly strike from below and seldom go down to chase a lure. If this is so, how could the ladderback atop the plug be influencing the catch? If the ladderback extends onto the sides of the lure, I can see that it may offer a little bit of visual appeal to a fish. For this reason, when I add prism tape, luminescent tape, or ladderback tape to plugs, I avoid the top of the lure and place it on the sides or bottom.

Questions seem to beget more questions and this issue leads to the query: Should lure color selection be based on light intensity? I once wrote that I often used light-colored lures on dark days and dark-colored lures on light days, and it brought some interesting comments. More and more I've been mixing this up, but I see a lot of reason to use a black spoon for salmon fishing when it is very sunny out, for example, especially in the early part of the season and when the fish are shallow. I think the dark color contrasts well with the brightness from above, yet there are many good fishermen who disagree with this. Dark days/dark lures, light days/light lures has been an angling dictum for decades, though it is occasionally allowed that fish sometimes break the rules.

I don't know that there are any rules where sport fish are concerned, but there are a few facts about light and color in aquatic environments, which you should know if you are going to make color work for you. The principal points to be aware of are the depth that you are to fish, the relative clarity of the water, and the intensity of the light.

Research work and conventional thought tell us that when light passes through water its intensity is reduced. This applies vertically as well as horizontally and is further influenced as the water moves from clear to stained or muddy conditions. Red and violet are the first to lose their distinctive color, followed by brown; ultimately these become black. Blue and green retain their visibility much longer, though they fade and don't appear as such. Their fluorescent counterparts remain highly visible at greater depths and distances, with fluorescent chartreuse being especially visible. No less an authority than the United States Navy, after testing the visibility of colors at various saltwater depths, concluded in a 1974 report that "fluorescent colors have been shown to be much more effective than regular paints of the same color under almost all conditions of underwater viewing." They also found that background contrast — dark water, sandy or vegetative bottom, and so forth — significantly affected visibility of all colors and that different times of the day produced different results. They noted, for example, that fluorescent orange was most visible early in the morning, decreasing thereafter, with fluorescent green exhibiting the reverse pattern (they did not test fluorescent chartreuse), and concluded that this had more to do with contrast against background colors than with differences in brightness contrast.

Color is an enhancement to action and vibration in lures, but ardent trollers know that it is sometimes essential for success to have a battery of different color lures to appeal to fish.

These points have to do with human visibility and perceptions, however. Dr. Loren Hill, chairman of the Zoology Department of the University of Oklahoma and director of its Biological Research Station, studied the reactions of largemouth bass to color and used a light meter to record light transmittance values under clear, stained, and muddy water conditions at specific times of the day and under both clear and overcast sky conditions. He not only discovered vast changes in the color preferences of bass based on the combined variables, but he shed some new light on what they perceive and maintains that these findings hold true for other game fish as well.

One of his findings was that the most visible color doesn't necessarily relate to contrasts in background, but with the way light disperses in the water. According to Dr. Hill, "If you have plankton or debris or sediment, these can have different affects on the scattering of light, either reflecting or refracting it, and this seems to modify things so that the consistency of background contrast is not always critical. Though it appears that red is the first color to fade, there are times that, because of the environment, red is extremely visible to the fish at depths you would not believe, and under conditions you would not believe."

Hill created a 9-volt battery-operated device, the Color-C-Lector, which is essentially a light intensity meter with a readout that corresponds to a color spectrum scale that he devised. It has clear, stained, and muddy water values and a probe that correlates light sensitivity to the exact conditions that he used in evaluating the fish's response to color.

The sequence of colors on each scale differs from the normal wavelength-visibility patterns in water, and Hill said that this surprised him. "If you look at the three scales, you'll see how the colors are changed and mixed up, and how long wavelength colors and short wavelength colors are mixed up. It doesn't necessarily go from bright light conditions and long wavelength colors to dim light conditions and short wavelengths. I think this also has to do with what happens to light in the water and the way it is affected. It's complicated and not predictable based on pure physics." Perhaps it is this way because it reflects the colors that are perceived by and most visible to fish under those conditions.

Although Dr. Hill, an ardent angler, agrees that color is generally an enhancement to action and vibration in lures, he departs from convention by stating that vision is the predominant sense of predatory fish. He has experienced times when the color of lure used, determined by his device, was more important to fishing success than the type of lure used. He also doesn't think that anglers should necessarily use either light or dark lures based on whether it is sunny or overcast. He says there isn't necessarily a correlation.

Surprisingly, his research showed that fish in muddy water have far better color visibility, up to 3 1/2 to 4 feet, than had been previously thought. Their distance visibility was a maximum of 10 to 12 feet in stained water and up to 40 feet in the clearest water. Great Lakes fishermen, who almost always troll under the clearest water conditions, can attest to the ability of salmon and trout to see lures from a great distance. That ability may account for the fish-catching productivity of brightly flashing, highly reflective silver and chrome colored spoons and plugs. It is common to catch fish that are not spotted below the boat on sonar equipment, because these fish must be attracted to and can see the lure from enough distance away yet are outside the cone angle of the transducer.

One of Dr. Hill's notable findings was that each particular color of the spectrum is camouflaged or highly visible at some time during the day or during a particular 24-hour period. He says that colors "fade in and out depending on the conditions of the environment. So if someone asks if there are some colors that fish can see better all of the time than others, every particular color appears to be camouflaged at one particular time associated with the conditions of that environment. And then it may come back in an hour and be visible. During my testing it was obvious that certain colors, according to conditions, would be camouflaged. Others came in bright. Modify that, they become camouflaged, then others come in. That seems to work as a regular phenomenon every day. But, it also makes sense, too. We can look at the biological interaction between a predator and preyfish such as shad, minnows, or sunfish as forage. If those forage organisms were highly visible all the time to predators, their population would be limited. But they're not. They're camouflaged a large part of the time. Only sometimes are their particular color patterns highly visible. It makes sense biologically if you stop and think about it."

If visibility is based upon water clarity, light penetration, depth, and time of day, then so must be color selection. With that in mind, I've tried to evaluate the usefulness of Dr. Hill's Color-C-Lector in trolling applications over the past few years. I have experienced some successful usage with that device, having tested its application for a variety of freshwater fish, though there have been times when I was able to catch fish using lure colors contrary to those it advocated. There have also been times, especially on the Great Lakes on bright days when fishing in clear water, that the recommended colors to fish seldom changed.

In using the Color-C-Lector, however, I did come to adopt Dr. Hill's basis for determining relative water clarity: lower the gray-white probe into the water. If you can't see it beyond 2 feet, the water is muddy; if you can't see it beyond 4 feet the water is stained; if you can see it beyond 4 feet the water is clear. At Hill's suggestion, if I didn't have the nonfluorescent color lure that the needle pointed to, I used a color next to it because it will still be in the range of high visibility. When the needle rests in the middle of a fluorescent band, that fluorescent color is dominant and the nonfluorescent colors below it are secondary, so this can serve to refine color selection still further. I also found that mixing colors of high visibility can be very beneficial. If you have stained water and the needle points to the middle of chartreuse, for example, try using a lure that combines purple (the secondary nonfluorescent color) with chartreuse.

You can be very effective at altering lure colors, especially spoons, if you keep a supply of different colored prism tape with you. This tape is sold in sparkle and reflective versions, in sheet form or precut into various patterns, including lightning bolt, ladderback, and angled strips. You can completely cover an old color with a new one, or add a strip of color to a lure to enhance it. I've found that it's best to keep a lure in the sun or in your pocket for a while to warm it up (in cold weather or when fishing cold water) before putting the tape on, so the tape will adhere better.

We can all think of moments when the determining factor in fishing success was either the overall color of a lure, a small strip of color or identifying characteristic on a lure, the precise size of a lure, the brand and action, or the particular way in which it was fished that alone contributed to success. Remember how prominent red and red and white were to fishermen decades ago before we all got studious? Surely those fishermen thought it was especially visible to fish. Today we not only have a tremendously greater range of colors, we even have lures that emit light when there is little or no natural light available. These are phosphorescent and luminescent products, and I've trolled them to catch fish under low light conditions.

Early morning, evening, night, and dark cloudy days lend themselves to the use of light-emitting lures or colors, as does fishing in very deep water. I've used chemiluminescent light sticks inside plugs to catch lake trout and salmon at night, in early morning, and in deep downrigger fishing. I'm convinced that their high visibility is the principal reason for their effectiveness. Primarily I've used Dandy-Glo plugs for this fishing; these are cut-plug baits that have a 4-inch chemiluminescent light stick inserted into the cavity of the lure. Light sticks are activated by snapping the sides and last between 5 and 12 hours, depending on water temperature. These particular lures with large light sticks seem to work best when the stick has been activated one or two hours before being used, to allow time for the brightness of the light stick to wane a bit. When Bob Scriver, maker of these plugs, and I fished Lake Michigan out of Manistee a few years ago, he lit a few sticks when we got up at 4 A.M. so they'd be activated for 90 minutes before we actually started fishing them. We caught some nice chinooks at dawn by trolling these lures at 70-foot depths.

In addition to these plugs, however, I've toyed with using the small 1 1/2-inch light sticks with small crankbaits and diving plugs. The plugs I've used include Rebel, Cordell, Bomber, Heddon, and Storm models, all of which are plastic. I've drilled small holes (the opening of which equals the diameter of the light stick) in these plugs from the rear of the back, front of the back, nose, and rear belly

Light sticks inserted into lures are proving to be of interest to some trollers. The Dandy-Glo, shown here, started this trend and has proven effective for a variety of fish, particularly for chinook salmon.

(location depends on the interior structure of the lure) and inserted activated light sticks in them, then covered the opening with a dab of silicone sealant. The silicone hardens in a few minutes and you then have a plug that glows. How much it glows depends on the basic color of the lure. Some of the light-colored or translucent lures work as is; darker lures can be scraped with a knife to peel off the outer paint and reveal a translucent gray or bone-white base color.

The insertion of these small light sticks has not affected the action or diving ability of the lures. Although I can't say that they have been wildly successful fish-catchers, they have caught fish. I suspect that if I used them more often and tested this idea further, I'd be able to make more definitive statements about their usefulness to other types of fishing besides trolling for trout and salmon.

When I first started this doctoring several years ago, these small light sticks were not available to the public and I had to beg American Cyanamid to send me some for experimentation purposes. Now, that company is selling them three to a pack at tackle stores, and these sticks can be incorporated into some spoons as well.

Another type of glowing lure is phosphorescent products, which have been available for quite a while. Heddon may have been among the first with its glow-in-the-dark Tadpolly, which is typical of this genre of plug. Phosphorescent paint is used on the exterior of these lures, although you can add phosphorescent tape to lures painted conventionally as well. You hold them close to a light source, such as a lantern or spotlight, to charge them up. The charge lasts for roughly 20 minutes, after which time you have to recharge the lure. This system is good for those who are casting and can recharge lures periodically in between casts, but for trollers who have to bring lines in to retrieve the lure for recharging, it isn't quite as convenient. It works, however, although lures with light sticks may be better because they don't require regular retrieval and charging.

All things considered, the unanswerable question in lure fishing remains whether the most significant factor is the action of the lure, the color of the lure, the proper presentation of the lure at the right time/right place, or an incalculable combination of these. It's easy to say that all these factors contribute to successful lure fishing. It's harder to prove that one is significantly more important than the others. There are already thousands of fishermen using a Color-C-Lector, either believing that it will unlock lure color selection secrets for them or help them through the hard times when they have to wet everything in the tackle box.

Must you have a Color-C-Lector or a light intensity meter to catch fish? I think not. Will it help? Sometimes. If you are an artificial lure troller, it can be a big help because it gets you thinking harder about the color that you are fishing and why you are fishing it, and it effectively demonstrates how light penetration affects visibility.

I think this entire matter of lure color selection and color visibility based on light intensity is an especially interesting subject for trollers because they are usually passing by fish fairly quickly and often don't have a chance to make repetitive presentations; because the fish are in all likelihood striking out of hunger and reflexive instinct, as opposed to being aggravated or coaxed; and because the ability to hear and see a prospective prey seems to be a particularly important aspect of foraging. If you adhere to the theory that fish won't strike trolled lures that they can't see, then you must play the color game fastidiously. Trout and salmon trollers, for instance, fish with some of the funkiest lure colors and lure color combinations imaginable and perhaps play to the fish's sense of vision more than any other trollers.

I adhere to the theory that visibility is an important aspect of all lure fishing, including trolling; that it can be the paramount factor in causing a fish to be attracted to your lure but that it is usually not the sole factor; and that a combination of factors, including the action of the lure, its speed, its color, the manner in which it is fished, and the place in which it is fished, all contribute to success. We may never know if one is a more dominant contributor than another, but I don't want to overlook any of them no matter what species of fish I'm trolling for.

Scents. Some of you may be disappointed to see how little attention I'm devoting to scents, particularly because I just said that I don't want to overlook any factor that helps make a fish strike. I don't dispute that fish have some olfactory ability. This is more acute in some species than in others. Migratory fish use some type of smelling power to distinguish their natal waters and to return to them to spawn.

The whole scent business has become a big part of the fishing equipment industry in recent years, and there are so many scent products around that it is hard to keep track of them. I have used many and have concluded that although they don't hurt your fishing, I cannot prove that they help it, particularly for trolling. People who are paid to use scent products and espouse their virtues would have you believe that this stuff adds to your catch, whether you cast or troll. I suspect that the use of scent products may improve the confidence of some anglers, and thereby help their catch, but in my experience, these products do not live up to their claims. I do not see that fish *are attracted* to your lure any more than they would be ordinarily because it has some nonalarming scent on it. The fact that the commercial fishing industry, especially fish farmers and hatchery operators — for whom it is important to get fish to eat plenty and grow fast — have not embraced this, makes me all the more suspicious of a scent's ability to cause fish to feed or strike.

Because there is so much that goes into fishing success — lure placement, lure color, lure size, presentation, speed, depth, and on and on — I cannot isolate scent alone as making the important contribution to fishing success that some people think. Not long ago while trolling for trout on Lake Ontario, I had a scent-related experience that would seem to have been precipitated by the use of a scent product. I had replaced an inside planer board lure with a fire dot shallow-running plug, a lure that my partner and I had not fished all day although we'd already boated half a dozen fish. I had rubbed this lure with Chummin' Rub sparkle-version scent — the only lure I'd done this to all day — and was setting it out. I'd just gotten it about 80 feet away, with the rod in my hand, and was about to put the rod down to place the line in the release, when a small brown trout took it. The lure hadn't trolled but a few feet.

It would be easy to say that the scent cause this. But did it? Obviously it didn't hurt. We never caught another fish the rest of the day on that scented lure, or on others that I tried the scent on, but we did catch two more trout on unscented lures. Was that strike a mere coincidence? I think so, but I can't prove that either. My guess is that this was simply a right time/right place accidental catch.

If you feel it's important to cut down on your odds and use scents to either mask potentially offensive odors, human smells, for instance, then try them. Most wash off after awhile in the water, so you'll need to reapply the stuff, and that can be a nuisance while using downriggers and slider rigs and the like. You may not like getting this stuff (most of which is rather greasey or oily) on your hands and ultimately transferring it to other lures, your clothes, and reel handles. I think that when trolling, fish primarily react to visual stimuli and sound, and I intend to focus my own trolling efforts on appealing to those fish senses.

Jointed plugs. I have a special fondness for trolling with jointed plugs. I especially like using them for trout, salmon, muskies, and pike; in cold water, particularly in early season and late fall; and in shallow water. The most notable aspect of jointed lures is their sex appeal. They wiggle and shimmy wilder than a belly dancer because they have two or three body segments rather than a straight, one-piece construction. The sinuous swimming action that such design causes, and the reaction from many species of fish, makes me a big fan of this genre of lure, and I feel compelled to devote a little space to their merits and use.

The stimulating action of jointed plugs has not been lost on fishermen since the early days of lure-making. Apparently the first "jointed animated minnow" lure was made by the K&K Manufacturing Company of Toledo, Ohio, which received a patent for a double-jointed "artificial minnow fishing bait" in June 1907. Jointed plugs were very popular in the 1920s and 1930s and were responsible for some significant world record catches, including the all-tackle world record largemouth bass in 1932 and apparently the all-tackle world record muskellunge in 1957, both of which stand.

The Creek Chub Pikie Minnow may be the most popular lure of this genre historically. It is the only one still being produced. Now it is made by Dura Pak in plastic, not in wood. The old jointed plugs were made of wood, often cedar, and herein lies one of the keys to the effectiveness of old plugs and of some modern-era jointed plugs: wood. In my opinion, and in the opinion of many knowledgeable anglers, wooden jointed lures simply "work" better than plastic ones.

That's not to say that some currently available jointed plugs made of plastic aren't fish-catchers. The plastic jointed Cordell Redfin, Rebel Minnow, Rebel Spoonbill Minnow, and Bill Norman Minnow are all good lures, but they have less action and vibration than their wooden counterparts because the joint is located far back, and they have a different buoyancy. The plastic jointed J-Plug by Luhr Jensen, which is a cut-plug-style lure for continuous trolling applications, is an extremely effective lure for salmon and steelhead and has good action even at relatively slow speeds. I have caught a lot of fish on this erratic swimmer and know that the jointed version works better than the unjointed model at slow speeds, giving it a distinct advantage in appealing to fish that don't want the faster speed. Also made of plastic is the jointed Pikie Minnow, which is still a popular lure; large versions of it see use in musky, pike, and striped bass fishing, and in saltwater.

In addition, Dura Pak makes a plastic jointed cut-plug lure called the Jointed FireFly, as well as a jointed Lazy Ike banana bait called the Flex Ike. Arbogast has a jointed Jitterbug called the Clicker, for surface fishing, which I have used successfully, but it is not nearly as popular as the unsegmented version. The Jointed Believer, a large plastic plug made by the Drifter Tackle Company, is known in musky casting and trolling circles. Bomber now has a jointed plastic minnow bait, and Cordell introduced a jointed version of its extraordinarily popular no-lipped sinking plastic plug, the Spot, a few years ago. In all likelihood, there are some other plastic jointed plugs in production, and at least one urethane foam jointed lure, the deep-diving Lindy Giant Shadling.

The lure that is probably the foremost commercially made jointed plug of modern vintage, however, is made of wood. This is the Rapala minnow. Rapala jointed minnow lures in three sizes are used for a broad range of casting and trolling applications in freshwater. The 4 1/2-inch-long, bronze-hooked J-11 floater is their premier jointed product. They did make a sinking (Countdown) version of this once but discontinued it, much to the unhappiness of some anglers. A Lake Michigan charter boat skipper recently told me that he wailed and begged for the return of the J-11 Countdown when the company suspended its production. He used it for long flat-line trolling because the lure got deeper than the floating model.

Fans of departed wooden lures know the feeling. Morey Wheeler, president of Dura Pak, told me that although his company doesn't make wooden Creek Chub products, they are continually asked to do so. I believe him. I have a friend, an unheralded but extraordinarily successful big musky troller, who went directly to Creek Chub years ago and bought cases of single- and double-jointed wooden Pikie Minnows in two or three specific colors, for his own use, when he learned that they were switching to plastic. Cases!

Although there are more models of plastic jointed plugs than wooden ones, fishermen who would rather use the latter have several options open to them. As mentioned, a few floating minnow plugs from Rapala have been in wide circulation. Rapala doesn't make a jointed crankbait or deep diver, however; also, the colors available are rather limited.

Some other, smaller manufacturers of jointed minnow plugs exist, but their products are less widely distributed. One of these is Nils Master, a prominent Finnish lure manufacturer whose wooden minnow-style plugs are characterized by a curved back. The company just recently began exporting its products to the United States.

If these don't fit your angling applications, however, you can make your own jointed wooden plugs by segmenting straight lures. You can't segment straight plastic lures, but you can segment wooden ones and you may improve them by doing so. Maybe some folks around the country have been tinkering with their wooden lures by segmenting them, but if they have, it isn't widely known. Furthermore, I suspect that many of the original jointed products got their start as cutup versions of the straight parent lure, so this isn't a totally new idea. I give my buddy Roger Tucker and his friend Charlie McNeer credit for not only coming up with the thought to do this with modern plugs, but also for doctoring some stupendous balsa wood lures.

Six or seven years ago, Tucker, who was then heavily into musky fishing and who had already doctored some Rapala lures, took deep-diving Bagley Bang-O-B crankbaits into his workshop and started modifying them. Working with 5- and 8-inch-long models, he and McNeer transformed them into single- and double-jointed versions. Tucker made some for me because I often cast and troll big deep-diving lures. I loved the way his jointed plugs swam, and I successfully used them for musky and northern Canada lake trout trolling. Then he did it with minnow plugs. One of his double-jointed minnows, a 7-inch Bagley Bang-O-Lure that had minimal life to it in the unadulterated form, became the slinkiest shallow-running lure I've ever slithered through the water. Right after he made one up for me, I took it to Lake of the Woods. When I came home and told him over the phone that it had caught a pair of muskies and drew follows from a few others, he almost sounded surprised.

The next winter he expanded the concept to include crankbaits and made up some single-jointed Bagley Small Fry minnows, lures that were merely 2 1/2 inches long and looked exactly like small alewives. That spring I took one of his adulterated little plugs out and had excellent results trolling it for brown trout, catching some of the biggest fish of the season on them. Everyone who saw the jointed lures wanted to know who made them and where they could get them. No one was the least bit happy to learn that this was strictly private enterprise.

You can segment lures yourself by making a judiciously placed cut through a wood-bodied plug with a fine-toothed hacksaw. Cut back all sides on an angle to allow for a wide wobble between segments, put a sufficiently long-stemmed wire loop into both segments (after linking them), and use slow-curing two-part epoxy to anchor the wire. You'll have to sacrifice a lure or two while experimenting with this. Make sure that the epoxy will hold at least 30 pounds of pulling strength (more if you're likely to use heavier line, though I have yet to pull one apart on a fish) and that you make the segments in the right areas to achieve optimum swimming action. Give the exposed raw wood a couple coats of black epoxy paint, cover it with clear lacquer, and you're in business.

One new lure company is getting into the jointed wooden lure field, and shows promise for the future. Lee Sisson Lures, owned and designed by Lee Sisson, who designed most of the popular Bagley balsa wood lures being used today, is mass-producing jointed wooden surface lures, minnow-style plugs, and crankbaits, as well as straight versions, that not only look outstanding but also fish outstandingly well. I've successfully used his Jointed Minnow Mates for Great Lakes and inland trout and know that they troll enticingly well.

Sisson's Jointed T-Shad, a 3 1/4-inch-long single-jointed diving plug, has worked for me on several species of fish. It is the only commercially made jointed crankbait and it's made of wood. In addition to having that critical belly dancer's shimmy, this lure also has a sound-chamber-enclosed BB inside it to make it rattle, which no other jointed wooden lures do, although some plastic jointed minnow-style lures do. Sisson says that the combination of the rattle and the enhanced action produced by the jointed tail section produce a whole different set of vibration patterns than a standard straight-bodied crankbait and provide more stimuli to appeal to fish.

If you're not that convinced about the usefulness of jointed plugs for trolling over their straight counterparts, try this experiment: Take a jointed plug and place it next to its unjointed counterpart in the water. Get the boat up to a speed that causes both lures to swim at a steady but highly active manner. Reduce speed and watch what happens. The unjointed lure will barely wobble while the jointed product will still have a seductive shimmy to it. The faster you go, the greater the vibration there is for the jointed lure. Make sure that you don't twist the connecting eyelets between body segments, however, or the jointed lure will not swim properly. Also note that most jointed plugs will dive as deep, or deeper, than their unjointed counterparts. I've conducted tests with deep divers and proved as much.

I'm a believer in jointed plugs for trolling, and often find myself reaching for a jointed version over a nonjointed one.

Whatever lures you troll, remember that the act of trolling is unlike the act of casting in that you do not physically "work" the lure with hand and wrist manipulation of your rod when you troll. *You* do not have direct contact with the lure to feel what it is doing or to choreograph its actions. But that is no excuse for simply tying on whatever appeals to you and dragging it around in the water. There are many nuances to using all types of lures in trolling applications. The more you know about what your lure is doing, how you can get the most out of it, and what to select, the better troller you'll be.

7

STRIPED BASS

Striped bass are one of the strongest fighting freshwater fish. They are predominantly open-water nomads that, in the summer, are best located and caught by trolling.

Locating stripers is the foremost task facing open-water anglers, yet this is generally not easy due to the nature of these fish. Inland stripers possess the hereditary traits of their ocean-dwelling brethren, and this influences their behavior in freshwater. The basic difference is that they are more confined in lake environs than they are in saltwater. Landlocked stripers possess the hereditary traits of their ocean-dwelling brethren, and this bears a marked influence on their behavior in freshwater environs and in the attempts of fishermen to catch them.

Striped bass characteristically have been vigorous eaters. Not surprisingly, the primary reason for the success of landlocked stripers has been the food found in the lakes where they have been introduced. Most striper lakes have large populations of shad, either gizzard or threadfin and occasionally both. Shad are basically an open-water fish, like stripers, and they congregate in large masses. Threadfin shad seem to be favored by stripers, especially by smaller ones, because they grow to an average length of only 5 inches. Their availability is sometimes adversely influenced by cold winters, however, so they may not always be plentiful. Gizzard shad provide suitable forage in the smaller sizes, but large specimens are only eaten occasionally by stripers.

Stripers gorge themselves on these creatures! Fisheries managers have reported finding stripers that had consumed between 40 and 70 small shad on a feeding binge just prior to capture. Stripers that are caught while schooling on the surface after shad may regurgitate bait fish right after being captured.

Some stripers, particularly hybrid stripers, may have been feeding before being caught but don't have anything in their stomachs. If you horse a fish and get it up in a real hurry before it can spit food out, you'll see the shad they've been feeding on. Or, if you see shad jump when being chased by hybrids, you have a good idea what size bait they're feeding on. The size of shad will give you a clue as to what size lure to use.

In some environments, shad are not present, thus stripers consume the bait fish that are most prominent. In many northern waters this is alewives, which vary from 2 1/2 to 6 inches in size and closely resemble threadfin shad in appearance. Small panfish, such as bluegills, also may be a major food source.

Stripers become active in the spring when they migrate up tributaries to spawn. Stripers need flowing water to hatch their eggs successfully, and they will migrate great distances up tributaries, and feeders to tributaries, about the time that the water temperature reaches 55 degrees. Spawning takes place in stages, generally from mid-April through mid-May, depending on geographic location.

The inside bend of major tributaries is often a hot spot to troll or cast for stripers in the spring. Most anglers are accustomed to working the outside bend at this time for largemouth bass, but stripers like a point where water rushes by, so they hold on the inside bend of a channel and use these spots to ambush whatever comes around.

After spawning, stripers are somewhat scattered. They do not travel in large schools but individually follow the tributary out to the lake, then traverse a migration route that often follows the path of channels and streambeds into deep water. From then through summer into fall, stripers school in fair groups of similarly sized fish, staying basically in open water. They will travel many miles and move around frequently and swiftly in pursuit of bait. Usually stripers are found at a depth between 20 and 40 feet at this time, sometimes suspended over much deeper water.

In the fall, stripers move into the shallow, flatter areas, and this is the prime time for them to chase schools of bait fish near the surface. They're on the move and vigorously following the bait. In the winter, stripers don't move as much, or so far, or so fast. They tend to stay deep but they also can be depended on to stick to their territory, which makes finding them a bit more reliable in the winter than at other times.

Joe Hughes took this large striper by trolling a jig behind a downrigger weight in November. Fall striper fishing is sometimes characterized by casting to a school of fish busting shad on the surface, but when schooling fish aren't around, trolling is a prime technique.

Though trolling for stripers is effective, it is far from being a perfected technique for many anglers. Some would-be inland striper catchers troll relatively aimlessly, without regard to method of presentation, depth their lures actually are running, and depth they should be working. This may, in part, be related to the fact that in many striper waters, particularly in the Southeast and Southwest, trolling is not a traditional fishing technique, or it has not been utilized for a species with the characteristics and size of the striper. Whatever the reason, fishermen should understand that there is more to trolling for stripers than simply dragging something behind the boat.

The prime considerations of any striper troller must be where to go and how deep to fish. In the summer, when the water is warm, stripers and bait fish are usually deep (roughly 20 feet to 50 feet depending on the characteristics of the lake), sometimes near the bottom, and other times suspended over considerably deeper water. They may be located over old creek beds and river channels, near sunken islands, along ridges with good drop-offs, at the deep ends of points, near bridges (especially if the bridges have long ripraps that extend far enough into the lake to make the area a funneling point for bait fish travel), and in the tops of submerged trees. These are the kinds of locales in which you should start fishing and in which you may expect to find stripers.

To pinpoint these areas, it is virtually essential to have some type of sonar. The object is to find the types of places that appeal to stripers and to locate fish. Often you won't catch the fish that you see on a depthfinder (or you will catch fish that were not seen on this device), but you will learn the all-important range of depth at which the stripers are holding. You can then attempt to place your lures at the right level.

In lakes that have stripers plus white bass and/or hybrid stripers — a cross between pure stripers and white bass, also called wipers and whiterock bass — you may find it hard to tell what fish you are viewing on your sonar. Sometimes these fish intermingle, especially in the fall, making species detection even tougher. Although I haven't been able to make the distinctions, friends who know say that by and large you'll view stripers below other fish, white bass above the stripers, and hybrid bass above the white bass.

Here's a tip on how to identify stripers on sonar, which was passed along to me by Texas striper guide Johnny Procell: "Stripers, if they're not feeding, form a lazy line. They might start, say, at 20 feet, then come up to 15 feet in a long line. Hybrids are not like that. There are seldom over twenty fish in a school of hybrids, and usually only eight or ten, and they get in a tight wad, nearly touching each other a few inches apart. You can almost tell every time that these tight-packed groups are hybrids. You can also tell if these fish are going to bite. Invariably they will be touching something, like a levee, a hump, an old dam from a pond or tank, or trees. If I go through an area watching my sonar and see fish 50 feet out from a tree line or levee or pond, I don't fool with them. I go and find another group of fish

Billy Murray hefts a striper caught by the author on Lake Ouachita in Arkansas. Note the downriggers and rail-mount rod holders used for striper trolling with a conventional bass boat. Although not the most convenient place for rigging, this tackle afforded us a chance to get lures down to just above the submerged treetop level where 20- to 30-pound stripers were holding.

because those hybrids away from structure usually don't bite, or at least are not as catchable as those touching something."

Though pure-strain stripers may often be scattered, you'll seldom find a single fish by itself in a particular spot. There are generally more in the area. Sometimes they'll be grouped fairly closely; characteristically, fish of similar sizes tend to band together.

Having determined the suitable depth to be fishing, you need to use lures or fishing techniques that will bring your offerings into that range. Stripers may be voracious feeders but they are not likely to move a significant distance to attack your bait. Some will, and via a graph recorder I've watched an occasional striper swim up and come behind a trolled lure, but it is usually necessary to get your offerings at or slightly above the holding level of the fish. This can be accomplished by using lead-core or wire line, which I find cumbersome and inhibiting, adding weight to your terminal tackle to help get it down, using a downrigger, or flat-lining your lure.

When stripers are within 25 feet of the surface, most trollers flat-line by tradition, though they needn't be restricted to this. When flat-lining for stripers, plugs, spoons, flies, and jigs can be used for shallow fishing, but only plugs have merit from 10 to 25 feet. Many striper trollers greatly overestimate the depth at which their lures are running, or the depth to which they are capable of diving. As a result, they often are not trolling at the proper level for success.

The nuances of trolled plugs are extensively detailed in the previous chapter, so I won't get into that subject again. Keep in mind, however, that some lures reaching great depths are those that are large in size. They may be significantly bigger than the normal bait consumed by stripers in that particular environment. If this is so, there must be a compromise among lure size, diving ability, and strength of line to be used. Sometimes standard black bass crankbaits, which are 2 to 2 1/2 inches long, are most representative of the size of local bait fish but require light line to get them down, which may not be feasible depending on local conditions. The point is that there are a lot of options available to you. Remember, a lure that dives 15 feet in a certain situation with one size of line can be made to dive deeper if you use a lighter line or troll a greater length of the same line.

Obviously it is important to know the abilities of your striper trolling lures if you will be flat-lining them very much. Downriggers are becoming an ever-greater force in striper trolling, however, and the use of these devices is affording deep striper trollers a greater range of lure presentation and more price lure placement and control. There are some places, however, where striper trollers are reluctant to use downriggers. Many southern impoundments that are home to large populations of pure-strain stripers or hybrid stripers have a significant amount of standing timber in them. This timber often holds bait fish and stripers and, obviously, poses certain hazards to anyone who would troll an 8- to 12-pound downrigger weight, not to mention a lure, in their midst.

I have done this and can say that it is not impossible to use a downrigger for striper trolling in these circumstances, providing you know your underwater terrain well, watch your sonar constantly, fish with another capable angler who is always ready to raise the weight, keep the clutch setting loose, and aren't afraid to lose some tackle now and then.

The last time I fished Arkansas' Lake Ouachita — a lake with plenty of submerged trees — friends and I caught fish 25 to 35 feet deep around the timber (it was in midfall). We marked many stripers on our graph recorder in that depth range. Some were holding in or just alongside of submerged trees, the tops of which came to within 30 feet of the surface, but their total depth was 65 to 70 feet. Others were suspended and schooled in open areas that were between tree-filled flats. We used a moderate trolling line length of 60 to 75 feet and were particularly attentive to raising or lowering the downrigger weight as necessary to keep the lures from getting hung as well as to keep them in front of fish as much as possible. We did hang our lure a couple of times on trees, and we did get the cannonball caught in the treetops a time or two, but we never lost it. We also caught a half-dozen fish between 20 and 28 pounds.

Even impoundments relatively devoid of timber have not seen the kind of downrigger use for striper trolling that you might think, or that might be similar to Great Lakes trolling, although the use of downriggers is spreading as anglers see the utility of this equipment. Less than a decade ago, not one out of several hundred boats trolling

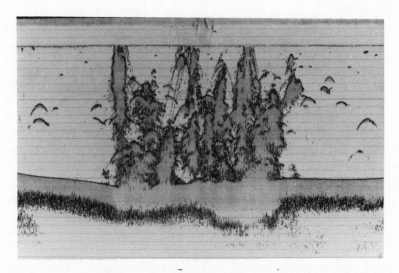

Many southern impoundments that have striped bass are also host to submerged trees. The author graphed these trees on the middle fork of the Red River on Greer's Ferry Lake, Arkansas, one March. The scale setting was 60 feet, so the bases of the trees are 40 feet deep. The inverted V marks are hybrid stripers; note that some fish are holding inside the trees.

for stripers would be sporting a downrigger. A few seasons ago in July on Oklahoma's Keystone Lake, I fished for stripers with friends and sorely missed not having downriggers or even rod holders. We made vain attempts at trolling, but our lures were not getting down consistently to the proper depth. We eventually caught some small stripers by jigging vertically amidst a few schools that were 25 feet deep, but I'm sure that downrigging would have expanded our presentation methods and would have resulted in more thorough and effective fishing. I did not even see another boat equipped with a downrigger. In sum, those who limit themselves to boat fishing for stripers without downriggers are missing something.

Finding stripers and presenting your lures at the appropriate level is more than half the battle in striper trolling, but accomplishing both of these is no guarantee that fish will take your offering. If there are bait fish near the stripers you mark on a depthfinder, the bass may be moving on quickly in pursuit of this bait. You'll find it extremely difficult to stay with them and continue to locate them.

Some of the stripers you find simply won't strike your lure for whatever reason, and still others may show only passing interest. Because you can never be sure when you'll have a strike, you should conduct your trolling with the thought that a fish is likely to hit at any moment. Every movement should be calculated to bring about a strike. The worst thing you can do is troll aimlessly for hours on end, even if your lures are at the proper depth.

For successful trolling, you must be conscious of where your lures are in relation to the position of the boat as well as in respect to depth. For instance, if you were to spot a school of fish and then turn the boat slightly, your lures would probably not come close to that school because the path of travel of the fish will be straighter than that of the boat. Keep this in mind when you are attempting to follow an underwater ridgeline or river channel closely, for instance. It is often necessary to steer your boat beyond or to the side of some object or fish in order to direct the path of travel of your following lures over it.

Many of the trolling tactics and boat manipulation skills employed when trolling for any species of fish work for striper fishing. These include avoiding trolling in open-water areas in a straight line for continuously long periods of time, alternating between heading upwind or downwind, making turns, changing speed, and so forth.

If you aren't running as many trolling lines as the law allows, you are not only decreasing your chances of taking fish, but you are missing an opportunity to experiment and determine what lures, lure colors, or depths should be fished. This is especially overlooked by striper fishermen, many of whom are not accustomed to trolling or spend a great deal of time casting for fish using only one rod at a time. I still see many southern impoundment striper trollers using one rod and holding it in their hand. Often this needn't be. Check the regulations in your area; most states permit the use of two rods per angler.

Where boat speed is concerned, you needn't travel especially slowly for stripers. These are strong-swimming fish and they are accustomed to chasing down prey in open water. That doesn't mean that they prefer to swim fast after a meal, only that they are capable of doing so. Nonetheless, a medium to medium-fast boat speed, as long as it is conducive to proper lure action, will get the job done.

For striper trolling it is best to have a long rod, preferably one of 7- to 8-foot length, with a moderate- to fast-action tip, the latter especially for use with downriggers. Reels may be spinning, bait-casting, or larger conventional levelwind models, but they should have a smooth and reliable drag and be capable of holding at least 120 yards of heavy line. A clicker is a desirable feature for the bait-casters and conventional reels. Largemouth bass fishing tackle may do at times, but the rods may be too short and the line capacity too little in situations where large fish are encountered or where there is heavy current or obstructions present.

Striper lures consist almost exclusively of deep-diving plugs, metal spoon-type jigs and hair jigs, and some surface lures although trolling products for stripers may be plugs, jigs, flies, and the occasional spoon or spinner. Plugs like the Whopper Stopper Hellbender and Bomber Waterdog are favorites in many striper lakes, and some anglers take the hooks off these plugs and use heavy line to attach a 1 1/2- to 2-ounce jig behind that. Of course, other diving plugs catch fish, too. Most striper anglers use 20- to 30-pound-test line; in my mind, 20 is more adequate. Twelve- to 17-pound-test line will do well in open-water circumstances, provided you fight a fish properly and you use the appropriate drag setting. An advantage to lighter line with stripers is that it can alarm fish less (stripers are a spooky fish) and draw more strikes, plus it gets lures deeper.

Although there are a variety of ways to fish for stripers, when the fish are deep in the summer and not as accessible, I think trolling is the best way to go.

The foregoing information applies to pure-strain striped bass, but because hybrid stripers have become a very popular sport fish in the United States and are offering good angling opportunities in lakes and states where pure-strain stripers are not present, I feel compelled to discuss the habits of these fish and trolling for them.

Hybrid stripers are a great fish to catch. When a hybrid strikes your lure, it really nails it. In small sizes a hybrid striper is tenacious. In medium sizes it is a football-shaped powerhouse. In large sizes it is prime bulldog. That it is a more aggressive bait and lure consumer than its striper parent, and grows to trophy sizes, further strengthens its appeal and in part explains why it has been introduced into over 30 states.

My first introduction to a good-sized hybrid striper impressed me greatly. Several years ago in mid-March, I was getting acquainted with my day-old boat on Greer's Ferry Lake in Arkansas by trolling the middle fork of the Red River for walleyes. At a heavily timbered flat along an inside channel bend, I was graphing scores of suspended white bass and bait fish when a trailing, deep-diving minnow plug was smashed by a fish that fought so hard it had me puzzled.

My quarry was one of Greer's fabled 15- to 20-pound spawning-run walleyes. At first I supposed that maybe I had one of these brutes, but I didn't imagine it would pull and run so doggedly. There were no stripers in that lake and white bass that could fight that well didn't exist. When my partner slipped the net under a 5-plus-pound hybrid striper we were both amazed.

It is characteristic for most hybrid fish to grow faster than one or both parent species. The hybrid striper, which is technically a cross between the female striped bass and the male white bass, puts on weight in a hurry. Stocked as a 3- to 4-inch fingerling, it may grow to 15 inches in a year. When 18 inches long, it will weigh at least 3 and perhaps as much as 5 pounds. To reach such desirable angling sizes so quickly, it eats prodigiously. This makes it fairly vulnerable to angling.

Hybrid stripers are recognized by broken spotted lines, or stripes, on their sides. White bass and pure stripers have continuous lines. Hybrid stripers may have a few continuous lines, but some will be all or partially broken, especially near the head. You can distinguish between white bass and hybrid bass by checking the tooth patch on each's tongue, the white bass having a single patch while the hybrid has a double.

In small sizes, hybrids look a lot like both parents and can be hard to distinguish from one another. It's important to be able to do so in some places, however. Hybrid stripers may have different size and creel restrictions than their parent species, especially in northern states and in areas where they are part of an experimental stocking program. A 15- or 18-inch size limit may be in effect here, as opposed to no minimum size for white bass, so it's advisable to check state fishing regulations.

Like their parents, hybrid stripers are an open-water species that does not relate to near-shore structure as many other popular warm-water game fish do. In many locales, particularly in large southern impoundments, the bulk of the warm-water game fish population (which is heavily pressured) is found inshore while the majority of forage exists offshore and is nomadic.

Threadfin and gizzard shad make up the primary forage in southern locales, alewives are the mainstay in some northern waters, and blue-gills or chubs or other species constitute main or secondary forage in other hybrid sites. Like pure-strain stripers, hybrids follow bait fish schools, feeding heavily on them.

The most popular season for hybrid striper fishing is spring, though good success can be had in all seasons if you spend a lot of time on the water and can track the movements of these fish. In spring, hybrids attempt to spawn in tributaries when the water temperature reaches the mid to upper 50s. They usually are right on the heels of white bass, and just before pure stripers, though in many of the lakes where hybrids are stocked, one or both of the parent species do not exist.

Hybrids travel in schools. When located, it's often possible to catch more than one or two. The most exciting fishing for them is the frenzied jump-fishing that occurs early and late in the day from late summer through fall when hybrids locate a school of bait fish, pin them against the bank, a sandbar, or the surface of the water, and pounce on them. Sea gulls at times can be seen hovering over this wild oceanlike marauding, and anglers use binoculars to spot the commotion, then race to the action to get a few casts in before the hybrids sound, often to reappear a few hundred yards away. When the school goes down, however, you may locate them by trolling, and you can

Roger Tucker holds a hybrid striper that took a trolled diving minnow plug. The broken lines on the fish indicate that this is a hybrid.

catch fish on the perimeter of the surface action by trolling, although stopping to rifle a lure into the melee is usually more productive.

Hybrids are primarily sight feeders. Lures that work well for them are those that imitate small bait fish, with white, silver, chrome, and clear or translucent finishes being favored. For trolling, diving minnow-shaped plugs, like a small Rebel Spoonbill Minnow or medium-to deep-diving crankbait, can do the job.

Places to locate hybrids include gravel and sandy bars, points, tailrace runs below dams, spillways, the mouth of rivers and creeks, between submerged or visible islands, along drop-offs, and above humps or levees. They are often found on humps, ledges, and points in the summer. In some really warm southern waters, hybrids will be down roughly at 21 to 22 feet around the thermocline. When trolling, be sure your lure runs at or above the level of these suspended fish.

Many of the places that attract white bass or pure stripers, detailed earlier, also attract hybrid stripers. In lakes where both are found, it's not uncommon to catch a hybrid in the midst of white bass. I've been into pods of small white bass and then found a hybrid mixed in with the catch later on, not having realized that a hybrid had been caught earlier during the flurry of fishing action. Many of the trolling techniques that apply to pure-strain stripers also apply to hybrids.

8

BLACK BASS

People always used to troll for bass in places where it was appropriate to do so, but in recent decades the pursuit of largemouth and small-mouth bass has swung almost entirely to casting. Better tackle and better understanding of the habits and habitat of bass have no doubt been the primary cause for this change. Most people who fish primarily or exclusively for bass don't want to have anything to do with trolling. Having written a book about bass fishing, I'd be one of the last to say that trolling was a primary way to catch bass, the best way to catch bass, or even the most enjoyable way to catch bass. Bass just aren't the roaming nomad that other fish, more suitable to trolling, are. Nonetheless, there are times and places in which trolling is a good way to get your lures in front of bass and a productive technique. The open-minded bass angler ought to know about this. Let's review some basic facts about bass and their habitat, and in so doing see why trolling for them can be an effective way to fish.

Like any other fish, bass react to natural aquatic changes in ac-cordance with the type of water they live in, the amount and location of food supplies, and the availability of cover. As the surface water surpasses 50 degrees, bass become a little active. When the shallows are warm enough, bass spawn; depending on latitude this occurs from midspring to early summer. Eventually the upper layers warm past the preferred temperature range of bass, and the fish begin to go deeper or seek heavy cover, where water temperatures are cooler. In the fall, the upper layers and the shallows cool off and are attractive to bass again.

On the whole, bass are basically found in relatively shallow water (not much deeper than 30 feet) and near shore or some protective cover. Though some bass do wander, the species is not a deep, open-water roamer like trout, salmon, or striped bass. They relate to objects, bottom, and specific water level zones as do their prey. Most of the food preferred by bass is found in or near cover of some form, so this, plus the need for security and protection from sunlight, is a factor in their specific habitat preferences.

Smallmouth bass have a much narrower habitat preference than largemouth bass do and are much more likely to be found in deep, open water. In their northernmost range, where water temperatures are unlikely to exceed the low 70s throughout the summer, small-mouths may be found in shallow to middepth environs throughout the fishing season. Where water temperatures in the shallow and near-shore areas exceed the low 70s for a long time, they move deeper. In some huge northern lakes, smallmouths may be 60 to 100 feet deep in the summer. Thus, they can be particularly appropriate for trolling, especially from late spring through fall.

Smallmouths typically inhabit rocky terrain. Their native range is typified by somewhat infertile, natural, rocky-shored northern lakes. Their expanded range includes southern impoundments with shoreline and deep-water rock structure. Smallmouths are located around rocky points, craggy clifflike shores, rocky islands and reefs, and ripraps near shores. They prefer golf ball- to brick-size rocks if they have a choice, but larger rocks, including boulders, are also suitable. The primary reason for the smallmouth's affection for rocks is that rocks harbor their principal food: crayfish.

In the spring prior to spawning, smallmouths in lakes that are completely rock-laden prefer to be near large rocks. When actually spawning, they like to be close to shore. These areas are often tough to troll unless you use sideplaner boards, or an electric motor and long flat lines. Prior to spawning, however, bass will be in slightly deeper water near potential spawning areas and can be trolled effectively there. After spawning, they will move out of the real skinny water, ultimately working to deep summer haunts where they also can be reached by trollers.

Largemouth bass have a much wider range of cover that they utilize, including vegetation, stumps, and timber. They usually are situated in places where they cannot be effectively trolled or where trolling is a much less practical technique than casting. Lakes without vegetation, with plenty of deep water, and without much submerged timber are more likely to yield largemouth bass to trollers, especially in the summer, because fish in these places exhibit somewhat similar behavior patterns to smallmouth bass, although largemouth don't necessarily go as deep.

There is a wide range of lure types that catch bass if you are casting, but the field is narrowed greatly when you talk trolling. The most successful and functional lure for bass trolling, exclusive of Lake Erie, is a small- to medium-size diving plug. Called crankbaits by the bass fishing fraternity, these relatively diminutive diving lures work well when cast but achieve much greater depths when trolled. A few versions are used for trout and/or salmon trolling, but most standard crankbaits are strictly thought of as bass (and walleye) lures. The action and vibration qualities of crankbaits are particularly appealing to the bottom and near cover dwelling nature of largemouth and smallmouth bass.

Although many northern waters are quite clear, the majority of bass lakes and reservoirs are on the slightly turbid side. It seems proper to say that in these places where human sight is limited to a few feet, vision is of restricted importance to a bass. In waters of marginal to poor visibility, the most important features of a lure will be its action and vibration patterns, not appearance, because the most acute sense of a bass is its hearing, thanks to its finely honed lateral line sensory mechanism.

Signals received through the displacement of water by bait fish are relative to the fish's shape and fin movement, so it is possible for bass not only to detect the presence of a fish (or lure) without seeing it but also to detect its approximate size and species. For most lures to be successful bass-catchers, it is important that they possess the properties that permit them to resemble bait in the way they appeal to the lateral line of the bass. The action of a constantly moving lure is critically important. A tight, fast wiggle in a crankbait is more desirable than a wide, slow action, because the former more closely mimics the body and tail movement activity of bait fish, especially wounded, erratic-swimming prey. Action and vibration are the choice assets of good bass-catching crankbaits, no matter whether they are used for casting or trolling.

Some crankbaits also possess rattle chambers within their bodies. Many plastic crankbaits, and at least one wooden one (Diving T-Shad by Sisson Lures), feature one or more BB-like spheres of varying size,

Crankbaits are a favorite casting lure for bass but also serve duty as trolling lures. Small boat fishermen who normally cast but who also troll from one area to another often pick up an extra bass or two.

which are free to move back and forth in the chamber thereby creating a rattling noise. That this sound can be produced is unquestionable. I realize that the food eaten by bass doesn't rattle; however, some prey do produce vibrations, and others, such as crayfish, may very well produce an audible "ticking" noise as they crawl over rocks. Most important is the fact that the rattle can draw the attention of a bass and make the lure more detectable under low light and turbid water conditions. Sometimes rattling crankbaits are more effective than non-rattlers, but many times there is no difference.

There is no doubt that bass strike some crankbaits they cannot see, such as in murky water or at night, because they have been able to detect that lure due to the water it displaced and the vibrations thereby produced. The better the overall action and vibration qualities, the more effective the lure can be at catching bass.

The primary forage for adult largemouth bass is bait fish and crayfish. Bait fish may take the form of shiners, bluegills (bream), shad, alewives (also called sawbellies or herring), minnows, and other small creatures, depending upon their abundance and accessibility in the particular body of water. Smallmouth show a marked preference for crayfish. Their bait fish preference runs to the fingerling-size shiners and minnows, and to a lesser extent alewives and small panfish. In streams, insects may make up a large part of the smallmouth's diet as well.

Crankbaits, called fat plugs or body baits by some hard-core trollers, imitate these small food items well. Although earlier models were rather bulbous in shape, newer ones are smaller in length and girth and have longer lips that allow for deep diving and more built-in action through a tighter, better controlled wiggling pattern.

Most crankbaits have clear plastic lips, which are presumably less visible to fish than metal lips, and they vary in length and shape. The larger the lip, the greater the trolling depth. The exception to this are lures that sink immediately to the bottom because they are not designed to float. These, too, may have smallish lips, but it is their weight, the amount of line you have out, and your boat speed that determine their working depth.

Depending upon lip size, crankbaits can be classified as shallow, medium, or deep diving, covering a range of depths from 2 to 12 feet. There are, incidentally, large crankbaits suitable for pike, musky, and striped bass angling. These will attain much greater depth when trolled but can occasionally be used for catching big largemouth bass as well. Ideally crankbaits should run on or close to the bottom, so it is clear that certain baits have applications for working specific bottom depths when you are flat-lining them. Of course, you can add weights to them as needed, use trolling sinkers, or employ downriggers. I discuss these points shortly.

One critically important aspect of crankbait fishing that is overlooked by many bass anglers, particularly if they are unaccustomed to trolling crankbaits, is the diving ability of the lure. Because you must fish specific near-bottom structure for bass, you must know how deep any diving plug runs to be effective with it. Diving abilities depend on the lure, the strength of your line, and the speed of your boat. These matters, especially as they pertain to diving plugs, are detailed in chapters 3 and 6.

You should know that there are a few lures that have little buoyancy or are neutral in buoyancy, and these can be good especially for near-bottom bass trolling. This genre of lure got its start with the Rebel Suspend-R a few years ago. Arbogast's Arby Hanger is a popular current suspension bait. These lures virtually remain stationary in the water when stopped. If you were casting one, you'd periodically stop your retrieve; when trolling, you would put the motor into neutral occasionally to stop the lure, which would neither sink nor rise.

The choice of color to use in a crankbait relates to the major forage of the bass where you are fishing and to the color and visibility of the water. Although there are as many different colors of crankbaits available as there are colors of automobiles, it is no coincidence that the best annual sellers are the silver, shad, and crayfish versions. These best resemble the predominant natural forage of bass. As long as you can determine what the primary forage of the fish you seek is, you have a headstart on color determination.

Water coloration is an influential factor, and here there are few guidelines. In blue-green water, chartreuse seems to stand out especially well. Crankbaits in this color, or with some chartreuse undercoating, are quite effective. In sand-colored or muddy water, I like light baits that have flash. In dark water influenced by tannic acid, a gold or chrome color in a plug has merit. In very clear water, darker colors seem to be less alarming to bass than light flashy ones. Depending on water color, a more subtle tone to a plug may be all that is needed; use, for instance, a lightly colored crayfish pattern rather than a dark one.

To be effective, crankbaits must run properly, and you should frequently check their operation. They must run straight, not lie on their side or swim off at an angle. Some lures will do this fresh out of the box and some will not; some are affected after catching a fish or having been snagged. You should always check the action of a crankbait beside your moving boat before letting it out to troll. If it's not running correctly, tune it to make it run true. How to tune trolling lures is reviewed in chapter 6.

The crankbait field is cluttered with good products, and I have used a wide array of these lures in trolling for many species of fish. Useful products for bass include those made by Rebel, Rapala, Sisson, Storm, Bomber, Bagley, Norman, Cordell, and Arbogast. Many of these manufacturers also produce 4- to 6-inch floating/diving minnow plugs that can be used for trolling. These lures don't dive appreciably, but if you flat-line them on a light line 150 to 225 feet behind the boat, you may be surprised to find that they'll get down to 5- to 8-foot depths. In the spring on large lakes, bass come out of their winter doldrums and orient from deep to shallow waters. I've caught a lot of bass, especially smallmouths, by trolling these lures then. These baits can also be fished deep for bass with the aid of weights or a downrigger, and I say more about that shortly.

Plugs aren't the only type of lure that will troll up bass. Spoons and spinners make their trolling mark, too. Spoons used for conventional bass fishing, however, are primarily lead-bodied jigging spoons or metal weedless spoons for vegetation fishing, and they will not do for trolling. The average diehard bass caster won't have a spoon in his tackle box that is appropriate for trolling. Such items include 1/8- to 1/4-ounce thick-bodied spoons up to 3 inches long, and lighter thin-metal spoons up to a similar length. The former can be cast or trolled while the latter are strictly for trolling. These are the same types of spoons used for trout trolling. In fact, in two-story lakes, hosting warm-water and cold-water species of fish, in which spoons are trolled for trout, smallmouth bass are often caught accidentally on them.

Spoons (and spinners) sink, of course, and this poses problems for trollers when they momentarily stop, because the lure sinks quickly to the bottom and invites a hang-up. Another key point to know about trolling spoons is that they are better fished on downriggers in deep or intermediate depth waters. Thin spoons don't achieve any depth when trolled, so they really must be fished behind a downrigger weight or some weighted-line system. Heavier spoons will achieve some depth, but it is much harder to discern diving depths with such

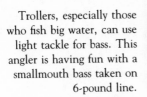

Trollers, especially those who fish big water, can use light tackle for bass. This angler is having fun with a smallmouth bass taken on 6-pound line.

a lure when flat-lined than it is with a plug. When bass are relatively shallow, flat-lining a spoon can have merit, but for deeper water trolling, you need a more controlled method of presentation at specific depths.

This seems to be a good time to note the merits of downriggers for bass trolling. Although it is far from being among the standard tool of a bass fisherman, a downrigger certainly can be used for bass, particularly for smallmouths, and especially where spoons and plugs are utilized. One of the best pieces of graph recorder paper that I ever ran was on Lake Ontario one summer while smallmouth bass fishing with downriggers. We trolled small crayfish plugs and spoons at 30 feet over a cobblestone bottom and watched smallmouths come up from the rocks, look at the downrigger weights, and strike the lures that were trailing a short distance behind the weights.

We had started our fishing by running plugs about 10 feet behind the weight, keeping the weight enough above the rocks to allow the trailing plug to scrape the bottom. By watching the graph recorder, we saw fish come up to look at the weight, so we shortened the lead and slightly lowered the weight. That caught fish, so we experimented

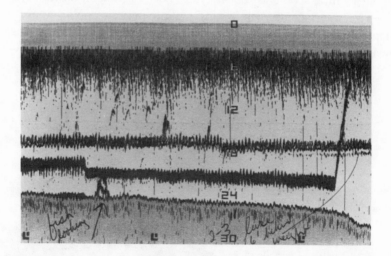

This graph paper, recorded on Lake Ontario one August, shows two downrigger weights being trolled for smallmouth bass. A 2- to 3-inch lure, being trolled 6 feet behind the upper weight, is visible on the graph paper. The lower weight attracted a fish that literally came from off the cobblestone bottom to inspect it. Some bass were caught in this manner.

further by dropping the weight a little closer to the bottom and running small spoons as close as 18 inches behind it. We caught smallmouth (and yellow perch) in this manner, and by watching the graph recorder we actually saw some fish strike.

I'm not going to deceive you and make you think that this was the best or only way to catch those smallmouths. The fish were in a cobblestone locale because of heavy crayfish presence. The day before this trolling took place, we'd absolutely clobbered them by drifting live softshell crabs across the bottom. Jigs, fished at the same time as bait, caught fish, too, but, like our trolling efforts, not nearly as successfully. The point, however, is that you can use downriggers to troll for bass. In places where you don't have such a fish concentration, it may be wise to do so. In large, clear lakes where bass are found very deep, fishermen equipped with a downrigger may have better action using this gear because they can cover a lot of ground, and can employ light line in the process. When a concentration of bass are found, stopping to jig or fish bait may have merit.

Spinners are not usually thought of as a bass lure by many anglers these days, particularly by those who chase largemouths exclusively or who never fish streams, but spinners are one of the most popular lure types in the world. Fishermen currently use spinners regularly to catch stream trout, pickerel, trout in lakes and ponds, panfish, muskies, walleyes, and smallmouth and largemouth bass. Plenty of other species — in fresh- and saltwater — also succumb to spinners every year under all kinds of circumstances. In this era of our trying to imitate game fish prey closely, spinners continue to be effective even though, as a lifeless object, they do not look anything like a fish. But in action, their wobbly flashy motion strongly suggests bait movement and offers an enticing temptation to many fish.

Though spinners are generally of minor value in largemouth bass fishing, they are quite valuable as stream smallmouth lures and are frequently successful for shallow water, early season smallmouth fishing in lakes. In both circumstances they can be cast or trolled, with 1/8- and 1/4-ounce sizes preferred. Good spinners for bass include Sheldon's Mepps, the Blue Fox Vibrax, the Harrison-Hoge Panther Martin, Burke's Abu Reflex, the C. P. Swing, and Cordell's spinner.

With these lures, blade design controls the action and the angle of blade revolution. The lighter the blade, the faster the spin, which is why round Colorado-bladed spinners are so popular; they are light, spin slowly, and work far from the shaft. The actual spinner blade is available in many colors, but silver, copper, and black are most popular. Spinners also produce vibration, which probably accounts for their success when used at night and under poor water-clarity conditions.

A favorite single-blade spinner for bait fishermen is the so-called June bug spinner, which features a long-shank hook and a single rotating blade with beads along the shaft. Variations of this are the most popular lure for smallmouth bass (and walleye) fishing on Lake Erie, where a Mepps Lusox, Earie Dearie, or similar products garnished with a live worm are drifted across reefs. Drifting with the wind is very much akin to slow trolling, and, as in motor trolling for bass, getting the lure down to the bottom and keeping it there are critically important.

One of the best times to fish spinners for smallmouths in lakes is just before spawning (provided the season is open, which it is not in some northern waters) and in the fall, when bass are just off rocky shorelines in 5 to 8 feet of water. Use a speed that is slow but fast enough to keep the blade turning and the lure from hanging bottom constantly. This is essentially flat-line trolling, although line is often weighted with split shot to help keep a trolled spinner down.

Using split shot or rubber-core sinkers is an oft-employed technique for flat-line trolling of minnow plugs, spoons, and sometimes diving plugs in addition to spinners. One of the better types of weights, especially for river trollers, is a bead-chain sinker. This is available in weights ranging from 1/4 ounce through 2 ounces, and it features a long barrellike weight on a snap swivel assembly. The device prevents line twist from occurring, does not get hung up too readily, and works with all types of lures. An 18- to 36-inch leader is utilized to connect the weight to the lure.

Another device that is extremely useful for getting lures deep for bass is the Gapen Bait Walker. This is a rig shaped like an open safety pin or a spinnerbait, with a lead body on the bottom and a swivel at the end of the top arm. Your fishing line is tied to the midsection, and a drop-back leader 18 to 48 inches long is attached to the swivel. This rig comes in a wide range of weights and can be used to cast (it's not easy but manageable if you use the smaller sizes) or troll lures. It is also remarkably snag free due to the shape of the lead weight and the angle of pull. A good use for the Gapen Bait Walker is in trolling small crankbaits, so that they will get down to a depth that is impossible

Dr. Mike Voiland of New York Sea Grant, with some nice smallmouth and a perch that he, the author, and two other fishermen caught on Lake Ontario. The Great Lakes, as well as smaller inland bodies of water, offer good opportunities for trollers to connect with bass.

for them to reach unaided. The biggest trick is selecting the right size weight for reaching the bottom.

I use these occasionally to catch smallmouths in 20 to 25 feet of water, primarily with floating/diving minnow-imitation plugs or shallow- to medium-depth crankbaits in crayfish and shad patterns. The Bait Walker keeps the lures right near the bottom and is good at avoiding hang-ups, although it is not completely snag free. Some of the recent Bait Walkers are gray and useful as is. Earlier models were painted bright orange, and I used to spray these with black paint to make them look a little less obtrusive in the water for bass. There are, incidentally, several other devices that work along the same principle. These are good systems for getting deep and covering a lot of potentially productive ground. Such devices are especially worth having if you are a person who ordinarily does very little trolling and doesn't have a downrigger or other trolling paraphernalia.

Whether fishermen cast or troll for bass, when they are unsuccessful it is because they fail to get their offerings down to the level at which their quarry is located. Accomplishing this is often more of a problem than getting bass to strike. When you are trolling for bass, always be cognizant of the bottom depth where you are fishing, the level at which you believe bass are located, and the level that your trolled lure is realistically working.

9

MUSKELLUNGE

Because of the nature of the quarry, musky fishing is one form of trolling in which you needn't feel disappointed if you haven't succeeded by the end of the day. I caution you that trolling for muskies is not a sure thing, and it amazes me that some anglers — including capable and diehard Midwestern musky fishing fanatics — consider it to be too easy, unsporting, and dangerous to the future of the fish.

What threatens muskies most is the mishandling and keeping of fish; I believe that the only muskies that should be kept are outstanding trophies. Someone who already has a wall mount or two doesn't need another. I'm a confirmed advocate of releasing muskies. Trolling detractors say that fast-paced trollers rip out the weed beds that muskies use for habitat. I think it's wrong to deliberately do so, but the merits of this argument escape me. What about all the casters who run lures through the weeds and rip them up? And what did the fish do before they had all these weeds? Most small lakes have become weedier over the years through eutrophication, and weed presence is greater now than in the old days when there were bigger fish and fewer fishermen. How can trolling for muskellunge be more or less sporting than trolling for walleyes, salmon, or trout? Objectors to trolling exist among the traditional cast-for-muskies fraternity, and I suspect they are just too set in their ways and their view of the sport of musky fishing to tolerate differing approaches. I cast and troll for muskies where legal and where either technique seems appropriate, and I consider neither method to be so easy; therefore, I can make no guarantees and flat-out assertions. So much for lecturing.

Every lake or river that holds muskies has a place where the musky activity gets hot at a certain time and the fever of fishermen rises to a boil. As much as anglers like to recount such exceptional moments and as much as experiencing those times fuels the desire to chase muskies, these fish are tough to land with consistency and deserve their reputation of being hard to catch and of having unpredictable behavior.

If constant action and numbers are your game, muskies aren't for you. On the other hand, if you rarely see a musky, let alone catch one, you're probably doing something wrong. I'm convinced that muskies are not as difficult to catch as the one-fish-per-ten-thousand-casts exponents would have us believe. Legends, myths, theories, and catch ratios aside, you can become a productive musky angler if you get away from haphazard fishing activities and develop a reasoned, knowledgeable approach to this sport. I have spent a lot of hours trolling for muskies and especially enjoy this particular hunt. I know that a savvy angler can have above-average success at trolling for muskies, and that trolling is productive for larger-than-average muskies. How you go about pursuing muskies greatly affects your ability to catch them. There is a distinction between catching these elusive creatures and fishing for them. Most anglers go equipped more with hope than with expectation.

The road to success begins by acquiring a fundamental understanding of the fish and its habitat. Muskies are primarily caught near some specific form of cover. It is arguable whether they always inhabit that particular locale or merely visit it frequently to feed. In some waters, especially in those that are shallow, small, and without great areas for muskies to wander, these fish will take up a station that is conducive to their feeding, security, and requirements for bodily comfort; they will stay in such locations until late in the season. In other waters, particularly in large lakes and rivers, some fish will stay in one locale while others will spend most of their time in deep-water sanctuaries, migrating into desirable locales to feed.

It isn't necessary to determine which of these conditions holds true where you are fishing for muskies, unless you'll be spending a great deal of time on that body of water and want to establish patterns of behavior to narrow down productive fishing times. What is important is to be able to identify and find the places that are likely to hold feeding muskies, particularly in the fall, when the best musky angling of the year is usually experienced and where there is an opportunity to catch really big muskies.

I saw this demonstrated conclusively a few years ago in October on a northern Wisconsin lake. Dick Rose and I launched his boat and then headed to a long sandbar and point, the edges of which we located on a depthfinder and pinpointed with marker buoys. We turned to make our first trolling pass when two friends in another boat, following our buoys and heading toward us, hooked and landed a 31-pound musky. We took photos of them, chatted for a few minutes, had coffee, and resumed trolling. Our friends hadn't been gone for five minutes when they were on another fish. That one turned out to be a 42-pound 12-ounce fish. Both of these giants were caught in almost the same place on the same lure (Cisco Kid) and were holding along the deep-water edge of the bar to feed. Dick knew where that spot was and marked it so we'd be able to fish it properly. A person who didn't know where that bar was or how to approach it might have trolled all day on that lake and never had a chance at those feeding fish.

Dick Rose (center), while fishing with the author, guided these two anglers to troll up 31-pound (left) and 42-pound (right) muskies within a half hour of each other on a Wisconsin Lake one snowy late October day.

Muskellunge are not characteristically prone to wandering in search of food. Instead, they lurk in or by places where food is abundant and where they can lie relatively concealed to pounce on appropriate-size forage. The angler seeking likely musky lairs should determine if prospective areas are conducive to good feeding opportunities. Veteran anglers refer to such musky feeding stations as ambush points. When you're pondering where to locate muskies, you should think in terms of the available forage and their habits and the muskies' predisposition toward ambush points.

Muskies often seem to have a preferred prey in every body of water, though it is sometimes hard to quantify this. Walleyes are undoubtedly one of their preferred foods, and you don't have to search hard to find an angler who has had a musky attempt to steal a walleye that was being brought to boat. Ciscoes, suckers, perch, golden shiners, and bass are also prime musky foods, and other species of forage and game fish enter into the equation in various areas. I am told of a taxidermist who mounted many muskies and reported finding bullheads in the stomachs of a lot of the muskies he prepared.

It is unlikely that muskies will consume a lot of small fish to make a meal or to chase abundant open-water prey such as shad or alewives, but a musky may take these tidbits if they wander near its selected ambush location. I have often wondered whether Great Lakes muskies prey upon the abundant alewives found in those lakes but can find no proof that they do so, although it is acknowledged that some of these muskies may inhabit open water at times. Despite the fact that some big water muskies may travel a fair distance, these fish by nature are not nomadic, like salmon or striped bass, which seems to indicate that they would not follow schools of bait fish endlessly in open water. The fact that few Great Lakes trout and salmon trollers rarely catch an accidental musky seems to support this.

Furthermore, consider that muskies are prone to taking big lures, perhaps because they are prone to eating big fish. There have been many documented instances of muskies consuming fish that are up to a third of their own length. A 15-inch walleye, for example, really isn't that big to a 40-inch muskellunge. It seems reasonable to assume that after a musky consumes a big meal, it will be fortified for a day or several days and may not need to move into an ambush spot to feed. It also wouldn't need to follow bait fish to be near a food source constantly. Realistically, this all adds up to a somewhat site-specific fish that utilizes certain areas to feed because they attract large enough forage to make an ambush attack worthwhile. The type of cover, the depth, and the presence of current will determine which places are better than others.

Submerged vegetation is a primary musky lair. Small muskies relate heavily to cover, and, in the case of vegetation, may lie in the midst of weed beds. But bigger muskies can't move within that cover well enough to forage, so they are attracted to the edges of that cover, at the break line where weeds end and deep water begins, and at the corners, pockets, or other irregular contour features. These places are suitable for trolling techniques. Because of the disposition of muskies to locate on the edges of such areas and because trollers have their lures in this water for a long period of time, this may explain why trollers catch more big muskies.

Another important musky locale is a point of land. Points, whether they extend from the contiguous shoreline or from islands, are natural impediments to fish movement and attractants to prey and predator alike for migration, home-area identification, and security. To a musky, the most attractive points will be those that have a long underwater slope and are adjacent to deep water, especially if they break sharply from 10 feet off to 20 or 25, those that have some form of heavy vegetation around their perimeter, or those that have rock piles on the underwater break lines.

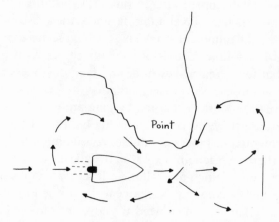

Points are particularly good places to fish for muskies and, where possible, should be trolled in a figure-eight pattern as shown to cover the water well.

Yet another prominent musky lair is an open-water shoal. An underwater mound or island, sandbars, and gravel bars are roughly the same thing. These locations may be rocky or boulder-strewn, or they may be sandy with moderate weed growth, but they attract small bait fish, which in turn attracts such fish as perch, smallmouths, or walleyes, which in turn makes them favorable feeding areas for muskies.

There are, of course, other places where muskies can be found, and you may have some situations in mind that don't conform to my descriptions. In all likelihood, however, those locations — for whatever reason — must hold feeding opportunities for muskies, and those opportunities may be peculiar to the aquatic conditions of that body of water.

In some musky waters, for instance, there are warm-water discharges in areas that may not otherwise seem to be top musky locales. In the fall, the immediate area near such a discharge is affected and may be attractive to forage fish and muskies. A feeder creek that is cool in the summer or one that is warm in the fall (both offering slight water temperature changes in the immediate tributary area) can spur feeding and fishing activity.

Current is also a big factor. A point or shoal that is washed by strong current is a prominent place to find muskies. A locale in which a strong current can bring bait washing by or retard the movement of weak, crippled, or wounded fish is another. Back eddies, slicks, and current edges are more good spots. Where a secondary tributary meets a major flow is also a promising locale, especially in summer when the secondary tributary may be dumping cooler and more oxygenated water into the main flow.

One of the most dynamic places I've ever seen for muskies was a shallow shoal on the St. Lawrence River in New York that was ringed with thick grass, sandwiched between two islands, and flushed by such a strong current flow that we could hardly make progress against it with a 24-volt electric motor on high speed. I caught a 28-pound musky off the tip of that shoal one morning, and friends caught three more there, ranging from 17 to 31 pounds, in the next day and a half. We rarely marked big fish on our graphs or flashers (although we did spy small fish), but it was a location obviously used by fish that came in from who knows where to feed. We hooked all four fish within yards of each other, all by trolling deep-diving plugs.

A 28-pound musky, caught by the author off a shoal on the St. Lawrence River in New York, is handled by a state fisheries biologist. The musky was given to the state fisheries agency for research work and was caught while trolling a black plug on 12-pound-test line.

Finding and catching muskies, then, requires attention to lake or river conditions just as much as it does to the tackle used and the places where it is used. The person who motors his way around a musky lake without regard to the type of water conditions there will most likely be unsuccessful and will have shortchanged himself.

Muskellunge are said to prefer a water temperature that ranges from the mid 50s to low 70s, which covers the usual water temperatures from late spring through early fall. They seem to adapt to the higher and lower ends of that range as local conditions warrant. They spawn in very shallow near-shore water in the spring, usually before the fishing season is open in northern states, stay around in the near-shore shallows for a while after spawning, then move out to deeper environs. Deep, however, is a relative term.

Most muskellunge are actually caught quite shallow, usually in less than 30 feet of water and primarily under 20 feet. This is a rather broad statement to make considering the wide variety of environments that muskies inhabit, but there is a lot of evidence to back it up. My own experiences have supported this, and an analysis of the methods of successful trollers shows that 10 to 20 feet is the predominant level at which muskies are caught in the summer and fall. This is as true on Lake of the Woods as it is on Lake St. Clair or on the St. Lawrence River, which are the three most reknowned musky producers, as well as on hundreds of smaller waters. In the summer on southern highland impoundments, however, muskies may suspend in deeper water over river channels and sharp drop-offs.

The most prominent and successful musky troller of all time was the late Arthur Lawton, who trolled the St. Lawrence River in the late 1950s and early 1960s with his wife Ruth. They caught an extraordinary number of muskies, including many that were more than 50 pounds, all by trolling. He caught the all-tackle 69-pound 15-ounce world record, and she caught the fourth largest documented musky, a 68-pound 5-ounce fish. In January 1977 in an interview with musky historian Larry Ramsell, Lawton said that he primarily caught his fish in 14 to 17 feet of water, following weed lines and getting his lures down to the bottom. He indicated that he could not remember ever catching a musky in 30 to 35 feet of water.

An almost equally successful husband-wife trolling team, Leonard and Betty Hartman, plied the St. Lawrence with awesome big fish success at about the same time as the Lawtons and set a host of big musky/light tackle records that may never be beaten. Leonard Hartman has been quoted as saying that he caught 90 percent of his muskies at 20 feet deep along weed edges or reefs. It is probably no coincidence that weeds often end around 12 feet and that the better producing weed lines are those where bottom depth at the edge of the weeds drops off quickly from 10 or 12 feet to 20 or 25 feet.

In recent years on the St. Lawrence, muskellunge over 40 pounds have been scarce, but the best guides are trolling deep lines 18 to 25 feet down and high lines 10 to 15 down. On Lake St. Clair, which is presently one of the premier all-size musky trolling waters and where reknowned musky troller and lure designer Homer LeBlanc put his popular Swim Whiz diving plug to work, most fish are trolled 10 to 15 feet deep. Many are caught shallower on short lines fished directly in the prop wash. The situation is much the same elsewhere. The bottom line is that you usually don't have to get very deep to be in musky territory.

The bread-and-butter musky trolling lure is a floating/diving plug that departs significantly from the traditionally successful casting lures: bucktails and jerk baits.

Bucktails, which are weighted in-line spinners heavily dressed with bucktail hair, are of primary use in shallow- to middepth casting, over the top of submerged cover, and along the edges of shallow submerged cover. Some people troll these over weed beds that come to within 2 feet of the surface, but I've never tried this and don't see how it can be done without motoring through the weeds, a tactic that may stir muskies up but does no good to the habitat or your motor. Weeds that cling to the intake will prevent water from entering and will cause an outboard to overheat. Nonetheless, there is no denying that bucktails — especially in black and including such lures as the Mepps Giant Killer, Blue Fox Vibrax, and Eppinger Buhl Spinner — are extremely effective casting lures, and it is natural that some fishermen will occasionally be successful at trolling with them.

Jerk baits are large wooden plugs, 6 to 10 inches long, that are very buoyant and are fished in a pull-pause retrieve. Few jerk baits do anything more than slip inactively through the water when pulled and bob up when paused. If ever there was a "do-nothing" lure, it is the jerk bait. Although casters have good success with this style of lure, I see no reason to troll such a lifeless blob.

In some musky-casting quarters, jigs are an oft-used lure, but they seldom get fished in musky trolling. Those who do troll jigs run fairly slowly with 5/8 to 1 ounce sizes adorned with soft-plastic single or twin-tailed bodies. Large spoons were once a prominent trolling and casting bait for muskies, but they have fallen into general disuse for these fish in deference to the more representative and active plug. Nonetheless, as with bucktails, there are some anglers who troll spoons over weed beds.

Because they are useful at slow to fast trolling speeds, exhibit plenty of action, and are well fished at relatively shallow depths, floating/diving plugs are called on for most musky trolling duty. This includes deep-diving plugs, in particular, and also shallow and inter- mediate divers depending on the strength of line to be used, the depth of water to be fished, and the utilization of sinkers, weighted lines, or downriggers.

I favor using 5- to 8-inch-long plugs for this, preferably in single- or double-jointed versions but also in unjointed models. Such lures include Bagley Deep-Diving Bang-O-Bs, Drifter Tackle's Believers, LeBlanc's Swim Whiz, Bomber Waterdogs, and Cisco Kids. Although I haven't had much success with them, I'd say that metal-lipped magnum Rapalas, and Whopper Stopper Hellbenders should be useful here, too. Creek Chub Pikie Minnows, in single- and double-jointed versions, have been perennially successful trolling plugs, and the former numbers Lawton's world record among its accomplishments.

For flat-line trolling, you must know how deep your lures are capable of running with the line you use, speed of boat, and length of line out. I discussed these points elsewhere in the book and won't reiterate them again here. Within the aforementioned group of intermediate and deep-diving plugs, however, there is a considerable difference in depth attainment. For instance, on a comparable line size/length/speed basis, Bang-O-Bs run the deepest, with Pikie Minnows and magnum Rapalas running the shallowest. With 75 feet of 12-pound line, for example, a Bang-O-B will dive about 18 feet deep; the magnum Rapala about 10; the Pikie a little less than the Rapala.

These lures are fished, incidentally, on short lines. There is seldom much reason to put out more than 75 feet of line, although there are some special-tackle trollers who do so, which I'll explain in a moment. Muskies are not spooked by boat noise, and some Midwestern trollers catch them right in the prop wash, within 10 to 25 feet of the boat and just a few feet below the surface. The prop wash apparently attracts or excites the fish. Except for prop wash trolling, line lengths normally vary between 40 and 75 or 80 feet.

Large straight and jointed plugs are the principal musky trolling lures.

Lures that won't achieve the desired depth on a flat-line troll need to be aided with keel or bead chain sinkers. Some prop wash fishermen use 4- to 16-ounce lead weights to get lures down quickly. Such heavy weights are needed because of the turbulence behind the boat and the fast speed (up to 5 mph) at which the lures are run. Others, trolling further behind the boat, use lighter weights. Arthur Lawton, for example, used 2- to 3-ounce weights with Pikie Minnows, let out 50 to 75 feet of line, and trolled on average at 2 to 3 mph but no more than 4 mph.

If you're trying to get down in that 10- to 17-foot range, you can do so with several of the aforementioned deep-diving plugs without weights, unless you use rope for fishing line. The 28 pounder that I mentioned having caught on the St. Lawrence was taken on an unweighted Bomber Waterdog behind about 75 feet of 12-pound nylon monofilament line. I believe the lure was getting down about 14 feet. To get it to the same depth with 30-pound line, however, I might have had to add a 1-ounce (or heavier) weight or let out twice the amount of line. Obviously you have to take several factors into consideration to determine the depth you want to achieve.

Downriggers are becoming more of a tool for musky trollers, as well they should. In 1979 I put downriggers on a bass boat and took it to the St. Lawrence River to fish for muskies. No one there had ever used a downrigger for musky trolling before, and not a single guide boat was outfitted with one, despite the proximity of the St. Lawrence to Lake Ontario and its well-known downrigger fishing for salmon and trout. In succeeding years, however, downriggers started appearing on boats there; now they're common and they account for some fish.

Downriggers do several good things for musky trollers. They allow you to fish light or heavy line without affecting the depth of the lure being used and without having to use lead weights on the fishing line; they make short-line prop wash fishing easier; they make it practical to troll spoons or spinners at precise depths; they make it practical to use shallow-running plugs, such as 6- to 8-inch "minnow" imitations (like a Rapala, A. C. Shiner, Rebel, or Bagley Bang-O-Lure) at specific depths; they keep you from having to check your lures often to see if they're clean (when flat-lining, especially near weeds and when leaves are dropping in the fall, you have to check your plugs often to see that no debris has gotten on them); and they allow lures to run shorter distances behind the boat or the weight, which makes turning and boat manipulation much easier when trolling at 12- to 20-foot depths.

Hook-setting while using downriggers can be a problem, however. Releases should require a lot of tension before they free the line, not only because the diving plugs being rolled pull hard but also because of the difficulty in setting the hook into the mouth of a musky under any circumstance. Only the best releases — ones that will handle heavy line and have adjustable tension settings — should be used, and it's a good idea to test the striking force needed to spring them. Those muskellunge that attack a lure sideways, which is how they usually strike their prey, clamp down with extraordinary viselike pressure and may never get firmly hooked. This is an endemic musky fishing problem that is made even tougher by not setting the hook directly, but rather by setting it indirectly via a downrigger release.

I'm not saying that hooking muskies is significantly easier when flat-line trolling. Essentially the rod, resting in a holder, sets the hook. When a musky strikes a trolled lure, get to the rod immediately and set the hook by hand. If the boat operator has enough presence of mind to think of this, he can aid hook-setting immediately after a strike by speeding the boat up for a moment, then throttling back as an angler grabs the rod (big-game saltwater boaters do this). Your tackle must be stout enough to handle this, however. And this still doesn't guarantee that you'll sink the hooks into a musky's bony, toothy maw. Muskies are hard to hook when casting or when flat-lining, and, as I was explaining, may be a little more so when using a downrigger and line release.

The same is true for those who might attempt using sideplaners for musky trolling. I have not done this but think it has merit. I can see sideplaners being applicable for getting lures over weed beds or right along weed edges, close to various shore structure, and near river locales that prevent boat passage or where it wouldn't be prudent to troll your boat. With sideplaners you can run relatively short dropback lines as well. However, hook-setting might pose difficulties.

Although few musky trollers that I am aware of presently use sideplaners, I mention this subject because these devices add another dimension to your presentation abilities. Presentation is critical especially when musky trolling, because any pass by an ambush point or feeding area must bring the lure along a specific contour and path of travel. Boat position and speed must be precise, and for this reason line lengths are fairly short. Where turns and frequent S-trolling maneuvers are necessary, short lines may make boat and lure manipulation easier. Anyone who has trolled the contours of weed beds, points, reefs, or islands appreciates this maneuverability to get lures in prime position.

You may be interested to know that Arthur Lawton maintained that he took most of his big muskellunge while making a turn. He thought that the change in bait movement, that is, the lure rising upward, triggered fish to strike. I agree. Muskies can be curious fish; they habitually follow a cast lure to the boat and are often excited into striking at the side of a boat by making frantic figure-eight movements with the lure. If they follow cast lures to a boat, why wouldn't they follow a trolled lure a modest distance? I'm guessing that they do and that the behavioral change of a lure when a turn is made may cause a following musky to pounce on the lure.

You can achieve a similar behavioral change of a lure in other ways. Speeding up or slowing down the boat for a few seconds is a good tactic. Using an oscillating downrigger is another. Keeping a trolling rod in your hand and either ripping the lure forward momentarily or pushing the freespool button momentarily will serve to speed up and slow down a lure for a sudden change of pace, which might make a following musky think this prospective prey is attempting to elude it.

Lure placement and arrangement while trolling is an important aspect of presentation and should be carefully thought out. The more people in your boat and the more rods you fish, the more important this becomes. I'm going to give you several multirod views of how this is approached by different fishermen in different waters.

On Lake St. Clair, big boats and open water are the order of the day. A guide boat might be arranged as follows. Two to three rods might be run in the prop wash. One would be directly behind the motor, running the lure about 6 to 10 feet back and a few feet under the surface. A second rod would be in a holder on the port side of the stern, facing out the stern and angled slightly toward the wake; the lure on this would be 15 to 20 feet back. A third rod would be in a holder on the starboard side of the stern, facing out the stern and angled slightly toward the wake; the lure would be 30 to 40 feet back in the wake. Depending on how many anglers were aboard, another

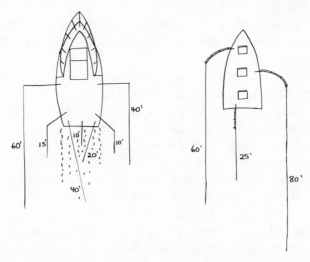

These are two multirod trolling systems for muskies. On the left is a big boat
setup, as might be used for shallow trolling on Lake St. Clair. On the right is a
Wisconsin guide boat setup for three fishermen. Short- and medium-length lines
are employed, the prop wash is trolled, and lures are well spread apart.

one to three or four rods might be fished. On both gunwales, slightly
ahead of the stern, a rod would be angled about 20 degrees away from
the stern, with lures 10 to 20 feet back. Further along both gunwales,
near midship, a rod perpendicular to the gunwale would be running
a lure 40 or more feet back.

A small Wisconsin guide boat fishing three lines might be arranged
like this. A stern rod would be placed in a transom rod holder pointed
directly at the prop wash, with 25 feet of line out and a lure running
6 feet deep. A port rod would be placed in a holder and laid perpendicular to the boat, with 60 feet of line out and a lure running 12 to
15 feet deep. A starboard rod, also perpendicular to the gunwale,
would have 80 feet of line out and a lure that runs 10 feet deep.

A traditional St. Lawrence River wire line troller running three
lines would set up as follows. Port and starboard rods would be at 90-
degree angles to the gunwale, running between 100 and 150 feet of
wire line and a jointed diving plug. A high line, of nylon monofilament, would be placed in the middle of the stern, running 200 to 300
feet back with a lure that dives 10 to 15 feet deep. I mention this
system because it diverges from the usual short-line trolling and also
because it illustrates wire line trolling. Most St. Lawrence River guides

today are running nylon monofilament flat-line lengths between 75 and 200 feet for open-water trolling, in part depending upon the lure they're using.

I don't have a musky trolling rod-setting system that I follow religiously. I tailor rod setting and lure placement to the conditions. When trolling the edges of weeds, sandbars, shoals, and so forth, I like to have a shallower running lure on the side of the boat nearest the edge and my deepest running lure on the opposite side. If fishing two lures off the same gunwale, I'd put a deep runner on the inside rod on a short- to medium-length line and a shallow runner on the outside position but on a longer length of line. It might get as deep as the other lure but be farther back to avoid tangling and also aid fish-playing and hook-setting. Or I'd use a lure on a short line behind a downrigger and a longer flat-lined plug.

You can see that there are plenty of variations to try. You just need the right equipment, good rod holder placement, and a knowledge of the depth you're trolling.

Although many of the biggest muskies were caught and the foremost musky fishermen were trolling when there was no sonar equipment, I wouldn't be without it. I want to know how deep the water is below me at all times and whether I'm encroaching on the shallows, or a reef, or weeds in time to be able to do something about it and to keep my lures from getting snagged. I don't think you necessarily find muskies on sonar, but you find places, define underwater terrain, and maybe locate smaller fish schools that might attract muskellunge (in which case you should troll around the school, not through it).

As for basic tackle, I differ from many tried-and-true trollers, so I'll give you both sides of the coin. Most musky anglers, whether they cast or troll, go armed for monsters. In their eyes, if you use 20-pound line, that's light; anything less is ultralight and foolhardy. Twenty-five to 40-pound line is standard musky line, and some use even heavier. There are still a fair number of musky anglers using braided Dacron instead of nylon monofilament for the no-stretch aspect it gives hook-setting efforts. They use big saltwater-size reels, and 4- to 5-foot trolling rods that you could beat the dust out of a rug with.

I don't own tackle like that and wouldn't use it if I did. I fish 12- to 20-pound nylon monofilament or cofilament line and troll even the hardest pulling, deepest diving lures with 12. I have caught some big fish — although no 40 pounders — on it without problems. Leon-

St. Lawrence River guide Jim Brabant, a musky trolling expert, with a 40-plus pounder taken on a jointed plug.

ard Hartman caught a 52 pounder on 12-pound line, a 51 pounder on 4-pound line, and a lot of 35- to 48-pound muskies on 4- to 8-pound line; however, it is unclear whether he caught some, or any, of these while casting or trolling. Lighter line makes plugs dive deeper and swim with great action. You can get more of it on a reel, which means that you can use a smaller and more comfortable reel. Muskies don't run like tuna or, in my experience, like a big salmon, so I don't see line capacity as being a great need in fighting muskies. A bait-casting reel that holds between 100 and 150 yards of 12- to 20-pound line is more than adequate. It should have an excellent drag system, however, and preferably a clicker. For rods, I like medium to medium-heavy duty 6 to 7 footers with a fast tip but lots of backbone, a rod you can cast or set in a downrigger or use to take the punishment of speed trolling with hard-pulling plugs. I sometimes use wire leaders with trolled plugs and sometimes don't. If I do, 12 inch is standard; some trollers use up to 30- and 36-inch wire leaders because they fear having large open-mouthed muskies roll on their line.

Lure colors, which I didn't discuss earlier, run the gamut. Based on my experience, however, I wouldn't be without a few lures in the following colors: all black; black and white; chartreuse; silver and black or a "shad" pattern; perch, walleye, largemouth bass, and musky patterns; and yellow with red or tiger stripes.

10
WALLEYE

If you've already read the chapters on trolling for bass and trolling for muskellunge, you know why trolling is a worthwhile secondary technique (bass) or an important primary technique (musky) for these warm-water species. Much of the same comments about the functionality of trolling for those fish also hold true for walleyes, which, not coincidentally, inhabit many of the same environments as smallmouth bass, some of the same environments as largemouth bass, and most of the same environments as musky because they are a food source for muskies. Trolling is not a secondary technique where walleyes are concerned. At times it is the best technique and at times it is less effective than other forms of fishing. Often, you may divide your walleye fishing efforts between trolling and other techniques.

The most prominent conventional methods of walleye fishing include casting jigs; casting or drifting with weight-forward spinners or so-called June bug style spinners; and still-fishing or drifting live bait. Additionally, some people cast crankbaits, and cast and slowly retrieve live bait rigs. Many walleye addicts won't troll at all, yet others use a controlled wind-drifting technique, employing an electric motor to keep the boat in proper position when conditions warrant. Some use an electric or outboard motor to move their boat in reverse, called backtrolling, to position jigs, live bait rigs, and spinners.

You should include trolling in your walleye fishing repertoire if for no other reason than to be versatile and adaptable to different situations. Modern trolling techniques, however, are coming on strong as important methods of catching bottom-hugging and suspended walleyes in natural lakes, in impoundments, and in the Great Lakes. Perhaps this is an outgrowth of the trout and salmon troll fishery on the Great Lakes. Anglers have been exposed to deep and shallow trolling strategies with plugs and spoons and have realized that they can efficiently cover a lot of territory by adapting trolling methods to the habitats in which they pursue walleyes, as well as utilize some of the same equipment that they have acquired for trout and salmon fishing.

There are several types of trolling techniques that can be used for walleyes. Downrigger fishing and weighted or unweighted flat-lining are the most prominent, but diving planer fishing is also possible. Sideplaner board fishing is showing lots of promise. Which of these to employ and what type of lure or bait to troll basically depends on the habitat and lures being fished and on the season.

Walleyes generally relate to structure, have light-sensitive eyes that make them primarily active in low-light and dark situations, are not particularly aggressive feeders, and do not usually inhabit extreme deep-water environs. They are schooling fish, so you can expect that when you catch one, more are nearby. Looking for walleyes, especially in big waters, may seem like a difficult task, but if you understand some basic aspects of walleye behavior and adapt your efforts accordingly, you can usually find them in time.

Sometimes the fastest fishing and the biggest walleyes, particularly in mid-South reservoirs, are caught when the fish are making their late winter/early spring spawning run. Walleyes begin spawning when the water temperature reaches the mid 40s. When good tributary streams and rivers are present, the males move up first followed by the females, which are larger. In big reservoirs, it takes a lot of warm weather and a heavy warm rain to influence the main lake temperature and activate the fish. Thus, a situation can occur where spawning is off again/on again, never happens, or is accomplished in a short period of time. In some lakes and in big rivers, walleyes have sufficient spawning areas and water conditions, so they don't make an official run. Nonetheless they are in very shallow water. In natural lakes, casting or still-fishing with bait may be a better technique at this time, but in large river systems and impoundments, trolling has merit. In areas with no closed season or an early opening season, you can capitalize on this; however, some northern states open their walleye fishing season after the run has ended, and the issue is moot.

After spawning, the water temperature is 45 to 55 degrees or so. Walleyes will inhabit areas adjacent to spawning grounds. A shallow bay or the mouth of a stream are examples. If there is water roughly 6 to 10 feet deep and a weedy bottom that is 2 to 4 feet below the surface, you can troll shallow-running lures over the tops of the weeds and catch walleyes. Boat speed will be slow, perhaps 1 to 1.5 mph, and line lengths approximately 60 to 80 feet back.

For most of the season, from late spring through summer and into fall, walleyes are attracted to specific types of cover. These include rock reefs, sandbars, gravel bars, points, weeds, rocky or riprap causeways or along shorelines, and creek channels. They are particularly known for congregating in or along the edges of vegetation. Weeds attract small bait fish and larger fish in the food chain, such as perch, and thus provide a food supply for walleyes. Weeds also offer protective cover. Fish that are deep in the weeds don't offer much of a trolling opportunity; even baits that are worked above such fish don't solicit strikes because walleyes don't move too far to take a lure. Trolling the weed lines, where the weeds end and the bottom begins to drop off to deeper water, is not only possible but is a prime fishing method because walleyes are often situated there.

Walleyes usually hug the bottom around favored haunts, therefore, it is almost a tenet of all kinds of walleye fishing that you have to get down to the bottom with your offering to be successful. This is more often true than not, especially on natural lakes with a lot of cover.

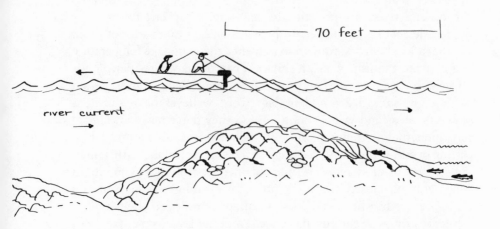

Slow trolling up a river and working a crankbait over shallow rocky shoals is a good bet for spring walleyes.

Walleyes do suspend off the bottom of some environments, including large impoundments and Lake Erie, the western basin of which may be the most productive walleye waters anywhere. In those environments, preferable water temperatures at upper water levels or abundant bait fish schools may be a factor in the suspending behavior of fish. Elsewhere, walleyes my suspend 2 to 3 feet off the bottom on weed lines, or even further off the bottom near underwater islands or reefs, or still further (as much as 12 feet over a bottom of 30) in completely open water.

On the whole, walleyes are not found particularly deep. They might be as deep as 25 to 30 feet on rocky reefs and as shallow as 4 or 5 feet when up near the surface. A depth of 6 to 8 feet is normal in spring, but 10 to 15 is more like the norm around weed beds, which usually don't grow much deeper than that range. This makes walleyes a good target for trollers, because there are many lures that work well within the 6- to 15-foot range on a flat line. In addition, lures can easily be weighted to get them down to that range, especially with the comparatively light line employed in walleye fishing. Four- to 10-pound-test is the line range, but 6 and 8 are standard. Six- to 7-foot rods, primarily spinning, are used, but bait-casting rods are also employed.

Trolling is essentially done with live bait rigs, weight-forward spinners, and various plugs. Because plugs have really been a major focus of walleye fishing attention in recent times, we'll review them first.

Walleye foods provide a good clue to lure sizes, at least where plugs are concerned. Natural forage includes yellow perch and small fingerling-size fish such as chubs, minnows (including fatheads), and various shiners. Walleye trolling plugs are 4- to 6-inch minnow imitations, 2- to 4-inch crankbaits, and 2- to 6-inch banana baits. The latter are trolling lures per se, while the others can be cast as well; all are floating/diving products.

Minnow imitators have shallow-running, medium- to deep-diving, and sinking versions. Shallow runners for walleye angling include the Sisson Minnow-Mate, Bagley Bang-O-Lure, Rebel Minnow, Rebel Fastrac Minnow, Rapala Minnow, Smithwick Rogue, Bomber Long A Minnow, Cordell Redfin, and others. These lures will dive 6 to 8 feet deep on a long (150-foot drop-back) light line. But because it's hard to maintain precise positioning with long lines while trolling

Diving minnow-imitation plugs, such as this Spoonbill Minnow, are noted for
trolling up large walleyes.

contours for walleyes and because long lines aren't usually needed
anyway, 50- to 80-foot lengths are employed and the lures run a bit
shallower. Sinking minnow imitators are typified by the Rapala Countdown Minnow; this type of plug can be good for cast-countdown-and-
retrieve fishing for suspended walleyes, but it is not particularly effective for slow trolling near the bottom because it invites debris pickup
and bottom snagging.

Diving minnow imitators include the Rebel Spoonbill Minnow,
Bagley Diving Bang-O-Lure, LeBlanc Swim Whiz, Drifter's Believer,
and Deep Smithwick Rogue. The diving minnow imitator is an overlooked bait type that is particularly good for big walleyes. It's the
favorite walleye lure on Greer's Ferry Reservoir in Arkansas, where
anglers catch monster walleyes on them every spring by trolling or
casting the tributaries. In addition to fishing them for Arkansas walleyes, I've used them on hard-fished and wilderness walleye waters to
search for lake and river fish. I consider the Spoonbill Minnow to be
my first choice for short-line flat-lining when I'm prospecting. That
bait will dive 9 to 10 feet on 12-pound-test line with just 75 feet of
it out, so an option is to use a shorter length of lighter line to achieve
at least the same running depth and maybe get the lure a little deeper.
Not all walleye trolling lures reach the same depth, however, so you
need to know their capabilities if you'll be switching between brands.

Crankbaits for walleye trolling may be the typical bulbous models prominent in bass fishing, particularly such lures as the Rapala Fat Rap, Storm Wiggle Wart, Storm Hot 'N Tot, Sisson's Ticker, Norman N series lures, and various Rebel crankbaits. Longer and slender versions that are sometimes called "shad" baits are slightly better, however. These are typified by Sisson T-Shad, Rapala Shad Rap, Bagley Bass 'N Shad, Rebel Deep Shad, and Lindy Shadling lures.

The so-called banana plugs are those with curvature of the spine. They include the Helin Flatfish, Luhr Jensen Fireplug, Dura Pak Lazy Ike, Heddon Tadpolly, and Bagley's Slo-Dancer, among others. These slow trolling, wide-wobbling lures don't achieve much depth and are often fished with a weight ahead of them.

There are many colors that have merit, but a perch pattern is a favorite with many anglers followed by silver and gold. Dark tops with light sides/ bellies are very effective; bright fluorescent colors may do the job in muddy water, silver in clear water, and gold in stained

Roger Tucker and the author took these walleyes on a variety of plugs that were slow trolled on Gouin Reservoir in Quebec.

water. Use this merely as a guideline, however, and don't be afraid to experiment.

The intricacies of trolling plugs such as these are thoroughly covered in previous chapters. It would be redundant to review those matters again here. Proper speed to get maximum lure action; a knowledge of the diving abilities of each plug based on speed, line size, and length of line trolled; and selection of the right lure to get to the necessary depth are the key elements in the successful usage of these lures. In most situations, plugs can be worked at slow speeds near the bottom, and in many lakes it is necessary to do so. However, fishing them off the bottom and at faster speeds sometimes is effective, especially in a body of water like Lake Erie, so don't assume that there are always hard-and-fast rules at work.

On a big lake like Erie, walleyes often suspend. Although casters use a countdown method to put weight-forward spinners at the right level while drifting, trollers cover a lot more territory with plugs they know will run at the appropriate nowhere-near-bottom level. On smaller natural lakes, too, suspending can be midsummer midday behavior for some walleyes. These fish will often be situated not far from shallower bars and points, and will be suspended at a 12-foot level over 30 or more feet of water. Walleyes are relatively inactive fish, but a lure that is brought right past their nose at an intermediate (1.5 to 2.5 mph) speed has a good chance of triggering a strike.

In the evening, however, those same walleyes will move shallower to the edges of the bar or a rock or gravel point that breaks sharply to deep water. Using plugs that dive to 8 or 10 feet deep, for example, troll from deep water to the point, then go along one side and work along the edge. Another approach is to pick a specific contour level, such as 10 or 12 feet, and keep your lures in that contour as you troll parallel to the edge of the structure.

If the lure you'd like to use won't achieve the necessary depth on an unweighted flat line, then weight it in some manner. Minnow imitations and banana plugs are often weighted. Rubber-core sinkers or pinch-on split shot, placed about 18 inches ahead of the lure, are standard, but you might want to try a small swiveling bead chain sinker. A bottom-walking sinker such as the Gapen Bait Walker is a very good option here as well, especially when fished with a minnow imitator set back on a 20- to 30-inch leader. The key is finding the right amount of weight to use. Split shot and rubber-core sinkers are also used to troll with weight-forward spinners and spinner/bait combinations.

These are flat-lining techniques, of course, but some walleye fishing situations can be met by using other trolling methods as well as flat-lining. Downrigging, for example, is gaining a foothold in walleye trolling circles, especially on large lakes. Now that anglers see they can still use 6- and 8-pound line with downriggers, they are giving it a go. Advantages to downrigger fishing for walleyes include the ability to run more lines by stacking two rods per downrigger or by using second-lure slider rigs; to cover a wide vertical range of water; to put any lure at a specific level; to appeal well to suspended walleyes; to get down to walleyes that are deeper than normally fished; and to overcome the problem of drift fishing when there is no wind. When fishing in deeper water, you can set lures just 6 to 15 feet behind the downrigger weight. For shallower fishing, put them 40 to 60 feet back.

Drawbacks to downrigger use for walleyes include the fact that you can't tell if a lure has picked up debris, such as weeds, and isn't working well. You also have to be careful about running depth, and may have to check lures periodically to see that they're running clean. Sometimes, small walleyes take a lure and don't exert enough force to trip the downrigger release, so you drag them around for a while. Because of this, you need to be precise about release tension. Some trollers employ light rubberband releases. If a small walleye doesn't break the rubberband upon striking the lure, it will usually bounce it enough to jiggle the fishing rod or downrigger cable so you know there's a fish on and can take the rod in hand and snap the rubberband yourself.

The use of sideplaners is also coming on in walleye fishing, particularly on Lake Erie. Although sideplaner boards may never be a superhot item on smaller inland lakes (if for no other reason than that the waters sometimes are crowded and boats are drifting or anchored in places you'd want to troll these boards), they can have merit in such a place, particularly when you don't know the lake well, don't have an idea where to fish, and are scouting for relatively shallow spring fish. In those shallows, sideplaners can help you get a lure well off to the side of the boat, if you have reason to believe that shallow boat passage might spook them.

It is not, however, a particularly easy chore to run a sideplaner board 60 to 80 feet off to the side of your boat and keep it next to an irregularly contoured submerged weed bed. Your boat is over open, deeper water, and you can't define the edge as well when you're not fairly close to it, meaning that you may often run your board too shallow or over the weed bed, instead of along it, and foul the lure. If you know the territory well, this is less of a problem. Keeping the sideplaner closer to the boat, say 30 feet away, is also a way to deal with this. When you aren't fishing such narrowly defined structure, however, such as when you are trolling for suspended walleyes in large lakes, you have the advantage of covering a broad horizontal distance by running several lures off sideplaners and potentially putting your lures in front of many more fish than if you were strictly flat-lining directly behind the boat, or drifting, or downrigging.

Although plugs are particularly useful for sideplaner board fishing and downrigging, and may be used most often, they aren't the only way to go. Spoons work fine on downriggers, of course. Light spoons that don't attain any depth may sometimes be preferable to plugs because they run at the level you set the weight. You have to account for the diving ability of any plug when set behind a downrigger, in addition to the depth at which the weight is set. Ditto for light weight-forward spinners that are tipped with bait. Many of the points previously mentioned about trolling for walleyes, particularly locations and depths to fish, are also applicable when these lures are used.

With weight-forward spinners (among which are the very popular Earie Dearie and Mepps Lusox) and spinner/ bait rigs, however, I think flat-lining, with and without sinkers on the line, at a slow speed is the best trolling technique. These and bottom-crawling live bait setups, such as the Lindy Rig, are probably the all-time favorite walleye lures, often fished by drifting, which is like trolling in a sense, but slower. Backtrolling with such lures is a premier walleye tactic for small boaters. A tiller-steered outboard motor in reverse or a transom-mounted electric motor, with lower unit turned so that the stern goes back when the motor is technically in a forward position, is used for backtrolling walleye. By moving very slowly stern first around points, reefs, weed lines, sandbars, and along drop-offs, you can maintain precise position.

By using some type of sonar unit, a backtroller can maintain position along specific depths, nearly hover over selected spots, and maneuver a boat to use whatever wind direction is present, positioning the boat in such a way as to keep any following bait in the proper

Weight-forward spinners tipped with a worm took these typical size Lake Erie walleyes being held by Darrell Lowrance. Such spinners and crankbaits account for a lot of trolled Great Lakes walleyes.

place. This is especially true when a school of walleyes are packed into one area — a spot that may be no larger than a small room. Using marker buoys, incidentally, particularly tossing one out in a place where you've caught your first walleye, is a good adjunct in this situation.

An ability to keep your boat and lure in productive water is absolutely essential. Controlled boat operation for precise lure placement is something that not enough walleye trollers master. Boat control and speed are the vital factors in trolling weight-forward spinners, spinner/ bait combos, and live bait rigs.

Trolling speeds with the aforementioned lures tend to be on the slow to superslow side. Superslow is just barely moving, although this isn't always the case. Speeds can change from day to day, but with weight-forward spinners, spinner combos, and live bait rigs, you seldom move fast. With plugs, you seldom move as slow as a crawl. Determining proper speed takes some experimentation and observation. When you troll for fish that you have not located and whose depth you are unsure of, it's best to maneuver your boat in S and zigzag patterns, watching your sonar to spot fish that are large enough to be walleyes or bait fish, which might mean that walleyes will be nearby, then concentrating on that depth. Work different speeds until

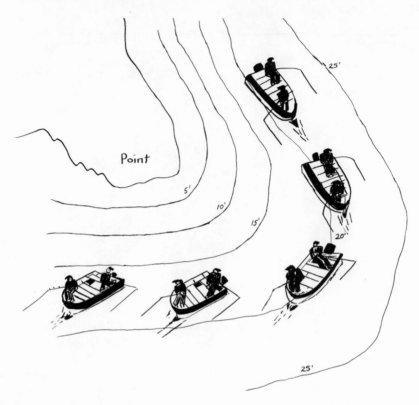

Backtrolling by moving slowly backward and allowing the boat to maneuver precisely to keep lures working along a specific contour is an oft-practiced walleye trolling method.

you catch a fish; you can maintain the same speed if fish continue to strike. If they don't, it may be that you caught one particularly aggressive walleye out of a school and need to go slower in the same area to appeal to the other fish.

Walleyes become most active during low-light and dark hours. Fishing at these times can increase your success. An hour before dark till 10 or 11 at night and early in the morning until an hour after daybreak are considered prime, although this is not carved in stone. On Lake Erie, good fishing can be had throughout the day. Anglers who work at deep-water trolling presentations on inland lakes can have nice catches. Trolling makes finding fish all the more feasible at those times.

11

SALMON

It's interesting to note that if this book on freshwater trolling were being written as recently as 1960, it would have only a little to say about salmon, principally landlocked Atlantic salmon. But the tremendously successful introduction of chinook and coho salmon to all of the Great Lakes not only requires that these fish now be the major focus of such a chapter, but also that the impact of this new fishery on methods of trolling and equipment employed since the early 1960s be recognized. From downriggers to brightly colored lures, from deepwater speed indicators to wafer-thin spoons, the art and science of trolling have been revolutionized, and these elusive big salmon prompted much of it.

Obviously salmon, particularly chinooks, are the premier Great Lakes fish. Chinooks, because of their size and tunalike fight, are revered by big water anglers more than any other fish. A broadshouldered chinook that runs and runs and runs will provide plenty of suspense. Coho, though not growing nearly as large as chinooks and not being able to fight as long or as hard, nonetheless fight very well. Their repeated and tiring aerial maneuvers are particularly exciting. A frisky coho, one that jumps repeatedly, crossing lines and confounding angler, boat operator, and prospective netter is a most entertaining salmon.

Obviously these nomadic swimmers are strong fish. They should be. A radiotelemetry study of Great Lakes salmon indicated that they travel an average of 7.8 miles a day in the spring and summer, and may travel as many as 20 miles in a day.

As fish that spend most of their adult lives roaming vast expanses of open water, salmon are especially compatible with the angling

Author's daughter, Kristen, who caught this chinook salmon but refused to hold it, smiles as Roger Lowden obliges. Although she's caught bigger salmon since this photo was taken, this was her largest fish at the time. For many anglers, chinook salmon are the biggest and strongest fish that they catch in freshwater, making them a truly coveted trophy.

technique of trolling, in which a lot of water is covered by fishermen in an effort to locate their quarry and to present lures to them in a controlled manner.

Coho and chinook salmon utilize the open-water areas of a lake to roam in search of food, returning after three to five years at large to the rivers and streams of their birth, where they spawn and die. Their movement in the open water is largely governed by water temperature and food availability. Biologists say that chinook, which live longer and grow much larger than cohos, eat three times more food than cohos. That they grow to sizes between 20 and 40 pounds in a few years indicates that they are veritable eating machines. Coho, which can grow to the mid-20-pound size, but are usually caught under 10 pounds these days, are not sluggish in the food-consumption category either. Both these fish put on many pounds from spring through summer, developing bulging bellies. They obviously eat heartily for most of the time that anglers pursue them.

The principal salmon forage is smelt and alewives. These bait fish, which mass in large schools, will come inshore to spawn when the water warms up in the 50s, and this will help draw salmon close to shore. Afterward, however, both smelt and alewives, which are cold-water fish, stay in the strata of water that are most conducive to their own comfort, roughly 48 degress for smelt and 54 degrees for alewives. These bait fish are also pelagic, and they range widely in search of plankton. The temperature-comfort requirements of salmon mix well with those of smelt and alewives. Salmon occupy roughly the same lake strata niche. In simplest terms, you could say that salmon follow bait fish and that the location of both is influenced by water temperature. Water temperature, in turn, is influenced by the weather and prevailing winds. Conditions that may be conducive to the presence of salmon in a particular place at one time can be markedly altered within a few days. This situation is decidedly different than that of fishing for species such as walleye, bass, muskies, striped bass, and, to a lesser extent, trout. Therefore, the vagaries of salmon combined with the changes in their environment make open-water fishing much like hunting.

The hunt begins in midspring, gains momentum in late spring and summer, and peaks in late summer and early fall. In pursuing spring salmon, anglers usually scour the water from top to bottom. Just as salmon range widely over a lake in the spring, so, too, are they dispersed at all water levels from the surface to 40 or 50 feet deep because of the uniformly cold water. Most spring (April through May) salmon are caught within 25 to 30 feet of the surface over a bottom depth that ranges from a few feet deep to as much as 100. They may move slightly offshore over this greater depth, yet are still close to the surface, when inshore boat activity and/or bright light in the spring forces them to relocate.

There are days when success comes consistently at a certain depth, but this depth may not be the same on the next day. It's a good idea to assume that conditions will change daily so that you are flexible enough to try various methods and to fish at differing water levels.

In salmon trolling, you have to work for your fish and keep trying different lures, depths, places, and boat speeds. This is true in any season. There are times when you catch all your fish at the same depth on the same type and color lure, but there are also times when you are forced to experiment because there is no consistent depth, lure type, or color pattern. Big boat anglers, such as charter boat skippers, have an advantage over small boaters and lone fishermen because they can run two lines per angler. With four or five anglers onboard, charter boat skippers can run eight to ten lines, not to mention the extra

lures that can be fished if slider rigs are added to lines set on downriggers. The water column can really be covered with an assortment
of lure types and colors.

Salmon are here today, gone tomorrow in the spring and summer.
Their unpredictable availability adds flavor to the hunt. Unlike fall
salmon, which cluster near tributaries and prepare to run upriver to
spawn, spring fish have no compulsion to linger and don't stage in
large schools or small pods. Passing through, they are temporarily
attracted to tributaries, power plant discharges, and the like because
of the warmer water and food to be found in these spots.

Usually the warming is precipitated by tributaries. When the water
temperature is in the low to mid 40s, a 50-degree day with rain might
send enough warmer water down a tributary to heat up the environs
of a tributary mouth a few notches. This could spur fish activity. Often
there will be a mud line created around tributary mouths, which results
from the stained or muddy spring runoff, and it may extend a short
distance to the east or west depending on lake currents. Salmon may
be caught on the edges of the mud line because there is usually a
thermal break here as well, with the inner edge being warmer.

Elsewhere, the upper layer of water may be warmed a bit on a
mild sunny day. Fish may be caught in very shallow water on these
days. As spring progresses, pockets of warm water or vertical separa-
tions of different temperature water away from immediate tributary
areas can produce fish. It's a good idea to keep monitoring shallow
water temperatures as you fish, to look for these things, and to determine if fish that you do catch are in a particular area because of
the temperature difference.

On all the Great Lakes, however, the bulk of inshore fishing
concentrates on immediate tributary environs. Good places to fish
here include heads of piers, river alleys between piers (nearest the lake
proper), harbors, breakwalls, troughs near shore, and nearby structures. These areas, however, are also most obvious and accessible to
other boaters and to shore-based fishermen. Although some fish can
be caught when angling pressure is intense, it's good to get away from
the crowd. Try fishing a mile or two down the shore and away from
the mouth. I try to fish tributary environs for the first hour or so of
the day. As traffic increases, I move off and look for nearby undisturbed
water or places that have been left alone for a few minutes. When
inshore traffic is heavy, other boaters zero in on the locale where

This bright, silvery spring chinook was taken on a surface thermal break on Lake Ontario.

someone is fighting a fish or was just observed to have landed a fish. This behavior often tends to cluster boats in certain places, if only for a relatively short period of time, therefore, you can be trolling the vacated spots.

Fishing away from the crowd works for trout as well as salmon trolling, and is a better tactic to adopt in fall rather than in spring if salmon are sought, because fall fish are in the area to stay whereas spring salmon are going to move on. Intense fishing pressure and heavy boat traffic cause spring salmon to leave, which are reasons why it pays to start early in the day. Salmon that have come into the near-tributary areas overnight may still be available for those first-light anglers. Low-light productivity with or without fishing pressure is actually a phenomenon that applies to salmon fishing all year long. I discuss the aspects of low light on salmon activity in more detail later in this chapter.

Spring salmon trolling can be accomplished by using flat lines, planer boards, downriggers, or diving planers. On the Great Lakes, most salmon trolling, even in the spring, is done with downriggers set shallow at first and then at intermediate depths; however, some people have success in using sideplaner boards to get lines away from the boat. I think running some flat-line plugs off sideplaner boards is especially worthwhile in early spring for coho or chinook salmon, and is a particularly good way to catch trout at the same time.

Early spring is about the only time of the salmon season when sonar instruments are not critically important. They are needed to tell you how deep you are, and they are needed when trolling with downriggers to make sure that you don't hang the weights up. Sonar also helps you locate pods of bait that might hold nearby salmon at this time of year. But from a fish-finding standpoint, sonar doesn't enter into the equation like it does when the water warms and you are hunting fish more than working localized areas. In my experience, the fish that are seen on sonar in early spring are usually not the fish that are caught. In the chapter on sonar, I note how you seldom see fish below the boat in shallow water. If I'm going to run a graph at this time, I often turn the paper speed down slow, mainly to conserve paper and to monitor bottom depth. Liquid crystal display recorders are particularly useful for this now.

Spring salmon, incidentally, are very beautiful fish. They are bright and healthy, black on top and silver-foiled on the sides. Coho and chinook, in contrast to their ever-darkening spawning brethren of late summer and fall, embody freshness and vitality. Their meat is excellent in spring, too. Fillets are pinkish or orange and firm. Spring salmon are fine eating and make better fare — whether canned, smoked, or cooked conventionally — than they do later in the season. Anglers who haven't tasted salmon through the winter months find a gastronomic incentive for the spring chase.

I give the nod to plugs for catching spring salmon on or near the

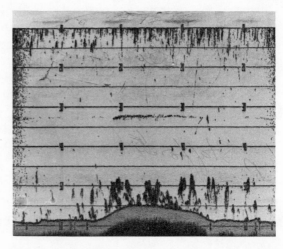

Schools of Lake Michigan alewives show up at the 50- to 55-foot level on this graph paper readout. Below the alewives are chinook salmon. Both are clustered in the thermocline offshore. This was recorded in late June, with a 10-foot upper scale setting and a 60-foot lower scale setting. Note that a very slow paper speed was used, which compresses the information tightly together. In reality, there are a lot of bait and salmon here.

surface and to spoons fished a little deeper via downriggers. Dodger and fly or spoon combos do the job later in the spring as the water warms. Plugs can be fished on flat lines, planer boards, and downriggers and usually exhibit good action even when worked at the moderately slow speed that cold-water spring fishing requires. Speed in spring may range from just below 2 to 3 mph, while later in the season it seldom will be at the lower end of that range and often will be greater.

As the shallow water warms up, bait fish and salmon move off-shore, depending on prevailing winds. Smelt are usually moving out of the inshore shallows by mid-May and alewives by the end of May or early June. Then, most fishing is accomplished with downriggers. Flat lines or planer board lines may catch fish on a thermal bar, of course, and sometimes diving planers, particularly the Dipsy Diver, are productive. Perhaps as much as 90 percent of the fish from here on in will be taken using downriggers fished at intermediate and deep depths, however.

In late spring and summer, the hunt is literally on for coho and chinook. You must *find* fish. The standard way to do this is to check water temperatures from the surface on down until you find water that is too cold for salmon to congregate. Set your lures in the 48- to 55-degree band of water and start covering a lot of territory, always watching your sonar instrument to note the presence and depth of bait fish schools and large individual fish that may be salmon. A device that gives you constant, deep temperature readouts is very valuable for this, but an alternative is to use a thermometer attached to a downrigger weight, preferably a manual model so you can raise it as quickly as possible to check the temperature at various depths.

As the water warms up, a thermocline is established, and salmon move deeper in the lake from late spring through early September. On the Great Lakes, you are usually fishing the thermocline in June, July, and most of August. It is a mistake, however, to strictly fish the thermocline band. Look for fish and bait on your sonar and note their depths. Deliberately fish a line or two (assuming you have enough lines to do this with) on either side of the thermocline. Look for 50- to 55-degree water but don't be afraid to work a bait in 48-degree water, especially for chinooks.

Now when you find fish, you're likely to see them in packs, not in large schools but in groups, more so than in the spring. Double-headers are a possibility. When you find salmon, you may want to slow down a bit (remember you've been moving and covering a lot of water), change lures if the fish don't respond to what you've been dragging, shorten the leads behind your downrigger, and bring lures closer together, packing them more tightly in the vertical space that the spotted fish occupy. Make a lot of turns, and include figure-eight patterns as part of your presentation repertoire. You may lose a school, but you may find another one. Depths at which lures are fished range from 30 feet to 50 or 60 in late spring and in early to midsummer, reaching 90 and 100 feet and even considerably deeper in late August. The bottom depth will range from 50 feet to several hundred.

This is precision trolling, truly controlled depth presentation, and the backbone of downrigger fishing. Really long drop-backs for salmon aren't necessary. Many times lures are run from a few feet behind the weight to 30 feet back, longer for shallow water and shorter for deeper water. With the depth of the lure assured because of short lines and downrigger weight settings, and with the speed of your boat known and the depth of fish marked on sonar, you might conclude that catching is a piece of cake. Sometimes it is, often it's not.

Remember that you do have to find the fish, then play with drop-back lengths, lure types, lure colors, speed, and so forth. The salmon you find are in the midst of an odyssey that will cause them to roam many miles on any given day. You're moving; they're moving. This is one reason why Loran is becoming a standard accessory on big Great Lakes boats, particularly on those belonging to charter captains. In the summer, you may have to go many miles offshore to locate salmon. Ten to twelve miles offshore is common in some places, but this depends on where you are on each of the lakes and from what direction is the prevailing wind. At times they are out "somewhere" in the middle of the lake, and for several midsummer weeks nobody can find them. That's when salmon-catching frustratingly grinds to a near halt.

On the other hand, summer salmon may be found in areas where there is some type of bottom structure different from the rest of the underwater terrain, such as reefs or rocky spots or troughs or sharp drop-offs, and where temperature is favorable. In some areas of the Great Lakes, such locales are not very far offshore, and salmon can be located fairly regularly and caught with some consistency. The Great Lakes, obviously, are huge waters. Although there are many similarities between the five lakes, there are also differences. These differences influence salmon behavior enough, so it would be inappropriate to state that these fish are basically caught at a certain depth on a certain lure at a certain distance from shore most of the time.

Much the same holds true for the types and colors of lures to fish. I'd like to tell you that a handful of specific lures are best for salmon, and I have made some references to certain lures I've had repeated success with. But there are many brands and types of lures that do the job, in fact, and you have to find what works for you under existing conditions on a day-to-day basis. One writer who surveyed charter boat captains for their salmon lure preferences wrote an article about the results of his survey according to each of the Great Lakes. The list of preferred lures that resulted included an incredible array of types and brands of lures and it seems like almost every manufacturer has a devotee. Let me cite a recent personal experience that illustrates how varied lure usage and success can be on a single day.

This April I made a day-and-a-half visit to Lake Ontario with a friend to troll for trout in the vicinity of the Oswego River. We hooked 15 fish and boated 11 of them, mostly brown trout but a laker, an

This small Lake Michigan coho took a fly trailed a short distance behind a dodger. This combination is one of the best coho salmon catchers.

Atlantic salmon, and a rainbow as well. All these fish were caught on colorful shallow-running plugs, albeit five different types of plugs, and all but one were caught off sideplaner boards. The exception was on a flat line. Most of the other people we spoke to lamented the poor fishing compared to a week earlier; other boats averaged just one to three fish per day.

The only other boat that had comparable success (although there were three anglers and thus more rods to fish) was pulling out of the launching area the same time as we were, and we talked at length. They'd caught six browns, a laker, and a coho that day, all on thin lightweight spoons fished off downriggers. They had tried plugs briefly but switched to all spoons; we'd tried a couple of spoons fished off a downrigger, but switched to all plugs. They were trolling fast; we were trolling slow. If someone had talked to each of us separately and learned what we did, they wouldn't have known what to make out of the information.

Similar experiences have happened to me in coho and chinook salmon fishing. My purpose in mentioning this is to emphasize that there are no hard-and-fast rules where lure choice is concerned. Moreover, there certainly are regional lure preferences. In salmon trolling, there are often hot colors and hot lure types just as there are times when people have success in doing quite different things. I still look at getting the right action out of my lures (regardless of type or color), being observant to details, and changing and experimenting as being the fundamental keys to catching trolled fish.

Having said that, let me give some general guidelines about lure selection for salmon trolling. The premier coho salmon catcher is a fly, spoon, or rubber squid fished behind a dodger. Dodgers serve as attractors and are used in a variety of colors and sizes. Popular colors include all silver, silver with assorted prism tape colors attached to it, fluorescent red, chartreuse, blue, and green, but there are others. Sizes vary, although smaller ones tend to see more use in the early part of the season, bigger ones later in the year. Spoons, flies, and squid are run 18 to 24 inches behind the dodger and are used in a wide range of colors. Coho also strike other lures fished without a dodger behind a downrigger, such as thin spoons and small casting spoons; however, this combination, fished primarily off a downrigger but also behind a diving planer, is a top producer perennially.

Cut plugs (above) and
lightweight spoons (right)
are the premier chinook
salmon lures, both fished
off downriggers.

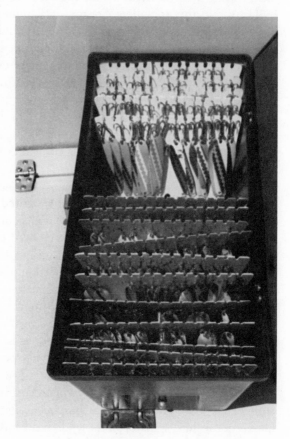

If I had to point to one lure type to use on chinooks, I would probably single out cut plugs. Typified by the single and jointed J-Plug, Silver Horde, Canadian Plug, Dandy Glo, Lucky Louie, and others, these erratic swimmers can sustain high trolling speeds and produce fish in summer and fall. Colors that I like include all silver, silver and blue, silver and green, green, and green and chartreuse. Other useful plugs, however, include jointed minnow imitations, such as the J-11 Rapala and Sisson Minnow-Mate in fluorescent colors, and small diving plugs, such as Hotshots, Tadpollys, and Hot 'N Tots in silver, blue and silver, chartreuse and red, and other colors.

As for spoons, the number of manufacturers is so great that it's hard to keep up with them. Some of the Eppinger products are well liked throughout the Great Lakes, and other very popular lures include Evil Eyes, Northport Nailers, Southport Slammers, Flutterspoons, Suttons, Andy Reekers, and on and on. You should realize that there are trolling spoons that cannot be cast without a weight and casting spoons that can be trolled but often are not as useful as trolling spoons. Few of the heavy, thick-bodied spoons are used routinely for salmon trolling because they sink too fast on turns, drop an indeterminate distance below a downrigger weight when trolled, and don't have the best action at slower speeds. However, thick-bodied spoons can be useful for surface flat-lining at times without the aid of weights because they do attain some depth while trolled.

Lightweight spoons, on the other hand, attain no depth unless fished with a weight, diving planer, or weighted line or trolled behind a downrigger weight. The wafer-thin models are made of light gauge metal and are so pliable that they can be bent to modify their action. They also bend readily when a fish thrashes in the net with one of these spoons in its mouth. They are predominantly worked slowly to achieve maximum action. The slightly heavier versions — still unsuitable for casting, however — are the foremost salmon spoon on the Great Lakes, and they have very good swimming action over the intermediate and fast ranges of trolling speeds.

An important point to remember about spoons — and this is true however they are trolled — is that each type of spoon has an optimum trolling speed and an acceptable range of trolling speed. When you troll below that range the lure has no action, and when you troll above it the lure spins or darts wildly and has an unnatural action. Therefore, when you are selecting a spoon to troll for salmon, make sure it is speed-compatible with the other spoons (and plugs) that you are already fishing. In general, make speed-related selections for salmon fishing based upon the design and thickness of the spoon.

One of the most interesting phenomena of salmon lures has been the emergence of products that emit light. Lures with phosphorescent paint have been around for some time, and have proven popular for low-light and deep-water salmon trolling. These lures must be held to a light source, such as a spotlight or lantern, to make them glow. Their illumination only lasts for 15 to 20 minutes, after which they must be recharged. Some lures have phosphorescent paint on them, but you can paint others yourself or use phosphorescent tape.

Chemiluminescent light sticks are another way to go. This field first got started with Dandy-Glo plugs, which are plastic cut-plug trolling lures that sport a 4-inch-long light stick inside them. I've used these for early morning downrigger trolling for chinooks in the summer and can attest to the fact that they work. It's important to activate the light stick for an hour or more before fishing, however, to let some of the brightness mellow. Using tape on translucent plugs or using darker colored plugs also helps diffuse brightness. Such newer products include small plugs and spoons that sport 1 1/2-inch light sticks. Although I haven't yet caught salmon while using them, I have taken trout. These high-visibility lures are particularly useful in low-light situations, such as on overcast, foggy, or early morning days or at night.

There is no question that salmon, especially chinook, are very sensitive to light. They are often found inshore in the wee hours of the morning and at dusk, moving offshore and getting progressively deeper as the sun rises. Getting out an hour before sunrise is usually a wise decision, not only because salmon may be closer to shore or shallower than later in the day but also because they are actively feeding and are more aggressive about striking lures just before daylight and at dusk. Salmon fishermen who are on the water day after day during the summer and early fall know that there is usually a one to three hour peak activity period in the morning and that catch rates almost invariably decline as light penetration increases. This is not to say that you can't catch fish during midday, but there are usually many slow stretches between midmorning and midafternoon. At dusk, however, the chance of renewed activity is increased.

Although I've spent many hours fishing in the dark, I haven't

The sun is just peeking over the horizon and this angler (above) is fast to a chinook salmon. Early in the morning and late in the day are prime times to catch salmon. The large coho taken by Marty Salovin (below) in the evening was, for a while, a line-class world record.

been salmon fishing through the night. I firmly believe that it's worth the effort, however. Certainly it can be exciting, and I suspect that it can be even more productive than dusk or daylight fishing because boat traffic is virtually nonexistent. The fish, which come inshore to feed, are less wary due to darkness and the lack of boat activity. I think light-emitting lures would be the ticket then, fished fairly shallow on downriggers and flat lines. Fog or rough water should be avoided, care should be exercised, and safety should be a foremost concern.

This fishing would be through the middle of the night till dawn in late spring and early summer, when the water temperature inshore is in the mid to upper 50s. When the inshore temperature is warmer in late summer, salmon may occasionally come in to foray, but they are not as likely to do so or to do so in numbers, because they are in a so-called staging disposition, schooling up in deep offshore water and beginning to undergo the physiological changes that will ultimately cause them to stop feeding and to come into the tributary regions. When they do come inshore preparing to spawn, there are usually plenty of fish, and the opportunities for catching trophy-size salmon are never greater.

The big fish and the swollen near-shore presence of salmon is what instills enthusiasm into fall anglers throughout the Great Lakes. Actually this begins in late August and extends through September and into October. Coho and chinook salmon return to natal streams during this period, eventually entering them, not en masse but sporadically when their biological clock nudges them to do so. Each new rainfall encourages their return also. This explains why mouths of rivers figure so prominently in the activities of late-season trollers.

Although large and small rivers attract fish, the entire tributary vicinity is likely to harbor salmon, and anglers may be more successful from a half-mile to several miles directly offshore, or relatively inshore yet several miles in either direction of tributaries. It is not uncommon to find a lot of fish close to a river mouth, but on the bottom and uncooperative. These are likely to be salmon that are almost ready to run the river; therefore, they are not interested in feeding. They may strike a lure, fly, or spawn sack later when they're in the river, if either is repeatedly dangled annoyingly in front of their snout, but an object passing by their nose in the lake doesn't antagonize them enough.

The surprise of fall fishing is that there are lake salmon that strike even though they are undergoing severe physiological changes that

In late summer and early fall, chinook and coho salmon move inshore near tribu-taries. This is when all the hardware comes out, boats are numerous, and the hunt for big fish is in full swing.

produce a kype (curled lower jaw), a darkening of body color, and an ultimate loss of appetite. Many fall salmon that will soon exhibit these traits are just on the verge of losing their appetite completely and probably strike more out of habit. Although the short-lived Great Lakes salmon are fish that grow so fast and seem to swim around like a bait fish vacuum, biologists' studies have shown that three out of four salmon caught in the fall have nothing in their stomachs.

This notwithstanding, coho and chinook strike plugs and spoons of varying sizes, colors, and shapes, and it is always a challenge to discover the kind, size, and color of lure that is successful. These patterns can remain constant for a season or a week, or change sud-denly, and they vary from year to year. Cut plugs, such as a J-Plug or Lucky Louie, have been good fall salmon-catchers for me, yet each year it seems the size that worked so well one autumn doesn't cut it the following year. Even smaller plugs, such as 2-inch-long wobbling crankbaits, like a Hotshot, Wiggle Wart, or Tadpolly, are effective. When you see a 30-pound chinook come into the boat with such a small lure in its mouth, you shake your head in amazement, but they can work wonders.

Of all the colors used in late-season Great Lakes salmon fishing, I wouldn't be without blue and silver. This color has produced more

Salmon lose their silvery sheen and become darker in the fall. This large chinook was turning reddish brown when caught in September and was just beginning to develop hooked jaws.

consistently for me than any other. It may not catch the most fish in a particular year or even the largest (though some years it will do both), but like the baseball player who hits for average, it's always in contention. I've also had fall success with some fluorescent colors, but silver, green and silver, chartreuse with red, and green and black have been most effective at this time. These colors apply to both spoons and plugs, although in general I find that plugs come into their own again as the more consistent salmon-catchers.

Running lures close to the downrigger weights have become the rule rather than the exception for me, and 6 to 8 feet back is normal in deep water in the fall. Occasionally I'll drop back from 12 to 20 feet for salmon. The downrigger weight piques the curiosity of salmon, or irritates them, and it apparently draws attention to the bait following it. I'll stack lines on the same downrigger, with the upper lure a few feet above the lower one and slightly further back. This puts two lures in the same zone and near one weight.

Despite the occasional presence of salmon near the surface, late-season fishermen should concentrate their efforts at deep levels. A high line may pick up the odd steelhead or brown trout, but salmon catches occur deep. This doesn't necessarily mean on the bottom, however. My records for early September in recent years show that I took big coho and chinook salmon at 20 feet over 30, 34 over 44, 40 over 80, 55 over 60, 55 over 150, 60 over 90, and 90 over 150. Sometimes I took them in the thermocline; other times I was above it. Sometimes I was a quarter-mile offshore; other times I was a mile or two offshore; once I was right in a harbor mouth. I was not in the same locales, so in a sense I'm comparing apples to oranges. My point is, you need to search for fish, which are invariably relatively deep, at specific levels using some type of sonar, and you need to utilize a downrigger to make a controlled presentation at these levels.

The water temperature at these depths may not be what is normally considered ideal for salmon, but temperature alone is not the guiding factor now. It's good if a thermocline is established near shore and salmon are holding in 50- to 55-degree water. The right wind, usually south or southwest, for several days can push warm water out, bring salmon closer to shore, and provide an explosion in fishing action. However, a strong north or northwest wind can alter the depth of fish near the tributaries; therefore, you need to assess the situation daily.

In late August or early September, you may see a lot of active fish on a graph recorder. These are streakers on the move and feeding, and you may get quite a few false releases (lines pulled out of the downrigger release device) as the result of fish striking your lures but not getting hooked. Streakers may be active fish that are more inclined to strike than stationary sulkers.

The concentration of near-shore fish at this season, whether due to spawning influence or thermocline presence, contrasts with spring and midsummer fishing in that salmon can be anywhere and at any depth in the early part of the season, and very deep and well offshore in summer, depending on the location of the thermocline and the prevailing wind. Although the first and last few hours of daylight remain good times to catch salmon, the fish don't necessarily disperse quite as readily as light penetration becomes greater. Some late-season salmon will disperse and others will stay in one area and be inactive.

Late-season salmon may be undergoing drastic changes that make them darker and more malevolent looking, but don't underestimate their pulling power or staying ability. Many autumn Great Lakes anglers have hooked up with fish that fatigued their wrists. Many salmon have gotten tougher near the boat and pulled free, or made netting awfully difficult. Of course, not all fish act the same, and some large late-season salmon are whipped pretty handily. Part of the fun at this time is not not knowing just when you'll get that tiger.

Irrespective of season, salmon, especially large chinooks, are among the most powerful fish in freshwater, and they have whipped many a fisherman's reel drag. I once heard a scientist say that a Great Lakes salmon was "as fast as any terrestrial animal in its ability to move in its environment." Though fall salmon may lose a fraction of their fighting vigor as they darken and get closer to running the rivers, they're no pussycats. I recall watching a 32-pound September chinook that ran like a tuna with the boat. Just when we thought it was near to landing, we had to steer furiously in circles to keep it out from

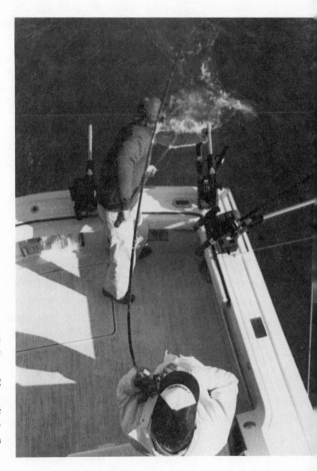

Battling a good-size salmon when it gets close to the boat is often an adventure. These strong-swimming fish often don't give up, and it's not unusual to lose them, for a variety of reasons, almost within reach of an outstretched net.

under the boat and off to starboard because it was intent on going past and below us. It's not uncommon to see nearby anglers frantically pull lines and downrigger weights, then chase after a salmon heading for the next county.

The possibility of hooking a real tackle-tester is one of the forces that keeps anglers after salmon, chinook especially, and late summer fish in particular. The fish will, of course, be larger in the fall, but a 20-pound spring chinook, not nearly ready to succumb to the physiological changes that will occur in fall, is still one broad-tailed Goliath. Many a spring pier fisherman, using light tackle for perch, has had his rod yanked off the pier by a salmon (or steelhead), or has been uncontrollably linked to a fish 25 times larger than what he was expecting. Trollers don't necessarily fare better even though their tackle is stouter. More than one boat angler has been despooled by a powerful chinook.

Obviously it takes some skill to land the bigger chinook, though this is something that an angler with adequate tackle can master quickly. A long rod, in at least the 8- to 9-foot range, is distinctly advantageous for use with downriggers and for playing fish. A reel should have plenty of line capacity (200 yards minimum) and a good drag. Levelwind reels are preferred for this, and line strength ranges from 14 to 25 pounds. Charter boat captains, who often have inexperienced anglers on board, seldom fish with less than 17-pound line for salmon. Many use 20 and some go to 25. I prefer light line because it's a challenge and thrill to play these strong fish in open water with it, though light line can be a problem when you hook a big fish that you have to wear down and other boats are in the immediate area. When boat traffic is not a problem, it's not hard to play a big fish in open water because there is nothing for it to snag your line on. The deck can be cleared and the boat maneuvered to your advantage. If the drag is set properly, the fish can take plenty of line and do its stuff. When conditions allow, I ordinarily prefer 12-pound line for salmon trolling, but I also fish with 6- and 8-pound line for trout and occasionally hook a salmon on a trout rod.

You may find it very exciting to fight these fish on ultralight tackle and superlong, so-called noodle rods. The first time I tried this, using a borrowed light and willowy 12 footer with a bait-casting reel spooled with 2-pound line, I carefully played a 12-pound chinook to the net on Lake Michigan near the Michigan City harbor. The fish didn't come in voluntarily, but it didn't take more than 12 minutes to land either. Anytime you are on a freshwater lake salmon for an honest 10 minutes or more, you know you've had a hold of something memorable.

The problem with using such gear, however, is that it does take a little more time than usual to land a fish. If a salmon runs a long way on the surface in a locale that is crowded with boats, there will be cutoffs and people who get upset because you're in their way. In the spring, when boats are clustered inshore, this is especially likely to be a problem. The solution is to fish the fringes of heavy traffic or use only the ultralight stuff when the water isn't crowded. My point in mentioning this light and ultralight tackle application for big and hard-pulling salmon is primarily to let you know that it can be done.

Oddly enough, some people using conventional strength tackle fight a big salmon for an interminable time. Although this has not happened to me, nor have I been on a boat where it has occurred, each year I am told of one or more instances in which big lake salmon — 25 to 40 pounds — have been played for over an hour and up to several hours by anglers using conventional strength tackle. This strikes me as being either a tall tale or the result of inept fish-playing, inept because the drag was too loosely set, the rod was too limber, or the angler did not know how to pressure a large fish. Apparently it happens. With light and ultralight tackle, there is no doubt that you can spend an hour on a really large fish, but if you know how to play a fish properly and use wind and boat position to your advantage, you needn't spend most of the day fighting Goliath.

Nobody talks about having a coho on for hours, though, if for no other reason than that the fish inevitably wears itself out by jumping and thrashing. This bundle of energy is a delight to catch and is especially welcome as the first salmon of the day because its antics get everyone fired up. If you happen to catch one on a short line, it may be up in the wake of the boat and leaping through the foam almost before you realize what's happening. So you hang onto the rod, reacting in amazement and perplexion as the fish whips about, then dashes away as line peels off the reel. How can you not be impressed with a fish like that?

Not to be overlooked in the admirable-qualities department is the landlocked Atlantic salmon. Known for leaping, running, and pressuring light tackle, the landlocked Atlantic is a salmon of grace,

Coho and chinook salmon are elusive in big bodies of water. Finding them and getting them to strike is half the challenge; landing them is the other half.

beauty, and maximum punch per pound. This fish has long been a troller's favorite in the Northeast.

Things are a bit different in landlocked Atlantic salmon fishing than they are in coho or chinook fishing. Landlocks are not quite as scattered as Great Lakes coho or chinook. Traditionally, landlocks are pursued by trollers using fly rods and weighted streamers, or lead-core line and either spoons or streamer flies. Downriggers and other Great Lakes salmon paraphernalia are still relatively new to the land-locked Atlantic salmon scene, although they are making inroads and are helping to extend what has been primarily a shallow spring fishery.

Although there is a more traditional attitude toward landlocked salmon trolling, the life cycle and behavioral pattern of these fish are very similar to that of coho and chinook salmon. Landlocks, for example, spawn in the fall, return to natal tributaries to do so, and live out their adult lives in the open water. Landlocks leave their natal waters as smolts and generally return to those tributaries two or three years later. Unlike coho or chinook salmon, Atlantics often survive the reproductive process and may spawn two or three times.

Landlocked Atlantic salmon inhabit large- and intermediate-size northern lakes, as well as small lakes or ponds in high-altitude areas. The predominant trolling fishery occurs in large lakes, such as George and Champlain in New York, Winnipesaukee and Squam in New Hampshire, Sebago in Maine, and Quabbin in Massachusetts. The principal fishing is in spring, beginning right after ice-out. Although some salmon may be caught when the ice is breaking up and the water temperature is in the 39- to 42-degree range, better action doesn't begin until the water hits the mid 40s. Landlocks are caught from the surface to 20 feet deep at this time, which is all uniform temperature, and can be found near shore over relatively shallow bottom or out in open water over deep water.

As the surface temperature increases, landlocks are more likely to be found near tributaries, if they attract large runs of spawning smelt, or inshore where schools of smelt or spawning alewives may be located. Water temperature then is in the low to mid 50s. This activity takes place in May and through June. By mid to late June in a normal year, the surface water will warm up and landlocked Atlantics will move to deeper water and locate in the thermocline, roughly staying in 52- to 57-degree water and roaming as widely as the size of lake and water temperature zones will allow.

Smelt are the foremost, and preferred, landlocked salmon food. Alewives are a major forage fish in a few locales that don't have a substantial smelt population. Elsewhere, ciscoes, shiners, and yellow perch make up part of their lake diet. Smelt are usually the bread-and-butter prey, and most landlocked salmon lures are meant to imitate smelt. These lures include minnow-imitating plugs in straight and jointed versions from 4 to 6 inches in length, long thin spoons, and single or tandem streamer flies.

The traditional and still widely practiced landlocked salmon trolling method is with a fly rod and a streamer. The fly rod is between 8 and 9 feet long and is equipped with a large-capacity fly reel loaded with 100 yards of backing, a level sinking line, and a long leader. The leader is about 20 to 30 feet long, and can be of one strength (6 to 10 pounds) or split into relatively equal sections of differing strengths (such as 10 and 6). Using one continuous section is preferable because it eliminates the potentially troublesome nylon-to-nylon knot. A streamer fly is tied to the end of the leader, and a split shot or two may be added a short distance ahead of it.

Another traditional method, used for getting to below-surface fish with either a fly or light spoon, is fishing with a fly rod or conventional rod, levelwind reel, and lead-core line. A long leader is again employed, and the issue is one of experimenting with how many colors to let out to get down to a certain depth. In both cases, where spoons or flies are fished, most successful anglers hold the rod in their hands, keep it parallel to the water and perpendicular to the gunwale of the boat, and sweep it back every few seconds. This pulsates the fly or spoon and causes it to surge forward and flutter back. The technique is an important aspect of appealing to landlocked salmon, so important, in fact, that electric devices to sweep the rod have been made locally and used for many years. These devices are essentially rod holders powered by windshield wiper motors timed to sweep the rod back and forth. Two or three small manufacturers make them, but they are not widely distributed, and I've found it hard to locate the products in stores or to get information from the manufacturers. Cannon recently unveiled such a product. Called the Excitor, it has a timed sweeping motion to jerk the rod back and forth and can be tilted to act as a vertical jigger as well.

Most of the traditional landlocked salmon trollers have not employed sonar devices, although more are doing so today. It makes sense to use them, however, not only to let you know when you are nearing potentially dangerous shallow waters (many natural northern lakes have submerged reefs), but also to help you pinpoint schools of salmon and the depth they are inhabiting. Pinpointing schools gives you a reference as to how much lead core you must let out in order to reach the fish-holding depth.

Downrigger fishing is growing each year on the landlocked salmon scene. Where spoons and plugs are used, downriggers are most beneficial. Spoons and plugs have an action of their own. Flies, on the other hand, need to be jerked to look more active when trolled. The only way to jerk flies is with an automatically oscillating downrigger, an expensive product that few landlocked salmon trollers, other than charter boat captains, are likely to buy because they are predominantly just spring fishermen.

Flies can catch salmon when used on downriggers, however, even though they may not be as active as you'd like. I've done it and can say that flies are most useful on windy days when boat movement through waves causes some natural up-and-down weight motion, thereby adding to streamer action. Downriggers can also be used for getting streamer flies down to a controlled trolling depth.

New Hampshire guide Pete Grasso holds a small Lake Winnipesaukee landlocked Atlantic salmon that took a spoon fished 20 feet deep off a downrigger.

The best fishing, especially in spring, is often in the first few hours of the day, with a late afternoon or evening flurry common. Midday, particularly under bluebird conditions, is dubious. A relatively fast trolling speed is employed for landlocks. Although lines are usually set from 75 to 200 feet behind the boat on flat lines and from 40 to 80 feet back on deep downrigger lines, some spring fish are literally caught in the prop wash.

Lure colors that work well include gray and black, gray and white, silver and black, silver, and copper, although streamers with a touch of red are sometimes the hot ticket. Gaudy colors, which are often so successful on Great Lakes salmon, just don't measure up when it comes to landlocks. I have caught them on spoons that had silver on one side and orange on the other, however; so maybe there is more room for color experimentation than I've experienced. Useful lures include Grey Ghost, Red Ghost, Ninethree, and Meredith Special streamers; Rebel, Rapala, Sisson, and Bagley minnow-imitation plugs; and Mooselook Wobbler, Sutton 44, and Flutterbelly spoons. There are other lures that will do the trick, too.

12

TROUT

I recently shot a group of photographs for an advertising and public relations agency. One of their requests was to take a photo of a small boat using downriggers while trolling for trout on a reservoir. They wanted the photo taken with a dam in the background because the downrigger manufacturer wanted to emphasize the use of its product for trout in smaller lakes, that is, in waters that weren't of the stature of the Great Lakes. That first struck me as being a little peculiar, but then I realized that a lot of folks associate modern trolling techniques with big water fishing and overlook the use of the same equipment for trout in smaller bodies of water. Many anglers have the impression that catching trout in smaller lakes is strictly a matter of early season luck and that if they want to catch trout their best bet is to stick with flowing water. My purpose in mentioning this is to note that there is plenty of reason to troll for trout in small- and medium-size bodies of water. Many of the same techniques that apply to trolling hold equally true for trout in the Great Lakes as for trout in inland lakes. We review trolling for brown trout, lake trout, rainbow trout, and steelhead in large and small waters in this chapter.

On balance, if you're interested in catching large trout, you should be plying the lakes. Naturally, size isn't everything. But with fishing for trout in lakes, you have a genuine angling challenge, plus the potential for catching big fish. Big lake trout, brown trout, and rainbows or steelhead are more likely to be found in lakes or reservoirs because such waters often provide suitable year-round water temperatures, have abundant forage fish opportunities, and readily accessible trout.

Accessibility is a prime issue in the matter of fishing for trout in lakes. It is because of better accessibility that so many Americans venture to locales in northern Canada each summer for lake trout; the water there is still cold and the fish aren't deep, meaning that they are available and catchable. It is because of accessibility that so many anglers from northern states flock to lakes and reservoirs after ice-out, when trout are on the prowl in shallow water and are more vulnerable than at other times of the season. It is because of the lack of accessibility — the fact that trout in lakes move a lot and aren't always confined to readily identifiable terrain — that many anglers don't want to pursue trout in lakes. After all, it's a lot easier to work a lure or fly for trout in flowing water because you can readily see the possible trout lies (if not, in fact, see the fish) and know that you are

Big waters with plenty of bait fish grow large trout. Most of the time, trolling is the way to have consistent success in obtaining trout in such places.

presenting your offering to a fish or working very good water. Many stream trout fishermen don't want to admit it, but few of them could find their way around and catch fish if deposited on a lake; it's often tough. For that matter, few still-water fishermen are really on top of their game when it comes to locating and catching trout in lakes.

Fishing for trout in lakes is like blind prospecting, and therein lies the challenge. To have regular success means covering a lot of water, hunting and pecking, eliminating places, lures, boat speeds, depths, and on and on until you unlock the secrets of those fish on that lake under those conditions and at that time of day. In some respects it is like hunting, if you're going to be aggressive about it, that is.

After ice-out or in late winter and early spring, trout lakes begin to warm on the surface. Trout may be found at any level at this time and are often within the upper strata, 20 feet or less, of a lake or in shallow water close to shore. Thermal discharges, tributaries, rocky shorelines, and the like contribute to warmer water locales. Warmer in this instance may be 46 degrees as opposed to 43 or 44 degrees throughout the rest of the lake. Pockets of water warmer than the rest of the lake may be found, and they can hold catchable fish.

In most big and small lakes and in many impoundments, tributaries play a critical role in trout behavior and therefore fishing success, especially in the spring when predator and prey species come into the near-shore areas influenced by tributaries because of the presence of food and more comfortable conditions.

In the spring, rivers, streams, and the outlets of upstream dams bear the rain and melted snow runoff that helps open up the lake, then the warm water that ultimately helps raise the temperature of the cold main lake. A warm rain is a blessing for a big body of water that is influenced by a major tributary, because it will stimulate activity, feeding, and possibly spawning, though it sometimes takes two or three days for a heavy warm rain to have an impact on a big lake system. Don't overlook the importance of fishing in and near tributaries and their environs for early season trout, and be alert to the influence of a warm rain on trout activity.

Ultimately the upper layer of water in a lake will warm to the point where trout are uncomfortable. Then they seek deeper, cooler environs. This seems rather obvious, but some anglers overlook the fact and continue to fish surface and shallow waters during the day at this time, when there is little hope of finding trout in such areas.

In the spring when lake water is still cold, tributaries and power plants (shown here) provide relatively warm water and are good places to seek trout.

Eventually a lake, with the exception of those in cold northern locales, will stratify and a thermocline will develop. The depth of the thermocline, which separates distinctly different temperatures of water, can range from 15 or 20 feet below the surface to 100 or more in very deep lakes with good oxygen content. Once a lake has stratified, you need to start looking for the thermocline and establishing the depths of the preferred temperature of trout. In the case of brown and rainbow trout, the place where those temperatures meet with the bottom of the lake can be a very strong locale for catching fish, especially if that place is a prominent aspect of underwater terrain, such as a point or near-shore ledge. Lake trout, which prefer temperatures below the thermocline, will orient to very deep water, often residing on or just above the bottom where they feed. They also foray into warmer water to shoals and reefs to feed, then depart for deeper environs again.

When trout are shallow and near the surface, they can be caught by trolling, casting from shore, or drifting with bait. I recommend trolling because it allows you to cover a lot of ground and look for active, aggressive fish, particularly trout that perhaps have not been spooked or otherwise bothered by other fishermen and boaters. Drift-fishing with a boat usually is a live-bait proposition. Many anglers are quite successful with this technique using the prominent forage, such as alewives, for bait, but it is slow and less productive than lure trolling where motors are permitted on lakes. If you cast from shore, you may simply be limited to one spot, such as a pier or breakwall, and must cast repeatedly in hope of attracting a moving, incoming fish to strike your lure. This can pay off in tributary areas where warm river water attracts a significant number of fish. In small lakes, however, it pays to be mobile, concentrating shore-casting efforts near prominent points, inlets, steep banks, rock- and boulder-studded shores, shorelines with sharp drop-offs to deep water, and warm bay and cove areas. These are the same places that you would work by trolling, the difference being that you can cover far more ground more thoroughly in a boat.

Line placement, lure presentation, and boat control are absolutely critical for shallow trout trolling success. Shallow fish are easily spooked. You can't motor through the shallows and expect fish to stay around and/or to be exceedingly receptive to the offering you trail behind. The simplest shallow trolling of any kind is to run a flat line straight out behind the boat. Whether you flat-line or not, remember that the clearer the water, the shallower the fish, the spookier the fish, and the more local boat activity, the longer the line you need.

Trout in shallow water near shore or close to the surface in open water move out of the boat's path of travel. That is one reason why you seldom see trout on sonar equipment in less than 15 feet of water. Proper boat manipulation can bring lures into the range of fish that may not have been in the boat's path or that have moved out of it, so be alert to this aspect of trolling and regularly alter the lure's path of travel by turning, steering in an S-shaped pattern, driving in other irregular ways, or increasing or decreasing the speed of the boat. It is also a good tactic to sweep in and out from shore, and plan strategically advantageous approaches to such areas as points, sandbars, islands, shoals, channels, and the like.

Fishing for shallow trout in lakes early in the season is a peculiar endeavor because the water is undergoing dramatic changes and because trout can be almost anywhere. To be successful, you should cover a lot of territory and make versatile presentations.

You can begin fishing as soon as the ice goes out. On inland lakes, I've found that good fishing occurs for several days immediately after ice-out. Success drops for a short while until the water stratifies. Then fish seek out the warmer surface water and angling success increases.

A warm rain and brisk winds can make ice disappear overnight, so it's a good idea to keep an eye on conditions in order to get on the water at the first opportunity.

One spring Saturday, I checked a local lake and found it mostly covered with thin ice. A warm front came through that night followed by a day of heavy rain, and the ice melted. Monday afternoon a friend and I spent an hour bypassing a washed-out road to reach the lake, but four hours of fishing yielded two 5-pound browns and a 12 pounder. We came back the following day and caught four more, the best of which topped 10 pounds. Fishing was hot for a week then slacked off temporarily. During that week, though, almost no one else was lake fishing, and they missed the fastest action.

Generally, and this is especially true of inland lakes, the most dependable angling doesn't begin until the surface water temperature reaches the mid 40s. Many of the lakes that I fish for ice-out trout are relatively small, a fraction of the size of the most prominent trout and salmon waters or any of the Great Lakes. Some are natural, some are manmade and used for water supply or hydroelectric purposes.

Inland lakes and reservoirs provide some excellent small boat trolling opportunities, particularly for brown trout.

They are good two-story lakes, having respectable warm-water fish populations as well as brown and lake trout and/or landlocked salmon. They all have cold-water environs, with the greatest depths ranging from 70 to 120 feet.

In the early spring, there are phenomenal concentrations of fish in 50 or more feet of water, often near the dams of these lakes and over the main channels. But the water temperature is only several degrees above freezing, while the surface temperature is 8 to 12 degrees above freezing. Though I've worked the deep fish very hard, they are disinterested and won't strike (besides trout these fish include perch, bass, panfish, and schools of bait). Despite the volume of deep fish, I concentrate on the upper layers of the lake. Trout individually move out of the deep levels to be in the more comfortable upper layer and to search for food. These fish are hungry and can be caught.

My boat is equipped with an electronic surface temperature gauge, that I refer to constantly. I look for warm water, which is often found around the river mouths and small tributaries. Sometimes the surface temperature can vary by as much as 4 to 6 degrees from the upper (main tributary area) end of the lake to the lower (near the dam), or from the upwind side to the downwind side. Shallow bays warm before the rest of the lake as do the shallows within several feet of shore, especially where there are rocks to retain the heat of the sun. Most trout are caught in the warmest surface waters.

If you don't have a surface temperature gauge, it's good to use a simple thermometer. I use a pool thermometer for checking deep temperatures or when I'm in a boat that doesn't have a surface temperature gauge. Immediately after ice-out, the water temperature is fairly uniform from the surface to the bottom. Soon it stratifies. The best condition exists when the top 20 feet of the lake is one temperature, with a distinct difference at deeper levels. Most ice-out trout angling is concentrated from the surface to 20 feet deep.

Because this early season fishing is primarily shallow, it can be accomplished without the aid of downriggers, wire line, lead-core line, diving planers, or heavy weights. I fish exclusively with 4-, 6-, and 8-pound lines and rarely use weights. I'll use downriggers occasionally to get certain shallow-running plugs down to a specific level, but 95 percent of my ice-out fishing is flat-lining.

Light line is necessary because trout are spooky, the water is very clear in the early season, and lure action is enhanced. I run the lures far behind the boat, a minimum of 100 feet and sometimes as much as 250 feet. This is to disassociate the appearance of the lure with the commotion of the recently passed boat. Motor noise in near-shore (and rocky) fishing situations is amplified and alarming to fish. I employ a long line in open-water areas, too.

The following lures have all been consistent early season coldwater trout-catchers: Rebel Floating Minnow; floating No. 11 Rapala and its jointed counterpart; Bagley shallow, supershallow, and deep-diving Small Fry plugs in shad or alewife imitations; 4-inch Rebel Spoonbill Minnow; Bagley Bang-O-Lure; jointed Sisson Minnow-Mate; and the Storm Thin Fin Shad.

These lures range from 3 to 5 inches in length, with either two or three sets of treble hooks. They are all floaters; sinking versions have not produced as well for me in the early season, although later in the year they can be productive for steelhead. Silver minnow, shad, alewife, smelt, dace, and rainbow trout patterns/colors have all been successful. Most of these lures closely represent some form of abundant natural forage. In some lakes, alewives are the principal trout food while in others, smelt are (chubs or ciscoes could be in your area). The stomachs of some of the larger fish have contained six to eight alewives or smelt. Others have contained unidentified small fish, though some contain yellow perch.

A sampling of spring trout trolling plugs and patterns.

The key to the effectiveness of these lures is twofold. Unlike spoons or flies, they sport numerous hooks. Ice-out trout don't often get caught on the rear hooks of the plugs, indicating that perhaps they strike from the side to injure or stun prey before consumption. A lot of fish fail to get hooked on spoons or flies because of this behavior. Secondly, plugs work well because trolling is done at the slowest possible speed. Trout don't want to chase a swiftly moving bait fish in this cold water. Most spoons don't work well at slow speeds, and few flies have the enticing action of good plugs. Additionally, these plugs float, so they rise slowly when you stop the motor or when you turn.

To a great extent much of the foregoing information is valid for Great Lakes trout, too, with exceptions being that the length of trolling lines is far shorter and the color of lures used is different. The same plug types and sizes are effective, as well as spoons, but colors run a more aesthetic gamut. Red, chartreuse, and fluorescent orange are hot Great Lakes trout colors in spring. Red with black, chartreuse with green, chartreuse with red (including the so-called fire dot pattern), orange and gold, and green with black have been particularly good colors in my experience. Blue and silver also gets a workout from me at times. I'm not sure I can explain why this is so, and why the same colors seem so outlandish on smaller inland trout waters. I don't do well with those colorful lures and rather prefer the more natural silver and black colors on small lakes and reservoirs. The reason, perhaps, may be because the color of the water is so different. Great Lakes water usually has a blue-green character, much like you see on the ocean, whereas inland waters have a blacker appearance. Both are usually very clear, so the difference is not so much one of clarity but shade.

In any event, Great Lakes trout are routinely caught on distances of 30- to 100-foot drop-backs on flat lines, downriggers, or sideplaners. Where boat traffic allows, I still like to get 70 to 150 feet of line back from my release to lure when flat-lining or using sideplaners. On a recent Lake Ontario outing in spring, a friend and I predominantly caught brown trout, but also lake and rainbow trout. Our success came to lures running 90 and 130 feet behind sideplaners. It appeared that most other fishermen, who didn't have the success we did, were using shorter lines. Many were not running sideplaners. Because we were fishing close to shore, catching fish 4 to 8 feet deep in 8 to 12 feet of water, I think the ability to spread our lures out and away from the

A fluorescent orange jointed plug, fished off a sideplaner board, took this hefty Lake Ontario brown trout in April.

boat (using 90 feet of sideplaner line), combined with comparatively lengthy drop-backs, helped us catch wary fish. Obviously, when the fish are abundant and action is hot, you can shorten up on drop-backs and still do well.

Whatever line length you use, it's wise to spice up your presentations frequently by making turns and increasing or decreasing boat speed. Some trout appear to be followers, swimming behind lures for considerable distances before losing interest or striking. Lakers are notorious for this. Vary your trolling routine by making turns or following S-shaped patterns. The variation throws a momentary change into the working of the lure and sometimes draws a strike.

Periodically I increase the throttle or put the motor into neutral for a few seconds, especially if I'm not catching anything and/or am marking fish on the graph recorder. Recently a friend and I caught three browns one day, and every fish struck after the motor had been placed in neutral. As soon as the motor was back in gear and the lures were moved forward, the fish were on.

When I first started trolling for trout in lakes, I simply ran my lines out the back of the boat. Then I tried to get them as far apart as possible to widen the territorial coverage. I seldom fish with more than two anglers in the boat, so the maximum number of lines that can be run is four (two per angler). Check the regulations in your area, as some states permit only one line per fisherman. When trolling three or four flat lines, it is helpful to use long spinning rods (7 to 9 feet). They help spread the lures out and also aid placement of shallow and deep-diving plugs to avoid tangling and to maximize coverage. Eventually I experimented with sideplaners and found them to work very well. I set the sideplaners about 60 to 80 feet out. The lures are run at varying distances behind the planer board and are connected to it via an adjustable tension line release.

As I mentioned earlier in the book, a host of deep and shallow fishing combinations are possible with sideplaners. When fishing near-shore areas, you can run two or three strategically spaced lines off the shoreside planer. On the open-water side of the boat, you have the option of running a surface or diving lure on a long flat line, running a lure deep via the downrigger, or running one or more lures off the other sideplaner. Moreover, the amount of territory that can be covered is vastly increased. If you run two sideplaners boards, each 60 feet to either side of the boat, and have two fishermen in the boat, you can run four lines over a 40-yard span of water. If the bottom drops off sharply near shore, as it does in many trout lakes, you could be working over a few feet of water on the near-shore side of the boat and over 40 feet on the opposite side, presenting your lures to fish that would not ordinarily see them. In this way, the fish would not be frightened by the passage of your boat either. On reservoirs, which often drop off sharply near some shore areas, I often fish the open-water side of the boat with a lure set behind a downrigger. Straight behind the boat I may run a shallow- or medium-running plug on a relatively long flat line. On the shore side, I'll run a planer board close to shore, using a shallow-running minnow plug nearest to shore on a moderate length line, and then either a similar plug or a spoon on the inside planer board line. This covers the close-to-shore environs in such a situation quite well.

Because early season trout roam in search of food, you stand a change of picking one up almost anywhere in a lake. It's best to concentrate on locales near deep-water areas that will likely be the summer refuge of these fish. Shallow flats and long sandy stretches of shoreline with a gradual drop-off don't produce many fish. The area near tributary creeks and streams can be good if there is a substantial flow that is warmer than the main body of the lake. Mainland points and long submerged points that drop off suddenly to deep water are productive locales, as are rocky shores with sharp drop-offs.

It is helpful to have a depthfinder or graph recorder to know the depth of water being fished. It is easy to spot fish on a graph because you don't have to watch it constantly as you do a digital or flashing depthfinder. A graph recorder also helps you determine if bait fish are in the area. Although you usually don't catch the shallow fish you see on a graph or depthfinder, there are times when you spot some fish, make an alteration in your presentation, go back over the school, and catch trout. When you are fishing shallow, incidentally, you seldom see fish on a graph or depthfinder because the cone angle of the transducer is too narrow for the depth or the fish simply move away from the path of the boat.

It isn't absolutely necessary to have a graph, sideplaner, temperature gauge, and the like to be successful. My first ice-out trout trolling was done in a 12-foot johnboat with a small outboard, using a portable depthfinder, short rods, and no rod holders. I caught fish. The difference was that my angling was more haphazard then, and I caught smaller trout. You can do well with small boats, even using electric motors, and a moderate amount of equipment, too, if you keep the principles of presentation and boat manipulation in mind.

I have emphasized shallow and early season trout trolling so far, partly because this is the best and most popular time to be fishing for trout. Keep in mind that some of the same techniques work for trout later in the season as well. Much of the same information about presentation, boat manipulation, and lure spreading applies, although trout are seldom found in the shallows.

When trout go deep, the boater with the ability to get lures down, to scout for fish with some type of sonar, and to ply a lot of water has a distinct advantage. Many methods have been employed to get lures deep for trout. These include using wire line, lead-core line, diving planers, heavily weighted nylon monofilament lines, and downriggers. Downriggers are suitable for fishing in nearly any lake that has trout. I've used them for trout on lakes that were only several hundred acres in size, and where I had to row or use an electric motor for propulsion. I can tell you that trying to set up a downrigger while you are alone in a boat and rowing — as I used to attempt on New York City's upstate reservoirs where all types of motors are prohibited — is a very trying and difficult procedure.

In fishing for trout in lakes, once you have established some idea of where and how deep to fish, the consideration becomes what type of lure to fish, what color, and at what speed. Spoons, plugs, and spinners all catch trout. Many flat-line trollers use fairly heavy spoons to help them get down, but light spoons, including the waferlike so-called flutter spoons, have really come on in recent years because they can be used so well with downriggers. They don't sink as fast on a turn, they run at the same depth as the downrigger, and they have an appealing wobbling action. These same flutter spoons can be used with bead chain sinkers or other types of weights as well.

Spoons are unquestionably the overall favorite trout-in-lakes lure, ranging all the way from the small, thin 2-inch-long models to the 2-ounce monsters trolled for giant lakers in the Northwest Territories. Spinners take some smaller trout, especially recently stocked trout, often near tributaries, but these lures don't represent as substantial a meal to larger and more savvy trout.

Plugs have a special appeal to trout in the spring and when they

Spoons are a favored trolling lure for trout in all locales. Mammoth spoons account for big lakers in northern Canada. The author made this catch while trolling on Great Slave Lake in the Northwest Territories.

are shallow, and at times produce deep-dwelling fish later in the season. The traditional minnow-imitation–style plugs do well for brown trout and steelhead, as do those fat-bodied plugs that may imitate alewives. Wide-wobbling cut plugs and erratic swimming plugs can be productive for steelhead, as well as lakers and browns, and they help emphasize the importance of lure action and behavior.

Trout, particularly lakers, are often very curious fish and may follow a lure for a considerable distance. Floating/diving-style plugs respond well to changes in boat speed, current, turns, or other factors that might influence or momentarily change the swimming pattern of a plug. These factors often cause a trout to strike. Of course, other lures respond to such factors as well, though they invariably sink when speed is decreased while plugs rise. This is an instance where spoon action is enhanced by a downrigger that oscillates your lure at regular intervals; any type of lure is automatically made to move up and down periodically.

When fish are deep, you may find success by trolling plugs and spoons, but spoons tend to win out more often. It seems that boat speed, which is greater for trout after the spring, bows in favor of spoons at this time. The exception to the higher speed rule, however, is lake trout, which are habitually a bottom-hugging and often structure-oriented fish from late spring through fall. They usually do not respond to the faster speed preferred by other trout and salmon, not to mention that they are often not at the same level. Usually you have to fish *for* lakers as opposed to fishing for any and all trout. If you find yourself catching lakers but not your targeted browns or rainbows, you may assume that you are going too slow for the latter. When fishing deep for salmon but catching lake trout, you are probably in water colder than salmon prefer, thus you are fishing too deep for them.

It is because of the laker's preference for slowly moving creatures that the most successful lake trout tactic on the Great Lakes is to run the so-called Peanut about 12 to 18 inches behind a dodger or cowbell attractor. Some spoons and small diving plugs are also worked in this fashion. In areas where there is a sandy bottom and where fish presumed to be lakers are spotted via sonar on the bottom in deep water (maybe 100 to 150 feet in summer), you can literally set your line by dropping the downrigger weight till it hits bottom, then raise it up a turn or two. The lead from weight to lure needn't be long.

Lakers do orient to structure, however, where it is available. Rocky islands and reefs are prime laker foraging grounds, and these fish characteristically move in to such spots to feed, then retreat to deeper (often significantly deeper) water. Remember that lake trout are great followers, therefore, it is to your advantage to try some tricks, such as oscillating a downrigger weight, pumping a rod to flutter a lure, increasing or decreasing speed, and the like, to encourage a strike. While trolling for lakers in deep, cold northern Canadian waters and holding a trolling rod in my hand (there were no rod holders on the boats), I could feel my lures get bumped by fish. The trout didn't often get hooked, however. I found that I could catch many of those fish by hitting the freespool button and letting the lure lay idle for a moment (as if the fish had stunned it), or by simply reaching back with my rod for a second or two, or by pumping the rod back and forth. Jigging or pumping the rod while trolling often elicited hookups even when a fish hadn't bumped the lure.

You can achieve similar behavioral changes in your lures, even if your rods are set in a holder and used with a downrigger. Remember the laker's penchant for this, and keep the speed down.

Some trout fishermen have been monitoring boat speed closely for several years, because they have learned how speed affects lure action and which species of fish relate to slow (lake trout), medium (browns and steelhead), and fast (salmon and sometimes steelhead) speeds. They are only now beginning to see that boat speed and lure speed may not be the same and to understand how this relates to fishing technique (see chapter 3). Keep in mind that all lures have a top speed, after which they no longer exhibit the action they were designed to have. Some lures are incompatible at specific speeds; in other words, the best speed for one lure may not be a desirable speed for another lure, and they should not be fished together. Always be alert to how each lure you use is working at the present boat speed, and check this before you start fishing it.

While lure speed is a recognizable phenomenon, lure color remains the big puzzle in trolling for deep trout. Matching the hatch, as one would by using a particular size and color of fly when stream trout fishing, can be the thing to do in smaller inland lakes but is seldom the way to go on large bodies of water. I've caught some exceptionally large brown trout in small reservoirs by using lures that closely resemble — in physical shape and size as well as in color — the prominent forage fish for those trout. By contrast, on the Great Lakes I've found that I may need to use lures that are smaller than the average prey fish, and nowhere near as representative in color.

Deep-color selection is becoming a more astute and closely followed aspect of fishing for trout in lakes, and usage depends not only on present forage but on clarity of the water, varying intensity of light, and depth to be fished (see chapter 4). The better trout fishermen are constantly changing colors, using lures that mix potentially productive colors, and switching lures to find what works. What works one day often doesn't work the next. Notice, however, that although fishermen are switching among spoons that have some blue or some green or some pink or some other attractive color to them (or a strip of prism tape on one side), they are combining this with silver or brass colors. As I mentioned before, the question becomes one of which color the fish are responding to.

I think it's best to keep experimenting and changing colors until you hit on something that seems to indicate a pattern. One fish on a particular color doesn't make a pattern, but two fish gets me putting out more lures in that color. Some fishermen, once they get three fish on one particular color, change all their lures to that color. This so-called monochromatic fishing obviously can be a self-fulfilling prophesy. I like to hedge my bets with at least one or two lures that are of a different color or shade of the hot color, especially when I am fishing deep enough with downriggers to allow the use of slider rigs. Theories on how to play the multilure color game for trout in lakes are interesting to explore.

In addition to speed and lure color, habitat and water temperature are factors that play an important role in the whereabouts of trout. I've paid a great deal of attention to temperatures, bait fish locations, and preferred trout habitat in lakes, and I've learned that if you're going to have success with trout in these environments, you can't be haphazard about your fishing. To cut down the job of locating and catching any species of trout, you have to formulate a relevant strategy based on the conditions. Throughout the summer and fall, it is especially important to pay attention to the depth of the preferred temperature of the various trout species.

Trout are essentially a cold-water fish, and they are most likely to be found and to be active in cool water levels, though if necessary they'll move into warm water for a while to feed. Cold water is 40 to

50 degrees for a lake trout, 55 to 60 for a brown trout, and slightly higher for a rainbow or steelhead, but these are only guidelines. If I had to pick temperatures to focus on in the summer for deep-water fishing, I would check the stated ranges but lean to the colder side of those ranges.

Checking the water with a thermometer at various levels is the only sure way to determine the depth of what may be suitable water. When you know what level this may be, start fishing your lures in and around that depth and pay close attention to your sonar to look for bait and/or trout at those levels, changing lure depths as necessary based on what you see below. I don't think it's sufficient to identify the ideal temperature zone and then relentlessly drag your lures in that depth of water. If you spot fish (on your sonar) other than bait schools at levels different from what you are trolling, alter your fishing depths and experiment with fishing zones. I have caught plenty of trout, including the cold-water laker, in much higher water temperatures than they supposedly prefer. The overriding determination in their behavior may very well be the presence and location of food.

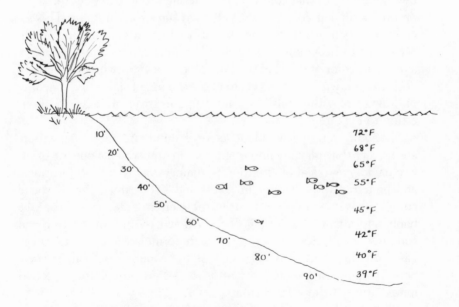

Searching for trout in the summer, when surface water is warm, cool water is deep, and a thermocline has been established, is often a matter of checking the depth of the preferred temperature of the trout species you seek.

When trout move out of their known, preferred temperature zones it is to feed, and foraging fish are active fish that can be caught. So be flexible; use preferred trout temperatures as a guideline, not as the last word.

Temperature, incidentally, enters the picture in a horizontal as well as a vertical sense in the early part of the season, where you might be looking for pockets of warm water (near a sun-bathed rocky shore, a tributary, or a warm shallow cove) or where there is a surface distinction between temperatures in larger lakes. The latter is likely to happen on huge bodies of water, such as the Great Lakes.

Lake Ontario, in particular, develops a vertical thermal barrier that is especially conducive to steelhead fishing, which is prominent in a typical year from mid-May through June. A few years ago, I fished that lake with charter boat captain Bill Kelley out of Rochester, New York, in early June to film a television show on offshore trout fishing. We ran north toward midlake for about 7 miles, constantly watching the surface temperature gauge on Bill's boat. Inshore the temperature was in the low 60s, but as we got far offshore it dropped through the 50s and 40s. Ultimately we came upon what is locally called the thermal bar, where the leading edge of cold surface water was 39 degrees. There was a visible scum line in which debris was trapped against the dense cold core.

We set up flat lines and shallow lines run off of planer boards and started fishing the warmer inside edge of the bar. It was not until we moved closer toward shore, however, and began working the temperature breaks around 44 degrees that we began to have success. As long as we stayed with thermal breaks — where there was a sudden change from one temperature to the next in the mid 40-degree range — we had success. We boated a bunch of steelhead on the surface in fairly short order, plus a pair of nice lakers.

Recently, also on Lake Ontario, friends and I experienced a similar phenomenon catching salmon, lake trout, and steelhead on the surface and within 30 feet of the surface, 4 to 8 miles offshore in 200 to 400 feet of water. Inshore water temperatures were 51 degrees and only an occasional brown trout was being taken there. Out where we were having success was on thermal breaks from 46 to 48 degrees. It was calm enough that you could literally see where surface water temperature breaks occurred, as well as warmer pockets of water.

This so-called thermal bar phenomenon was previously thought

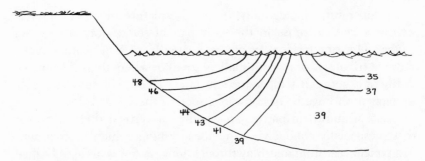

Great Lakes Thermal Bar
Several Miles Offshore

A thermal bar starts at the edge of a mass of 39-degree water, but the breaks to troll are where there is a jump of several degrees in temperature. The area between 44 and 48 degrees in this illustration typifies the locale to fish. Note how temperatures vary at below-surface levels as well; often it is more pronounced than this example illustrates.

to be a separation between warm and cold air masses, but it has recently been scientifically viewed as a mixing of water temperatures leading to the development of a thermocline. The important point is that the surface temperature breaks attract trout, and an occasional salmon also, as do more traditionally explored bands of temperature deep in the water column.

It is interesting to note that steelhead, which are ocean- or big lake-running versions of rainbow trout, can be present and active in mid 40-degree water although theoretically they ought to be inshore where their warmer, preferred temperature is located. This seems to contradict the notion that temperature preference is of paramount concern. As I've said, temperatures are only a guideline for your fishing efforts. Trout will inhabit warmer or cooler water if other factors, particularly forage presence, warrant it.

Thus, another couple of clues to solving the mysteries of fishing for trout in lakes is to know what trout feed on in a lake environment and where that forage is likely to be located.

Forage foods in lakes include alewives, smelt, ciscoes, chubs, sculpin, assorted species of shiners and darters, insects, and even yellow perch, crayfish, and other trout. It is usually a certainty that the prominent forage species in any environment constitutes the major part of the diet of a trout. In most large lakes and reservoirs, this is alewives or smelt. Lake trout, however, which spend a lot of midsummer time in deep environs, may feed primarily on sculpin and deviate from the relative-abundance generality.

In far-northern waters that are fairly sterile, there is no great concentration of bait fish. Lake trout in these waters eat whitefish or other trout. I've had good success using dark-colored plugs that I thought imitated the darkly colored lakers. In those same environments, I've caught small lakers with stomachs completely full of mosquitoes. It takes a lot of cruising to fill the belly of a 5-pound trout with insects, so you have to suspect that there was a lack of bait fish forage in that environment.

On the other hand, there are many situations in which trout in lakes are extraordinarily difficult to catch because there is such an abundance of bait fish available to them. When there is a plethora of bait in the active temperature band of trout, your offerings pall in comparison, and trout can be extremely selective. It's your lure — which vaguely looks like bait — versus millions of the real McCoys, and trout in popularly fished lakes are remarkably adept at making the distinction.

To make this information work for you, it pays to know whether that prominent forage is found deep or shallow at various times of the year. How do their temperature preferences relate to those of the trout? Smelt and alewives, for instance, respectively prefer 48- and 54-degree water, plus or minus a few degrees. Because there is reason to suspect that trout sometimes prefer food over temperature (within reason, of course), it makes sense to be fishing in places and at depth levels where both food and temperature requirements are met.

Such a dynamic place is where bait fish get funneled or where they routinely pass by. That's why reefs are attractive to lake trout; lakers can come out of deep water and stay by a reef to feed, then return to the depths. The deep-water/shallow water interface near islands can be similarly productive. In addition to such deep- or open-water structures, a sharply sloping shoreline often provides foraging opportunities, especially for brown trout. The edges of long underwater bars or shoals are places where bait migrate by naturally and logically present feeding opportunities for trout. These are the kinds of places where trout may be located, and they form another part of the puzzle of where to find and catch trout in lakes.

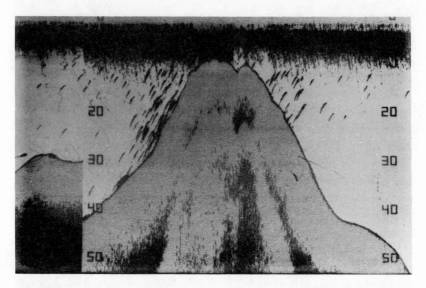

This reef, graphed in an open-water area of Great Slave Lake, was host to a lot of lake trout. Note that the fish are clustered between 10 and 30 feet along the edges of the reef. The author drove a boat fairly slowly directly over the top of this reef, with the paper speed setting on high, so this area isn't as big as it might appear to be; yet the recording demonstrates how trout are attracted to such structure.

An ideal situation for deep-trout prospecting in large lakes is to find a place in which all three criteria of temperature, forage, and shore structure coincide. If you are looking for schools of bait fish and monitoring preferred water temperature, you could do no better than to find both of these where the thermocline intersects the bottom. This would be a prime place to begin looking for trout, especially browns, in the summer on large lakes. Brown trout don't generally inhabit and widely roam the vast expanse of open water after late spring, and they seem to gravitate toward places where shallow areas meet deep areas, places where they can be comfortable and expect to ambush prey. If you're fishing open, midlake areas and not finding trout, look for fish closer to the bottom near sharply sloping shorelines. Trout may be more concentrated, incidentally, along a sharply sloped shoreline than along a moderately sloped shoreline that has a wider band of preferable temperatures; that's one advantage of the sharper bottom contour. In midsummer, deep trout may cruise over a large area in the horizontal strata of their active preferred temperature range, so in large lakes you may have a lot of scouring to do.

One thing that you'll find true about fishing for trout in confined bodies of water, like small lakes or reservoirs, is that the places that produce trout will repeatedly produce trout over time. This is one instance in which trout in lakes are like their flowing-water brethren.

The more you fish a particular body of water, the more you'll discover the nuances of that lake's fish and begin to put some of the puzzle together. You may well find that bigger, older fish seem to have a stronger orientation toward temperature than smaller, younger fish; small fish seem likely to visit higher temperature zones to feed and then return to colder water more readily than canny older fish. Fish in their active preferred temperature range are quite likely to be active feeders, which you observe sometimes on sonar equipment. In nutrient-rich lakes where there is deep cold water but an absence of oxygen at deeper levels, trout may be driven to seek relief in the tributaries during the summer. The direction and velocity of wind also may have a marked affect on the location of bait and/or trout.

Perhaps the most remarkable deviation from preferred temperature occurs with summer-run steelhead in the Great Lakes. The Skamania is currently a prime example, but additional summer-run strains of steelhead may be present shortly in the Great Lakes and also offer inshore midsummer fishing to trollers at a time when other salmonids are very deep and well offshore.

Skamania come into relatively shallow near-shore areas from late June through September prior to running up tributaries, where they stay and spawn in late winter. This means that they are accessible to shore and pier fishermen as well as to boaters and anglers in boats that are too small to explore the offshore waters for salmon and other trout. Angling in shorts and T-shirts when the water is warm enough to swim in (60 to 70 degrees inshore) seems a bit incongruous with the pursuit of steelhead, but not when the quarry is these remarkable Skamania.

These steelhead are caught routinely during the middle of the day, a time that is traditionally slow for salmon and only fair for catching trout, as well as early and late in the day. Most lake fishing for Skamania is done within a half-mile of shore and around tributaries. Some summertime trolling for Skamania takes place within a stone's throw of shore. Although you can occasionally catch Skamania on a flat line trolled fairly close to the surface, the bulk of the midsummer fish are taken with downriggers in water not much deeper than 60 feet. The most recent Skamania fishing I did was on Lake Michigan

This Skamania steelhead, taken in July on Lake Michigan, is relatively small, but it was still a spectacular jumper.

in July, and I caught Skamania up to 22 pounds on plugs fished 48 to 54 feet deep over 60 feet of water, using downriggers.

Lure speed is very important in Skamania trolling, and some veterans prefer a faster clip — around 3 mph — for these steelhead than for other trout and salmon. Orange and red are generally accepted as being the most successful lure colors, with thin spoons and small diving plugs the predominant trolling lures, although cut-plug lures in blue and silver and green and silver can be highly effective, as can dodger-and-fly combinations.

In case you aren't familiar with these up-and-coming fish, I should point out that steelhead in general are known as hard-fighting fish prone to jumping. Skamania, however, jump as much as or more than any other steelhead, seemingly leap higher, and have a curious knack for twisting as they do so. They often break a light line by landing on it or toss the hook through their aerial contortions, making landing one challenging. Furthermore, it is common, and fascinating, to have a Skamania strike a lure trolled 50 feet deep yet take to the air before the fishing line has popped out of the downrigger release. Skamania grow particularly large. In recent years, it has been common to catch fish over 10 pounds, close to shore, in the summer. You'll be hearing more about these and other summer-run steelhead as their range spreads throughout the Great Lakes. Small boat trollers will find them especially appealing.

13

POTPOURRI

Although I've tried to be thorough in presenting information about various aspects of trolling, there are some matters that don't fit into standard pegholes, that are applicable to many types of fishing, or that I didn't want to explore in greater depth when they were mentioned in other chapters of this book. This includes such trolling products, techniques, and incidentals as diving planers, attractors, wire and lead-core line, noodle rods, the Seth Green rig, spoon-plugging, nonmotor trolling, trolling sinkers, river trolling, and maps. These subjects are detailed in this chapter.

Diving planers. Diving planers are objects that attach to fishing line a few feet ahead of a lure and dive deeply. There are no weights used to get the lure down; the resistance of the planer makes it dive. When a fish strikes, it trips a release mechanism that allows the diver to offer minimal water resistance as the fish is played.

The earliest diving planers, which predate the era of downriggers, were nondirectional and dove only straight down. Such products included the Deep Six, formerly made by Les Davis and then acquired by Luhr Jensen, and the Pink Lady, the Dolphin, and the Jet Planer, all made by Luhr Jensen. For those without downriggers and for those who wished to avoid wire or lead-core line or the use of heavy weights to get deep, these planers offered an alternative.

As downriggers became more widespread, people abandoned diving planers. A few years ago, however, Luhr Jensen started manufacturing the Dipsy Diver, a directional diving planer that could be run not only straight down but also — and most preferably — off to the left or the right of a straight path and still get deep. This was followed

Lake Michigan captain Bob Kimble holds a laker taken on a dodger-fly combo trolled behind a Dipsy Diver planer.

by another directional diving planer, the Jons Diver from Big Jon. Now these products, particularly the Dipsy Diver, have nearly made the use of nondirectional divers obsolete.

Diving planers offer several benefits besides taking lures deep. They can serve as attractors to trout and salmon by their very size, color, and swimming motion. They offer an action that lures set behind downriggers don't get; the divers are more responsive to boat movement (turns and wave effects, for example). Because the lures are set a short distance behind them, they respond similarly. Directional divers, however, take lures down and *out away* from the boat. This latter point is the basis for the new popularity of directional planers, and explains why many big boaters are using them in conjunction with downrigger-set lines. Some fish that are in the path of the boat are spooked by downrigger weights and move down or out away from them. Directional diving planers bring lures off to the side of other presentations. They help you to cover more deep territory and, as a result, offer further presentation opportunities to shores, piers, and the like.

To determine the depth that divers will run, consult the chart supplied with them by the manufacturer. Because divers run deep, you cannot estimate the amount of line let out, but you must use the pull or pass system of line-length determination. According to the manufacturers, for example, 50 feet of 20-pound-test line will get a size 0 Pink Lady down 32 feet and a size 0 Dolphin down 24 feet. The Dipsy, which has four different base plate settings (size 0 being straight down and size 3 being furthest out to the side) runs a little shallower the more the diver runs to port or starboard. A size 0 Dipsy (size 1 is a larger version), for example, will run 25 feet deep when 45 feet of line is let out with a 0 setting or when 59 feet is let out with a 3 setting. Furthermore, there is a large plastic O ring that attaches around the collar of the Dipsy Diver and allows this planer to get 20 percent deeper.

If this sounds complicated, rest assured it isn't. The manufacturer's directions, which come with the product, give you good information that get you started in using this device. One drawback to planer use is that you aren't always certain of the depth the planer (and your lure) is running. Boat manipulation patterns affect its depth; you know approximate depth, not actual, as in downrigging. Therefore, it's important to judge accurately how much line you've let out, especially if you catch fish off a planer and want to reset it at the same level.

The Dipsy Diver has an adjustable trip tension screw, and you need to have this just right for the strength of line you are using and the depth to which you're going. This, and other divers pull awfully hard. If you want to retrieve one and the release won't trip (or, worse, if a small fish is on and the release won't trip), it's hard work bringing it in. The Jons Diver, incidentally, is the only diving planer that can be reset without retrieving the planer, although you still need to watch line length in order to get it at the desired depth.

The lures to be fished behind a diving planer are quite broad. Spoons and cut plugs are especially favored because these devices are primarily used for trout and salmon. Minnow-imitating plugs of various sizes also get the nod, as do dodger and fly or squid combinations. Diving plugs aren't usually worked unless they are very shallow runners and can withstand sometimes erratic planer action. Three to 5 feet is a common setback length. I prefer leaders on the short side because of the difficulty of netting a fish that is 5 or so feet behind a diving planer. Leader strength should be as strong or stronger than the main fishing line, preferably 17 to 20 pounds if big fish are likely to be encountered and perhaps 25 to 30 if a dodger is trolled. The main fishing line should be strong, at least 14 pounds; most people use 20.

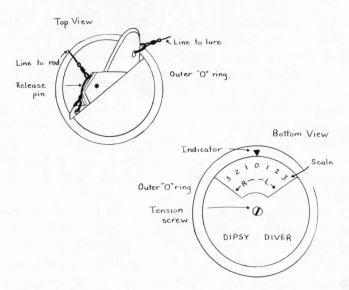

The Dipsy Diver sports a release pin that trips when a fish strikes the trailing lure, so the planer stops diving. It also has a weighted keel that can be adjusted to make the planer swim to either side of the boat.

Long, stout rods are the order of the day for diving planer use. On big boats, beefy 9 to 10 footers are used, and on smaller ones, beefy 7 or 8 footers are worked. Because diving planers pull so hard, a good rod holder is necessary, preferably one that is adjustable, that can take a lot of handle torque, and that isn't difficult to get a rod out of. It's better to place diving planer rods on the gunwale, several feet ahead of the transom, and have them angled low and perpendicular to the water.

A criticism of diving planers is that they inhibit the fight of a fish a little. This is true, but the extent depends on the fish. Large fish still pull very hard, and some, including cohos and steelhead, still jump out of the water, although not quite as often. When fighting a fish, you know that the planer, even though it has tripped, is there. This is not quite as satisfactory as fighting the fish on an unencumbered line. A way to get around this interference is to use a diving planer in the same manner as a downrigger; that is, attach a release clip to the diving planer, attach a hand line or separate rod to the diving planer, and attach the actual fishing rod and line to the release clip. Few people do this, but it is a way to fight a fish on a free line. In any event, diving planers can account for an extra fish or two during the course of a day's trolling (where trout and salmon are concerned, these may be fish that are out of the preferred temperature zone or the thermocline), and merit consideration to round out your trolling presentation abilities.

Attractors. As you've seen and read earlier in this book, fish can be attracted to other trolled objects besides lures. Downrigger weights and diving planers, for example, can get the attention of fish although their purpose is to carry lures to a specific depth. There are some devices that have the primary function of getting the attention of fish in mid to deep environs, because their vibration causes fish to hear them and/or their appearance provides visual stimuli, causing fish to be drawn to them and possibly striking a lure that trails behind them. Attractors include dodgers, flashers, and cowbells and are primarily of value when fishing for trout and salmon.

Dodgers and flashers are similar, but not the same. Both are thin-metal objects, rounded at the ends, and shaped like the inside of a 1/4-mile running track. They are 2 to 3 inches wide and 5 to 10 inches long. Dodgers sway from side to side and, although capable of rotating, do not rotate unless run too fast. They are more widely trolled than flashers, which are meant to rotate not sway. Both sport swivels at either end, come in various sizes and colors, and can be altered in appearance with the application of prism tape.

Plugs, spoons, flies, and imitation squid are fished behind dodgers and flashers. Flies and squid are the most popular trailing lures, particularly for steelhead trout and coho salmon, and are run 12 to 18 inches behind the attractor. Plugs, primarily cut plugs, and spoons are run 18 to 30 inches back. Because dodgers and flashers are attractors, there is no need to use long leads; also, short leads make netting fish easier.

These attractors don't have any weight to attain depth, so they are primarily fished behind a downrigger, but they are also used in conjunction with diving planers and heavy sinkers. The distance from these objects to the dodger is 2 to 6 feet. Short leads to the attractor improve its action. When attractors are trolled with a downrigger, it's important to have a fairly tight tension setting on the line release, because attractors pull fairly hard and often pull the line out of a lightly set release.

"Cowbells" is more of a term to describe a multibladed attractor

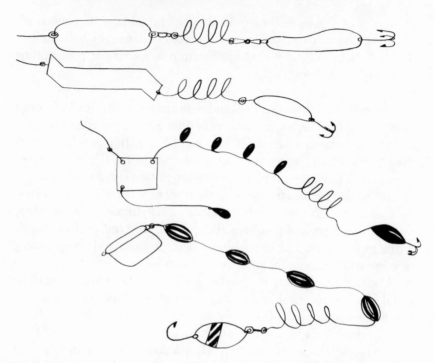

Shown from the top are a dodger, flasher, and two cowbells, all followed by a short leader and spoon.

than it is a specific product. Such attractors are a series of lightweight spoons, or blades, spaced at intervals over a short to medium length of wire line. There are many versions of this device. Some feature a rudder at the head, to which fishing line is attached, and all feature a swivel to prevent line twist. At the end of the rig, you attach a short leader (6 to 24 inches) and your lure. The idea is not only to attract fish but also to imitate a school of bait fish, with the trailing member being the one that doesn't swim the same therefore it appears to be vulnerable. Usually bait, a spoon, or a fly is attached to cowbells, but sometimes a plug is used.

The size and shape of the blades are the big differences among cowbells. Shape includes willowleaf, Colorado, Indiana, and more. Lengths may be 1 1/2 to 5 inches long, although only a few anglers use the larger sizes. Blades are predominantly silver, but they can be painted or taped.

Cowbells are largely used in deep lake trout trolling. A few fishermen use them with downriggers, but traditionally they have been fished on wire or lead-core line or on lines weighted with a heavy

Captain Skip Stafford took this Lake Michigan lake trout in deep water on the bottom using the big-bladed cowbell attractor held in his right hand.

sinker. One novel deep-fishing use I've seen and think has merit is a string of fairly large-bladed cowbells snapped to a downrigger weight, with a lure running slightly above and behind them and attached to a line release located on the downrigger cable just above the weight.

Weighted lines. I'm not a fan of wire or lead-core line fishing. I don't own an outfit for either and shun opportunities to troll with them, especially with wire. I've trolled wire for lake trout, musky, and striped bass and lead core for trout and salmon, so I have some experience with it, but I don't find the use of these to be as satisfying as other trolling techniques. I'm not saying that it's unsporting, just that I prefer to use lighter and more modern tackle. The problem is that weighted lines make fish-landing mostly a reel-cranking, winch-the-fish-up affair. If you catch a giant, it will surely fight well enough for you to know it's there. But for every giant you hook, you'll catch a hundred (or more) small- to medium-size fish, which just don't give as good an account of themselves as they do on finer line because they must resist the bulky drag of the weighted line (and there is usually a lot of it out) in the water. In defense of wire, however, it doesn't stretch, so on shorter lengths it does transmit some of the fish's movement. It also makes hookups a little surer. Having confessed my bias, let's review the basic aspects of weighted line trolling.

The value of both wire and lead-core line is that they are heavy and sink. The amount of line set out determines how deep your offering will be. Before modern trolling systems came along, these were the principal methods of fishing deep, especially for lake trout, brown trout, and landlocked salmon.

Wire lines are primarily made of single or multiple strands in Monel or stainless steel. Monel is more expensive and kinks less. Multistrand is easier to handle but poses difficulties when burrs develop. Because it sinks less readily than single-strand wire, it is less used.

Wire sinks 10 feet for every 100 feet let out, so use this formula for attaining depth with wire. To get down 30 feet, therefore, you'd have to let out 300 feet of wire, although you can obtain more depth also by using some weight and fishing slowly or making turns. Most wire lining is done for deep lake trout fishing, and weights up to 1 pound are used. Because of the weight, the amount of line out isn't as great even though the depth achieved is far greater. The tactic here is to troll very slowly and let line out until you feel the sinker hit the bottom. Reel up a turn or two and set the rod in a holder. Remember that you can't freespool wire out when you set it or you'll get a terrible tangle, so you must release line out slowly under tension, with your thumb controlling the reel spool.

This is heavy tackle fishing, and big star drag reels and stout rods with carbide guides are necessary. There is no levelwind on the reels because wire would cut it, so you must use your thumb to guide the wire back evenly on the spool. This is something that few freshwater fishermen have experience at doing these days. Because there is no levelwind, you can't count passes, and the pull system isn't practical with such heavy gear, so you'll have to mark wire in specific intervals, starting at 100 feet, to know how much you've set out. One way to do this is to put a colored adhesive wrap around it.

Lead-core line doesn't sink as readily as wire, especially at high speeds and where there is current. It is color-coded every 10 yards so you can determine how much is let out, although this doesn't necessarily tell you how deep the lure is. No special tackle is required for it, although the rod should be relatively stout and the reel large enough to hold this bulky product and some backing. Levelwind reels can be used.

Light tackle trolling. I've noted elsewhere in this book that light lines can be used for flat line, sideplaner board, and downrigger trolling. In fact, it's a lot of fun to do so. So-called noodle-rod fishing has taken hold in some big waters as a transfer from stream steelheading applications, so there has been more emphasis on this in recent times, although light-lining has been going on for years. Light line may be considered as 8-pound-test when fishing for large (20 pounds and up) fall salmon or big striped bass, although you might ordinarily troll that strength of line for walleyes. Or it might be 2- or 4-pound line for smallmouth bass because you might ordinarily troll for them with 6- or 8-pound line. Given the broad range of trolling that is possible, I consider 2- through 8-pound line to be light or ultralight, depending on the circumstances.

Here's a synopsis of the fine points of light-line trolling:

1. *Be sensible.* It would be foolish to troll 6-pound line over the tops of submerged trees for striped bass. When you hook a fish in this environment, you need to be able to muscle it away from that cover. You simply cannot do this with light line when the fish is relatively large. Trolling with light line in these circumstances is not just a matter of losing lures or fish; it's not fair to the fish that has a hook in it for a while and that may trail some line behind it. Light line is great to use in open water, especially if there are no obstructions for hooked fish to break off on. Open water is where light line has it greatest trolling application, no matter what species or size of fish is pursued.

2. *Be considerate of other fishermen.* When fish are clustered in one area and when that area is plowed with a lot of boat traffic, no one wants a light-lining angler tied up to a fish in the midst of the best water. The angler will be on the fish for a long time and have a lot of line out, thereby inhibiting other trollers. That leads to cutoffs, angry words, and bad feelings. Use heavier tackle in such circumstances, or get out and away from the crowd by trolling the perimeter of the congested area.

3. *Use long rods.* Long rods provide more leverage for playing fish. Because they are fairly limber, they absorb a lot of punishment and are forgiving. Long rods are also helpful for maneuvering fish near the boat, as fish caught on light line often give a surge near the boat and try to dive under it. I've been using 7- to 9-foot rods for light-line trolling for years. Lately, some fishermen have gone to 12-foot noodle rods for 2- and 4-pound-test line use. The guides on these are not arranged in the conventional aligned fashion, but

This angler is using a 12-foot noodle rod and 4-pound line to battle a Lake Michigan salmon that was caught using a downrigger. In open water and where boat traffic is minimal, light tackle trolling is practical and a lot of fun.

twist around the rod to help keep the line from contacting the wall of the rod in a bent-over position. The rod should have a long handle and plenty of guides and mustn't provide too much tension when bowed over for downrigging.

4. *Use a good-quality release.* Line releases used in sideplaner or down-rigger light-line trolling must be able to be adjusted for light-line use, so striking fish don't break the line and so the trailing lure doesn't pull free. There is a very fine working point here, and many releases that work well with heavy lines do not work well with the lightest lines.

5. *Clear the boat.* When you are trolling with light line, it's imperative to clear all other trolled lines, weights, and planers as quickly as possible after the fish has been hooked. You don't have a lot of control over the fish on light tackle. It may take a lot of line off the reel and/or circle around the boat, so you need to be able to react properly. Boat manipulation is also critical because big fish will run all over the lake. It's to the angler's fish-playing advantage if the boat operator keeps the fish off the transom or the back quarters of the boat until it's time to land the fish.

6. *You need an excellent drag and line.* Big fish and light line are a great combination, but there is a lot of stress put on light line and your

tackle must be up to it. The drag must be smooth and not hesitating, and the line must be of top quality. There is no margin for error in light-line trolling.

The Seth Green rig. One of the oldest methods of deep trolling and also a method of multilure presentation was developed by renowned New York fish culturist Seth Green a 100 years ago. There are some deep-water trollers still using this technique, principally as an adjunct to other styles of deep trolling, but I mention it here as food for thought.

The Seth Green rig features five to eight lures, usually spoons or flies, on individual leaders that snap to the main fishing line and stay at a constant position in the main fishing line because they are attached to swivels. A heavy lead weight is used to get the rig down. Leaders are separated by a 10- to 20-foot distance. To fish it, you lower the weight and line into the water until the first barrel swivel is reached, then you take a leader and snap it to the barrel swivel. Slowly lower it in the water until you reach the next swivel, and attach another leader. Continue in this fashion until all lures are out.

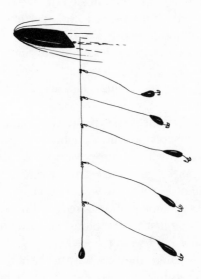

The Seth Green rig is an old-time way to use many lures on one main fishing line, although it's a chore to set out and to retrieve.

This requires a heavy rod and reel and some adroit manipulation to retrieve. When you reel in, you must stop to remove each of the snapped-on leaders. Leader length varies; old-timers used 15- to 30-foot leaders but I'd opt for much shorter ones. This setup has also been called a thermal rig and is primarily used in deep midsummer trout and salmon fishing for covering a wide spectrum of water. It was adapted from commercial fishing applications. Sport fishermen should check state fishing regulations to be sure that they can use this many lures or hook points on one fishing line.

Spoonplugging. Spoonplugging isn't new, but you'll be hard pressed to find many practitioners, particularly outside of the upper Midwest. You just about have to refer to a mail-order tackle supplier to find them because so few tackle shops have them on hand. Spoonplugs are sinking lures stamped from brass into a slightly arched position. There are seven models, all of which are used solely for trolling. A good feature about these lures is that they can take a lot of abuse; they can be run into all kinds of objects but still hold their form without needing further tuning adjustments.

As with other trolling baits, the size of the lure and the amount and strength (diameter) of line out determine how deep it will run. Spoonplugs are noted for high-speed work, particularly by people who are new to an area and are both scouting for fish and trying to learn the bottom contours and structures of a lake. Spoonplug practitioners often use No-Bo, a supposedly low-stretch premeasured nylon monofilament line that, like spoonplugs, is tough to find.

Nonmotor trolling. If you own a rowboat and have read through this book, you'll probably be a little slighted because so much of what I've written has to do with motor-powered boats and motor trolling, whether the motors be gas or electric powered. Much of it is also applicable to nonmotor trolling as well, although it's admittedly harder to accomplish. As someone who started trolling on small lakes with oar power, and whose first trout trolling was done on reservoirs where no outboards of any kind were allowed, I am sympathetic to anglers who troll in places where they cannot, or do not, use motors.

Rowers have their trolling work cut out for them. Because so much of trolling is a matter of covering a lot of territory and making repeated presentations to fish or along certain terrain, rowers obviously get a lot of exercise. Nonmotor trollers can benefit from the use of a 6-volt battery-powered portable depthfinder, as it is important to know what is below you and how deep you are no matter how you troll. Row-trolling is basically a matter of making slow and superslow presentations, especially when headed into the wind, so you should choose lures that work well at slow speeds. Downriggers can be worked by rowing, especially if there are two people in a boat, and this is the best way to go. However, when I row-trolled reservoirs, I found it awfully difficult to set a downrigger when fishing alone and to have forward momentum. Still, lone rowers can accomplish it. Many row-trollers use wire or lead-core line, cowbells, and bait or light spoons for deep fishing. This setup works well at slow speeds and is good for the frequent surge-pause efforts that are generated by trollers. Rod holders are needed, incidentally, as they are in motor trolling, and they should be located near enough to the angler so that he doesn't have to reach for the rod, but not so near as to interfere with oar movement. Without rod holders, you'll have to lay the rod in front of you and keep the ball of your foot on the butt of the rod.

Rowers who are simply moving from one place to another should lay out a trolling line as they go, simply on the chance that they might hook onto something. In my early rowing days when bass fishing, I would always troll a line or two as I headed from one spot on the lake to the next, no matter how fast or slow I was rowing. I frequently picked up a nice bass (or other fish) this way and found a new place to fish in the process. This is one thing that motorized fishermen often don't do. Because they can get from one spot to another quickly, they are most likely to pick up their lines, throttle down, and speed off to the next hot spot. A nonmotor angler doesn't have that luxury, but he can often make the disadvantage pay off by trolling between locales.

Trolling sinkers. Elsewhere in this book, I mention the use of weights or sinkers for getting lines down to depths they would be unable to achieve if unweighted. Weighted flat-line trolling involves the use of some type of light sinker, either to get a lure down because it achieves no depth on it's own when trolled (like a light spoon) or to get a diving plug deeper.

Such sinkers include a torpedo sinker, which has minimal drag or water resistance because of its shape; a torpedo-style bead chain sinker, which swivels and prevents line twist; a keel-style bead chain sinker, which tracks well with little swaying motion; a planing sinker, which dives; a clinch sinker, which is simple to add to or remove from the

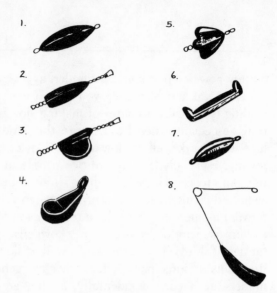

Sinkers used in trolling include: 1. torpedo; 2. torpedo-shaped bead chain; 3. keel-shaped bead chain; 4. bottom-walking; 5. planing; 6. clinch; 7. rubber core; 8. Bait Walker.

line; and a rubber-core sinker, which is also simple to add to or remove from the line and does not abrade it. There are many sizes and weights of these available. These sinkers are all fastened in line, either being affixed on the main fishing line or tied to a leader. The bead chain styles prevent line twist and, with a snap, aid leader and lure changing.

Some sliding or slip sinkers are used for slow trolling with bait. These include ball, egg or barrel, cone or bullet, and walking. Egg and ball sinkers slide freely on the line, are often stopped by a small split shot or a barrel swivel, and are preferred for open water. Cone-shaped sinkers provide minimal drag and are relatively weedless. Walking sinkers are used with a stopper when casting or trolling with bait along the bottom; they remain upright when a fish runs with the bait.

River trolling. Many of the trolling aspects previously addressed in this book also apply to big rivers, although current flow and strength is always a factor to be reckoned with and has a large bearing on the direction in which you troll and the speed at which you troll. In smaller rivers or in large but relatively shallow rivers, however, there is not the room for maneuverability nor the depth of water to be worked as there is in large, deep rivers and lakes. Such species as American shad, walleye, smallmouth bass, steelhead, coho and chinook salmon, and brown trout are all fishing targets for those who troll in the traditional forward fashion or slowly backward.

The latter technique is especially noteworthy in rivers. In some quarters it is referred to as backtrolling, although it is different from the form of backtrolling on lakes as practiced by walleye anglers. In other circles, backtrolling is called Hotshotting, a term derived from the West Coast technique of using a Hotshot plug for river trout and salmon, or pulling plugs; and in others, it is referred to as slipping, a term coined by my friend Dan Gapen, an extremely competent river fisherman. I like the term *slipping*, because it is nongeneric, descriptive, and doesn't conflict with other trolling terminology.

Whatever you call it, the idea is to have the bow of your boat pointed upstream, using motor or oars to control the downstream progression of the boat. The boat moves very slowly — it actually drifts — downstream. At times, it remains stationary in the current, and some boaters anchor once they have caught fish in a spot. Lures are fished at 50- to 80-foot distances behind the boat. The lures dangle in front of fish that the boat has not yet passed over, which is a big difference compared to upstream trolling, where the boat passes over fish and alerts them to your presence, possibly spooking them. Additionally, lures that are slipped downstream ahead of the boat approach fish from the front, instead of coming from behind them and swimming past their head. Lures are usually fished in the channels and deep pools where bigger fish lie. They waver in front of fish for a much longer period than they would if cast and retrieved or if trolled upstream and away. The fact that fish have a better chance of being undisturbed and of seeing a more natural presentation makes this a

An extremely effective method of river trolling by slowly moving downstream is to keep the motor in forward gear, allowing the boat to slip backward or to veer from side to side. Pools can be worked with deep-running plugs or weighted lures, and fish can be approached naturally from ahead.

highly effective river fishing technique. A small fish, for instance, struggles against the current and is slowly swept downward without being spooked.

Most of this downstream drift trolling is done with diving plugs for fish that take them. Some fish, such as shad, don't take plugs; therefore, you must use shad darts (a form of jig) or tiny spoons fished behind a torpedo-shaped bead chain sinker. Others respond well to bait. Winter-run steelhead, for example, are caught with pencil lead-weighted spawn sacks or single-hook salmon eggs. Many different attractions, including plugs, spoons, spinners, flies, and bait, can be used in slipping, depending on the circumstances.

When slipping, it's important to manipulate the boat properly in order to maintain precise lure position. The location and depth of your offering is critical to river fishing success. The lure must be on or close to the bottom, so you need to use the appropriate amount of weight or design of lure that will achieve this.

Pools are the major locale fished with this technique, and often the boat needs to be positioned far enough upriver so the lure slowly works from the head of a pool down through the tail of it. It's not good enough to boat down to a pool then hold position, because the fish you seek may have been located at the head of the pool. When working from side to side across the river, you should realize that it takes awhile for a trailing lure to catch up to the boat position. When you sweep close to a bank, for instance, hold that position because it takes time for the lure to get over to the bank. If you were to sweep in and out quickly, the lure wouldn't get as far to either side as you might like.

Another point to remember is that you want to slip backward in a slow, controlled fashion. When you stop rowing or throttle the motor back, a floating plug rises, a spinner doesn't spin, and weights sink because there is now less pressure against those objects. Slow, controlled slipping keeps lures working best and draws more strikes.

Boat control is maintained with oars, especially in rafts, johnboats, and river drift boats (McKenzie River style dories), or with small tiller-steered outboard motors. Last season I started using Mercury's new 9.9 outboard for this type of fishing and found it to be more adaptable than the small outboards I'd previously used, especially because of its handle-tilt operation. Where motors are used, they should be small enough to operate well at the slowest forward setting.

Pools and channels are the primary river trolling locations.

River trollers may find it worthwhile to use some type of speed indicator. Last spring I used a speed gauge for river fishing for the first time when pursuing shad. I have decided that it's something I want to experiment with more. You'd be surprised at how much the flow varies in places that don't visually seem to be very different and at how fast you are actually moving upstream against the current when trolling upriver. I used the speed indicator for checking my boat speed when forward trolling and slipping. I also measured the flow of current with the speed indicator when my boat was stationary. This prompted me to avoid some areas that I might have fished and to try some that I would not have been inclined to work.

There are, incidentally, opportunities to experiment with downriggers and sideplaner boards in small- and medium-size rivers. Downriggers are a vastly overlooked aspect of river angling. This is essentially a two-angler operation because of the extra safety precaution that must be taken in river boating. Slipping and forward trolling with these devices are possible.

Underwater contour maps. Every angler who trolls a large and/or unfamiliar body of water should have a good map of that place. Maps, especially those that show underwater contours and hydrographic features, will help you navigate without getting lost or possibly running into obstructions. You will also be able to find areas that may provide good fishing. By pinpointing the location of islands, mounds, shoals, reefs, drop-offs, roadbeds, channels, river and creek beds, and the like — plus depths — you can troll the particular places that are most likely to harbor the fish you seek. Furthermore, by having such maps before visiting a lake or river, you can study them and pinpoint areas to try without having to spend time scouting on the water.

Underwater contour (hydrographic) maps and navigational charts are distinguished from topographic maps. The latter seldom denote water depth or location of reefs, rocks, shallows, and such, while the former do and are preferable. Underwater contour maps are available for many large bodies of water, and these can be particularly useful because their high level of detail pinpoints important hydrographic features. When used in conjunction with a compass, they help you maintain course, especially in fog, low-light conditions, or at night.

Topographic maps and navigational charts are produced by American and Canadian federal agencies and are available at some sporting goods stores, marinas, and map stores in major cities. They cost a few dollars apiece. Dealers usually stock local maps and can order others for you. To order maps yourself, obtain a map index from the appropriate government agency.

For U.S. topographical maps of areas east of the Mississippi, write U.S. Geological Survey, Branch of Distribution, 1200 S. Eads St., Arlington, VA 22202. For areas west of the Mississippi, write U.S. Geological Survey, Branch of Distribution, Box 25286, Denver Federal Center, Denver, CO 80225.

For navigational charts of U.S. waters, contact National Oceanic and Atmospheric Administration, National Ocean Survey, Distribution Division (C44), Riverdale, MD 20840 (301-436-6990).

For Canadian topographic maps, contact Canada Map Office, Surveys and Mapping Branch, Department of Energy, Mines and Resources, 615 Booth St., Ottawa, Ontario K1A 0E9 (613-998-9900). For navigational charts of Canadian waters, contact Chart Distribution Office, Department of Fisheries and Oceans, P. O. Box 8080, 1675 Russell Rd., Ottawa, Ontario K1G 3H6 (613-998-4931).

There is no charge to receive a map index or chart catalog from any of these agencies. Order maps long before you expect to depart on a trip. Remember that the larger the scale, the more detail is provided. Other maps of big waters may be available from jurisdictional agencies, such as the Corps of Engineers or the Tennessee Valley Authority (TVA), although their maps are rarely detailed enough to give you more than general information.

Maps supplied by private firms, however, are often geared to fishermen's interests and provide a great deal of underwater contour information. Their size and scale level will determine how helpful they are as boating and fishing aids. Many good maps are available at tackle shops, sporting goods stores, and marinas near popular waterways. In addition, state fisheries agencies often have contour maps, ranging from large scale to reduced size on an 8 1/2 × 11 sheet of paper, particularly for smaller lakes and ponds. You should check with these agencies for such availability.

Not all the information on lake maps is necessarily 100 percent accurate. In fact, it is not uncommon to find particular structures not indicated on underwater contour maps or navigational charts. These products are substantial aids to fishermen who know their quarry and can identify areas that are likely to be productive, however. This is particularly so where big lakes and rivers are concerned.

It's a good idea, incidentally, to store maps in a large, clear, sealable plastic pouch or treat them with a waterproofing material to help them last in marine environments. Color-coding the different contour levels, or marking certain areas/places with indelible markers, is also worthwhile.

I hope that in reading this book you've come to realize that trolling is a worthwhile, challenging, and effective method of angling; that there are ways to troll for and catch fish that seem to be out of reach; and that you can enjoy finding them and be successful at catching them.

As I mentioned in the Introduction, to most fishermen, trolling is the art of dragging any old lure or bait at an indeterminate distance behind a boat at an unknown depth, in an unplanned fashion. And with generally unproductive results. That's a description that I've coined because it represents my opinion of a rather prevalent attitude, although it does not accurately depict the art of trolling that is possible in the modern era and that has been detailed in this book. There's nothing wrong with laid-back absent-minded trolling — as long as you want to kick up your feet, take a boat ride, and maybe catch a fish or two. Many people want more out of angling, however, than that. They feel compelled to conscientiously search for and find fish. They feel compelled to know exactly where their lures are and to scour the water column for their quarry. They feel compelled to make a calculated, determined effort to entice fish that they rarely see until it is hoisted out of the water in a landing net.

I felt compelled to write this book and thereby share information on modern freshwater trolling equipment and techniques with you. I know that when you use the information detailed here to troll and the cry goes out "Fish on!" you'll feel especially delighted.

INDEX